MW01050133

Security Metrics
A Beginner's Guide

"An extraordinarily thorough and sophisticated explanation of why you need to measure the effectiveness of your security program and how to do it. A must have for any quality security program!"

—*Dave Cullinane, CISSP, CISO & VP*
Global Fraud, Risk & Security, eBay

"Beginners in security need a guide that manages complexity without sacrificing detail. Wong's remarkably clear, comprehensive manual delivers what they need."

—*Richard Thieme*
Author of *Mind Games and Islands in the Clickstream*
and global speaker on the impact of technology

About the Author

Caroline Wong, CISSP, was formerly the Chief of Staff for the Global Information Security Team at eBay, where she built the security metrics program from the ground up. She is well known for her expertise in the area of security metrics and has been a featured speaker at industry functions, including RSA (USA and Europe), ITWeb Summit (South Africa), Metricon, the Executive Women's Forum, ISC2, and the Information Security Forum. Caroline contributed as a technical reviewer to the Center for Information Security Consensus Metrics Definitions. She has also worked with the Cloud Security Alliance to define metrics for the cloud computing space.

Caroline graduated from U.C. Berkeley with a B.S. in Electrical Engineering and Computer Sciences, has a Certificate in Finance and Accounting from Stanford's Executive Education Program, and is CISSP certified. She was awarded the 2010 Women of Influence "One to Watch" Award by the Executive Women's Forum.

About the Contributors

Betsy Nichols is the CTO and Co-Founder of PlexLogic LLC, which offers a Metrics-On-Demand service called MetricsCenter, and is the original creator of MetricML. MetricsCenter implements both a for-profit security metrics web site at www.metricscenter.net as well as an open and free public resource for security metrics at www.MetricsCenter.org. MetricML is an open, web services–based framework for creating, collaborating, and sharing metric definitions and data. Betsy is an active participant in many public, community, and private enterprise security metrics projects in addition to helping initiate the CSA working group. Betsy earned her Ph.D. in Mathematics at Duke University and her undergraduate degree at Vassar College.

Lynn Terwoerds is the Director of Compliance at Microsoft Corporation. Highly respected in both business and technical circles, Lynn is an active member of the Cloud Security Alliance and leads its Cloud Security Metrics working group.

Before joining Microsoft, Lynn was Vice President of Business Development for SafeMashups, where she maintained a focus on developing and managing strategic relationships. She was the head of Security Architecture and Standards for Barclay's global retail and commercial bank based in London. Prior to that, she spent more than eight years with Microsoft, leading efforts in security response, Trustworthy Computing, and critical infrastructure protection. Before entering the software industry, she worked with various solutions integrators, providing consulting services to Fortune 100 companies, giving her 20 years overall IT industry experience. Lynn is a CISSP, CEH, and holds a master's degree in Classics.

About the Technical Editors

Jim Reavis is the President of Reavis Consulting Group, LLC, where he advises security companies, large enterprises, and other organizations on the implications of new trends, such as cloud computing, and how to take advantage of them. Jim has previously been an international board member of the ISSA, a global not-for-profit association of information security professionals, and formerly served as the association's Executive Director. Jim was a co-founder of the Alliance for Enterprise Security Risk Management, a partnership among the ISSA, ISACA, and ASIS, formed to address the enterprise risk issues associated with the convergence of logical and traditional security. Jim is helping shape the future of information security as co-founder, executive director, and driving force of the Cloud Security Alliance. Jim was recently named as one of the Top 10 Cloud Computing Leaders by SearchCloudComputing.com.

Tara Darbyshire is a founding board member of the Archer Foundation, a nonprofit charitable organization whose mission is to advance entrepreneurial achievement in Kansas, extend the reach of community service programs, and foster educational opportunities for students and single mothers. Prior to joining the Archer Foundation, Tara was a co-founder and the Executive Vice President of Business Development and Sales for Archer Technologies. Tara set the strategic direction for all sales programs and business development activities for the company since early 2001. Prior to joining Archer, Tara held the positions of Vice President of Sales and Marketing for eSecurityOnline, National Director of Sales for the Information Security practice of Ernst & Young, and Senior Sales Manager for MCI Telecommunications. Tara has more than 15 years of experience in strategic sales and business development with Fortune 500 companies and in managing and implementing successful sales programs.

Security Metrics
A Beginner's Guide

Caroline Wong

New York   Chicago   San Francisco
Lisbon   London   Madrid   Mexico City
Milan   New Delhi   San Juan
Seoul   Singapore   Sydney   Toronto

The McGraw·Hill Companies

Library of Congress Cataloging-in-Publication Data

Wong, Caroline.
    Security metrics : a beginner's guide / Caroline Wong.
        p. cm.
    ISBN 978-0-07-174400-3 (alk. paper)
    1. Data protection—Standards.   2. Microcomputers—Access control.   3. Computer
security—Evaluation.   4. Computer crimes—Prevention.   I. Title.
    QA76.9.A25W658 2012
    005.8—dc23

                                                                              2011043857

McGraw-Hill books are available at special quantity discounts to use as premiums and sales promotions, or for use in corporate training programs. To contact a representative, please e-mail us at bulksales@mcgraw-hill.com.

Security Metrics: A Beginner's Guide

Copyright © 2012 by The McGraw-Hill Companies. All rights reserved. Printed in the United States of America. Except as permitted under the Copyright Act of 1976, no part of this publication may be reproduced or distributed in any form or by any means, or stored in a database or retrieval system, without the prior written permission of publisher, with the exception that the program listings may be entered, stored, and executed in a computer system, but they may not be reproduced for publication.

All trademarks or copyrights mentioned herein are the possession of their respective owners and McGraw-Hill makes no claim of ownership by the mention of products that contain these marks.

1234567890   QFR QFR   10987654321

ISBN   978-0-07-174400-3
MHID   0-07-174400-2

Sponsoring Editor   Megg Morin

Editorial Supervisor   Janet Walden

Project Editor   LeeAnn Pickrell

Acquisitions Coordinator   Joya Anthony

Technical Editors   Jim Reavis, Betsy Nichols, Tara Darbyshire

Copy Editor   William McManus

Proofreader   Paul Tyler

Indexer   Karin Arrigoni

Production Supervisor   George Anderson

Composition   Cenveo Publisher Services

Illustration   Cenveo Publisher Services

Art Director, Cover   Jeff Weeks

Cover Designer   Jeff Weeks

Information has been obtained by McGraw-Hill from sources believed to be reliable. However, because of the possibility of human or mechanical error by our sources, McGraw-Hill, or others, McGraw-Hill does not guarantee the accuracy, adequacy, or completeness of any information and is not responsible for any errors or omissions or the results obtained from the use of such information.

This book is dedicated to Dave Cullinane. Thank you for teaching me.

Contents at a Glance

Contents

Foreword

Information security is one of those funny disciplines where the best outcome in a given day is ... nothing. Nothing bad happens. No hackers break in, no data vanishes, no viruses wreak havoc, and no threats—advanced or persistent—cause the CEO to light up his teams' pagers.

I've often written that security is about nothing. But security is about more than that. It's probably more accurate to say that security is just as much about the loud interruptions that punctuate the apparent silence. When things work the way they should, your colleagues and friends don't notice anything at all. But when something bad happens, everyone notices. And pagers ring.

These two opposing tendencies of information security—silence and its interruptions— are the yin and yang that power our industry, condition our expectations, and drive our budgets. They are what make information security the most dynamic sector of IT.

Of course, acknowledging that break-ins, fear, and perfidy power our industry isn't news. It does tell us why managers buy security gear with business cases flimsier than Donald Trump's casino restructuring plans. And it explains why it is often easier to chase the threats *du jour* than to pull back and try to answer the most important question: are we more secure today than we were yesterday? (Whatever "secure" means.)

Fear-driven security programs are fundamentally about manipulating emotions, not marshaling facts. Five years ago, I set out to bring some analytical rigor to information security and wrote *Security Metrics: Replacing Fear, Uncertainty and Doubt*. It was my first book. I enjoyed writing it, although it was a challenge. When I started out, my book outline called for sixteen chapters, starting with definitions and background, proceeding through visualization, breezing through the Balanced Scorecard, and finally getting to the good stuff: case studies and lessons learned.

But as with many first-time authors unaccustomed to writing deadlines and page counts, my ambition exceeded my reach. I fell behind schedule. At a certain point, my editor tapped me on the shoulder and gently reminded me that I needed to, you know, finish the book. So I did what any self-respecting software engineering manager would do: I cut features until the darn thing shipped. Sadly, the least-developed parts of my outline—the case studies and lessons learned—were the first parts to get the chop. As a result, my book became mostly about what security metrics are and less about how to make them.

The question of how to make security metrics goes well beyond academic exercises. A wise man once said that "amateurs think about *what;* professionals think about *how*." Suppose you've created a terrifically insightful metric about the effectiveness of your fraud detection system. A pro knows it will lose its credibility if the underlying sources are suspect. Perhaps you possess statistics that show why antivirus systems aren't working well. A pro knows they will only spur corrective action if the numbers are presented in a manner that aligns with the executive team's frame of reference—and their incentives. Or suppose you have printed scores of factoids on stacks of paper. A pro understands that senior managers who are deluged with data have one more foolproof reason to throw their hands up and not decide something.

Understanding not just what to do, but how to do it, is what separates the professionals from the punters. Caroline's book, *Security Metrics: A Beginner's Guide,* takes on such challenging and necessary endeavors as project management, prioritizing efforts, obtaining stakeholder buy-in, communicating with management—and oh, a trunkful of actual security stuff too. Succeeding at these tasks is important in any initiative that results in enterprise change. But information security is a special case, precisely because of the yin, yang, interruptions, and silences that make security more emotional and less rational than most other areas of IT. That's why we need to know *how. This book gives you the foundation you need to move from punter to pro status and understand what's needed to set up a security metrics program of your own.*

Earlier this year, Caroline asked me to serve as a guest panelist for a session she led at the annual RSA Security Conference in San Francisco, called "Security Metrics: A Beginner's Guide." The evening before the session, the panel spent time brainstorming zany, pithy, and funny elevator pitches to summarize and advertise the panel's objectives. After an extended, logical, reasoned debate, and a few beers, the group agreed that the objective could be reduced down to a simple imperative: "get your ass off of the couch."

Knowing the best ways to understand and measure your information security program is a good thing. Good enough, even, to get you to lean forward on the couch. Knowing how to do these things does more, though. It gets your keister off of it.

May Caroline's book interrupt your silence and propel you off of your own couch.

~Andrew
Andrew Jaquith
Chief Technology Officer, Perimeter E-Security
Boston, April 2011

Acknowledgments

This book was created by a team of amazing people. Big hugs and much gratitude go to

- Betsy and Lynn for their expert contributions
- Jim, Tara, and Betsy for their thoughtful review and feedback
- Megg, Amy, Joya, LeeAnn, and Jane for their faith, leadership, and patience
- My family and friends for their love, support, and encouragement
- Andy Jaquith and Dan Geer for leading the way

Introduction

Security is hard to measure. With limited resources and budgets and an endless list of problems to solve, as security practitioners we need the visibility of security metrics to enable better decision-making and drive change throughout our organizations.

A few years ago when I began to build a security metrics program at eBay, I did what any enterprise practitioner would do. I searched for industry case studies and playbooks to learn from those who had done this before me. I found many great ideas and concepts but fewer "how-to" manuals.

This book is the one I wish I had come across at that time. It's intended to be extremely practical, so you can read it and immediately begin implementing a security metrics program. This book doesn't have a top-ten list of security metrics that will apply to every security organization in every situation; it's intended to be a guide to help you ask the right questions to design the right approach for what you need.

About the Book

This book is written in the order of the steps you should take when building your own security metrics program. My recommendation is to read the book straight through, and then go back and refer to specific chapters as you are working on a particular piece. The next sections give you a chapter-by-chapter overview of what you'll learn from this book.

Part I, "Why Security Metrics?"

Chapter 1, "Why Measure Security?"

The purpose of an information security program is to protect information and information systems from unauthorized access, use, disclosure, modification, or destruction. Chapter 1 looks at the three benefits of measuring security: measurement provides visibility, educates and provides a common language for understanding the information security program, and improves the information security program by enabling investment planning and decision making and driving organizational change. I also look at the inherent challenges of creating a security metrics program.

Chapter 2, "Why Security Metrics Are Needed Now"

Today's constantly changing technology and threat landscape means organizational assets must often be protected outside of traditional organizational boundaries. This chapter examines today's cybercriminals and their motivation, as well as how security work is currently performed. The chapter also looks at the value of security practices and controls and standards frameworks.

Part II, "Essential Components of an Effective Security Metrics Practitioner"

Chapter 3, "Analytics"

Chapter 3 delves into the nuts and bolts of analytics, beginning with a definition of analytics and moving on to interpretation and the tools you can use to generate analytics for your security metrics program. Finally, this chapter explores some examples of analytics and how their interpretation enriches metrics.

Chapter 4, "Commitment to Project Management"

This chapter reviews a specific project management methodology and framework. Using a project management methodology that incorporates specific objectives, problem and solution statements, roles and responsibilities, success criteria and metrics, and resource allocations allows you to get the most value from limited resources for an information security program.

Part III, "Decide What to Measure"

Chapter 5, "Identify Core Competencies, Information Security Work, and Resourcing Options"

Chapter 5 examines information security core competencies and the analysis of core competencies for security metrics. This chapter discusses what a security metrics program should measure and for what purpose. I also look at the various resourcing options available.

Chapter 6, "Identify Targets"

In this chapter, I discuss the very first step to starting any security metrics initiative or project: selecting a target for measurement, analysis, and reporting. This chapter looks at the various approaches that will guide you in identifying these targets. No specific set of metrics will fit every situation, so here I focus on the general categories of questions you can use to determine targets.

Part IV, "Get Started"

Chapter 7, "Define Project Objectives"

Chapter 7 reviews the benefits of a security metrics program and what it means to have an objective tied to a metrics project. This chapter discusses how to define your objectives clearly and focuses on practical tips for succeeding in a metrics project once a goal has been defined.

Chapter 8, "Define Your Priorities"

Chapter 8 focuses on the importance of prioritizing your security metrics projects. Prioritizing is necessary to focus limited resources on the most critical activities. I discuss key factors to consider when prioritizing your metrics projects and techniques for prioritizing.

Chapter 9, "Identify Key Messages and Key Audiences"

Chapter 9 shows you how to identify key messages for key audiences. Stakeholder engagement is critical to the success of any security metrics project. This chapter includes advice for determining what you will say, who you will say it to, what security metrics you will present, and what issues you'll discuss.

Chapter 10, "Obtain Buy-In from Stakeholders"

Now that you know what you want to say and who you want to say it to, this chapter will help you prepare for meeting with stakeholders by exploring why buy-in is needed for the success of your security metrics project. This chapter then walks you through a step-by-step process for effectively obtaining buy-in for security metrics projects.

Part V, "Toolkit"

Chapter 11, "Automation"

This chapter reviews the benefits of automating a metrics program. This discussion is followed by a general workflow for metrics automation and the functions that typically comprise a metrics automation workflow.

Chapter 12, "Analysis Technologies and a Case Study"

Chapter 12 covers analysis technologies that can be used to automate each functional area in an automated metrics program. This chapter examines the advantages and disadvantages of each option. In particular, the chapters looks at the strengths and weaknesses of security metrics programs implemented with spreadsheets, homegrown systems, and a purpose-built commercially available metrics cloud service.

Part VI, "Creating the Best Environment for Healthy Metrics"

Chapter 13, "Define a Communications Strategy"

Chapter 13 explores techniques for communicating the importance of a security metrics program more effectively. I offer tips on how to tailor your message to specific audiences, using multiple communication formats.

Chapter 14, "Drive an Action Plan: The Importance of Project Management"

This chapter focuses on project management and the project manager. The best project managers are detail oriented and able to grasp dependencies. They know how to manage change. This chapter looks at the role of the project manager in shepherding a security metrics project through to completion.

Part VII, "Secret Sauce: Lessons Learned from an Enterprise Practitioner"

Chapter 15, "Improving Data Quality and Presentation"
Chapter 15 is about creating useful data out of useless data. Unfortunately, most security metrics reported by raw data generators "out of the box" are not helpful. Better data quality requires cleansing the data that you've already got, including removing false positives and repeats. The best data comes from clean and simple processes that are clearly defined and well understood by the people implementing the processes. This chapter discusses the effort required to obtain "clean" data.

Chapter 16, "Resourcing and Security Metrics Projects"
Getting people to do security work is not always easy. This chapter focuses on how to alleviate this problem. I look at options for resourcing security metrics projects and how you can use metrics to justify more resources for your projects.

Part VIII, "Looking Forward"

Chapter 17, "Security Metrics for Cloud Computing"
Chapter 17 begins with a definition of cloud computing and the common business drivers that are motivating organizations to move to the cloud. This chapter then looks at common security metrics in the context of cloud computing and finishes with a discussion of major cloud industry groups, especially the Cloud Security Alliance, and the efforts to describe cloud controls and related metrics.

Part IX, "Appendix and Glossary"
The Appendix is a summary of some of the key points covered in various chapters along with important tables and a template, so you don't have to take notes as you work through each chapter. The glossary defines many of the terms used throughout the book.

About the Series
I worked with the publisher to develop several special editorial elements for this series, which I hope you'll find helpful while navigating the book—and furthering your career.

Lingo

The Lingo boxes are designed to help you familiarize yourself with common security terminology so that you're never held back by an unfamiliar word or expression.

IMHO (In My Humble Opinion)

When you come across an IMHO, you'll be reading my frank, personal opinion based on experiences in the security industry.

Budget Note

The Budget Notes are designed to help increase your ease while discussing security budget needs within your organization, and to provide tips and ideas for initiating successful, informed conversations about budgets.

In Actual Practice

Theory might teach us smart tactics for business, but there are in-the-trenches exceptions to every rule. The In Actual Practice feature highlights how things actually get done in the real world at times—exceptions to the rules—and why.

Your Plan

The Your Plan feature offers strategic ideas that can be helpful to review as you get into planning mode, as you refine a plan outline, and are embarking on a final course of action.

Into Action

The Into Action lists are get-going tips to support you in taking action on the job. These lists contain steps, tips, and ideas to help you plan, prioritize, and work as effectively as possible.

I hope that this book gives you the tools you need to create and manage a security metrics program. I hope that your security metrics program gives you control in a world of chaos and brings you and your team success in your information security professional endeavors.

PART I

Why Security Metrics?

CHAPTER 1

Why Measure Security?

We'll Cover

● The purpose of an information security program

● The three benefits of a security metrics program

● The inherent challenges of creating a security metrics program

This chapter begins with a discussion of the purpose of an information security program and reviews different ways to think about that purpose. Determining the purpose of an information security program can be facilitated by defining a mission statement and a charter for that program, by evaluating the functional components of an information security program, and by analyzing a predictive security model to determine how the functional components should work together. The three primary benefits of measuring security (visibility, education, and improvement) are described and discussed. The most important benefit of measuring security—improvement—is discussed in further detail, highlighting the three key ways in which measurement improves an information security program (enables better management of the program, supports investment planning and decision making, and drives organizational change). Finally, the inherent challenges of creating a security metrics program, a key component of any information security program, are discussed and addressed.

Purpose of an Information Security Program

Before I discuss in detail the specific benefits of introducing metrics into an information security program, I'll explain the purpose of an information security program as well as a few different ways to determine the purpose of such a program. To best understand the point of security metrics, you must first understand the point of information security.

LINGO
Throughout this book, I use the term **information security** for what may otherwise be called *data security, computer security,* or *IT security.*

The purpose of an information security program is to protect information and information systems from unauthorized access, use, disclosure, modification, or destruction. Specifically, the three key components of information to protect are its *confidentiality, integrity,* and *availability*:

● *Confidentiality* refers to the prevention of disclosure of information to unauthorized parties.

- *Integrity* refers to the prevention of data modification by unauthorized parties.
- *Availability* means that information must be available when it is needed by authorized parties.

Protecting these three components has been a core principle of the information security field for over 20 years.

Today, authorized parties, which can also be thought of as information protectors, include governments, corporations, financial institutions, hospitals, academic institutions, and others. These organizations collect, process, and store information electronically.

Unauthorized parties, also referred to as *attackers,* can also be thought of as information stealers or information abusers. Information security professionals work to protect information and systems from attackers, and must constantly be on guard for new and evolving threats while also preserving usability. Confidentiality, integrity, and availability are the key values protected by an information security program.

Define a Mission Statement and a Charter for the Information Security Program

One very useful way to analyze the purpose of an information security program is to go through the exercise of defining a mission statement and a charter. To give you an example from another security field, the mission statement of the U.S. Department of Homeland Security Strategic Plan (Fiscal Years 2008–2013) states, "We will lead the unified national effort to secure America. We will prevent and deter terrorist attacks and protect against and respond to threats and hazards to the Nation. We will secure our national borders while welcoming lawful immigrants, visitors, and trade." The charter is also referenced in this DHS Strategic Plan: "While the Department was created to secure our country against those who seek to disrupt the American way of life, our charter also includes preparation for and response to all hazards and disasters."

> **LINGO**
> A **mission statement** outlines an information security program's overall goals and provides guidelines for its strategic direction. A **charter** for an information security program describes the specific rights and privileges granted from the organization to the information security team.

Both the mission statement and the charter guide an organization and can be used to resolve conflict when issues arise between teams with similar or shared roles and responsibilities. For an information security program, these documents may do the following:

- Describe how the information security program relates to and supports the success of the business or organization.

- Describe how the information security program relates to, provides for, and supports key stakeholders in the business or organization, such as customers.

- Define what the information security program provides for key stakeholders such as customers. This may include education and providing for the security needs of key stakeholders.

- Define areas of leadership for the information security program.

- Define the scope of the information security program.

- Address the relationship between the information security program and its intent to respond to constantly evolving unauthorized uses, attackers, and information stealers.

- Define the role of the information security program in managing crises and ensuring critical business operations.

- Define the primary capabilities of the information security program, including incident response, investigations, and intelligence, and how they will be used to defend against unauthorized users, attackers, and information stealers.

- Describe how the information security program will support the business or organization as it changes and grows.

- Describe the impact of the information security program on the company's or organization's culture and mindset.

- Describe the services provided to stakeholders by the information security program.

- Describe the relationship and collaboration between the information security program and stakeholders external to the organization. These stakeholders may include government agencies, industry partners, research communities, and academia. This description may also include any necessary compliance with local, national, and international regulations.

- Describe (at a high level) how the information security program utilizes technologies and practices to accomplish the goals of the program.

IMHO

If your organization has not already done so, I highly recommend writing a mission statement and a charter for your information security program. If your team already has these documents, it is worthwhile to review them annually. This will ensure that as the business and the organization you operate within changes, your team remains relevant, valuable, and properly aligned. A mission statement is very different from quarterly or even annual goals for an organization. Both the mission statement and the charter will remain the same for years, outlast changes on the team, and keep everyone on the same page and marching toward the same goal in their work.

Evaluate the Components of an Information Security Program

Understanding the purpose of an information security program requires that you review and understand each of the different functional components of the program. These are also considered the roles and responsibilities of the program. An information security program consists of several different functional components. These functional components operate in conjunction with one another and depend on each other for critical information needed to keep the whole program running smoothly.

Incident Response

The incident response functional component develops the incident response process and runs it in the event of a security incident.

Compliance and Audit

The compliance functional component ensures that the organization acts and behaves in compliance with any regulatory requirements as well as information security policy. The audit functional component evaluates controls specified in the regulatory requirements and information security policy to assess compliance.

Testing and Monitoring

The testing and monitoring functional component evaluates information systems and technologies for confidentiality, integrity, availability, proper authentication and authorization, and nonrepudiation. This may be done using scanning technologies on the network and application, or via penetration testing or other means. It also includes vendor security assessments.

Information Risk Management

The information risk management functional component is responsible for identifying, assessing, and prioritizing risks related to information security as well as coordinating the activities required to minimize and manage the risks.

Information Security Architecture

The information security architecture functional component is responsible for ensuring secure design of an organization's products and information systems. This functional component must be aligned with the overall business goals and needs so that it can incorporate security into the design at the beginning of the design process.

Business Continuity and Disaster Recovery

The business continuity functional component is responsible for ensuring that critical business functional components will be available as needed. Disaster recovery is a related functional component that is responsible for ensuring that critical applications and infrastructure can recover in a timely manner following a disastrous event.

Information Training and Communication

The information training and communication functional component is responsible for ensuring appropriate awareness and education throughout the organization, in particular for key stakeholders and sponsors. This may include customers.

Information Security Policies and Standards

The information security policies and standards functional component is responsible for writing and distributing information security policies and standards to inform and guide key stakeholders (employees, customers, and so forth) on secure behaviors and practices.

Physical Security

The physical security functional component is responsible for managing physical access control systems and security systems, including surveillance and burglar alarm systems. Guards maintain safety of employees and physical property. This functional component may also provide executive protection consulting services to top management and key staff members.

Personnel Security

The personnel security functional component is responsible for managing overall company and organizational policies, including a code of conduct and a disciplinary process with penalties for employees who are not in compliance with internal policies and standards.

This team also screens prospective workers (by conducting background checks, for example) to ensure they will be suitable employees.

ISO/IEC 27001 Standard Domains

The set of functional components described in the previous section comprises only one such possible set for an information security program. ISO/IEC 27001 provides a standardized view of these functional components, including Human Resources Security, Physical and Environmental Security, Communication and Operational Management, Access Control, Systems Development and Maintenance, Information Security and Incident Management, Business Continuity Planning, and Compliance.

ISO/IEC recommends a Plan-Do-Check-Act cycle for continuous improvement. In the Plan phase, you determine what to do and how to do it. In the Do phase, you execute the plan. The Check phase involves validating that everything went according to plan, and the Act phase is where plans are improved to achieve better results next time. Metrics help to strengthen and formalize this process framework and can be incorporated at each step of the process. Metrics should be defined in the Plan phase, collected in the Do phase, validated in the Check phase, and used to drive innovation and improvement during the Act phase.

Review the Predictive Security Model

The predictive security model describes the role that security metrics play within an information security program and how this role relates to the other functional areas.

The predictive security model is one way of looking at the interaction among different components of an information security program. It is called "predictive" because, when done correctly, the functional components will work together in a continuous feedback loop to show where the data is gathered and how it can be integrated back into the process to evolve the design of the overall security program, producing the most effective outcomes based on an organization's security needs. The predictive security model is shown in Figure 1-1.

The predictive security model framework can be broken down into three stages, starting with information gathering functional components on the left, which feed information reporting and processing functional components in the middle, which impact information security outcomes on the right. The following sections walk through the flow of information between components and describe how all the different functional components work together.

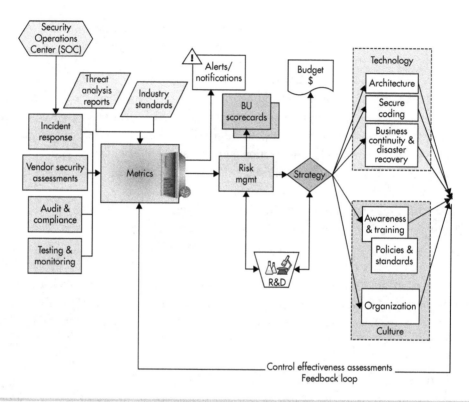

Figure 1-1   Predictive security model

In Actual Practice

These functional components may be, but are not necessarily, reflected in the actual organizational structure in terms of subteams within the information security team. Often, related functional components are combined within a subteam. Some functional components may be heavily staffed and others may not. Some functional components may be outsourced or offshored. Organizational structure must be determined by the chief information security officer (CISO) based on an organization's specific business model, security needs, and level of investment.

Information Gathering

The predictive security model starts on the left side with the components of an information security program that perform information gathering, as shown in Figure 1-2. This includes the testing and monitoring functional component, which continually evaluates information systems for security vulnerabilities and risks. Activities performed as part of this functional component may include vulnerability scans at the application and network layers, penetration testing of high risk applications, and other testing and monitoring activities. It also includes reactive information gathering, which occurs as part of the incident response functional component.

Tip

An important part of information gathering is to develop baselines so that you understand what type of behavior is typical (for comparison to behavior that is not typical, which can be used in alerting and kicking off an incident response process).

In Figure 1-2, you can see that the Security Operations Center (SOC) feeds the incident response process with alerts based on first-line-of-defense monitoring. Technology may be deployed and team members may monitor feeds to look out for any unusual behavior that might kick off the incident response process. During a security incident, the information

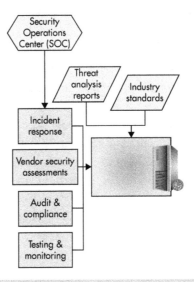

Figure 1-2   Information gathering stage

security team members involved in the incident response process are responsible for finding out what happened, containing and remediating the issue at hand, and conducting postmortems to address any fundamental issues that may have allowed the incident to occur. Information discovered in this process should be shared with other functional components in the information security team to prevent similar incidents from happening in the future.

IMHO

Sometimes difficult decisions are required in response situations. One example is the decision of whether to recover and, by doing so, destroy forensic evidence (to support ongoing operations) or to preserve evidence for forensic analysis (but delay ongoing operations). These decisions must be made based on each individual situation. Saving data for metrics may or may not be the right decision, depending on the business criticality of a system. Remember that although this is a book about security metrics, and security metrics are important, security metrics exist to serve security programs, and security programs exist to serve the business.

Another information gathering functional component is vendor security assessments. This testing functional component involves the evaluation of vendors and other partners outside of the direct organization who may be storing, processing, or transferring sensitive or confidential employee or customer data. This information can be used by the information security team in a proactive manner to clean up security issues before connecting and starting projects with higher-risk vendor partners to ensure that information is being protected properly even outside of the direct organization. This functional component is particularly important in this age of increased outsourcing and offshoring of business functional components and will continue to grow in importance with the move toward cloud computing.

The audit and compliance functional component is a big part of information gathering. Here, formal testing of security controls takes place to evaluate or confirm their effectiveness. Testing and documenting the results of testing for security controls will be useful for determining where investments should be made to affect information security outcomes.

Threat analysis reporting and other intelligence reporting is also a part of information gathering. These reports may be available to an information security team from a specialized vendor, or as a subscription to online resources and feeds. Intelligence reporting enables an information security team to understand what threats are current and relevant on a global level.

The final component to information gathering is to refer to industry standards. Industry standards are continually being published and revised and are used by an information security team to ensure a comprehensive approach to running the information security program.

Information Reporting and Processing

The information reporting and processing stage of the predictive security model, shown in Figure 1-3, is where the management of the overall program and decision making happens. Security metrics play a huge role here, particularly in quantifying the results of the information gathering functional components. This information is then passed on to the risk management functional component, which filters the information discovered in the information gathering stage to match the organization's risk tolerance. This leads to information security strategy, where prioritization of issues and projects takes place. The information reporting and processing stage is also where budget justifications are made, and where budget decisions in terms of areas of investment are weighed against one another and made.

Research and development is an area of information security that differs from the other areas in that there may not necessarily be as many well-defined outcomes. Research and development receives ideas and high-level requirements from the risk management and strategy functional components, and this is how an organization determines what areas to look into. Research and development also transmits information to the strategic

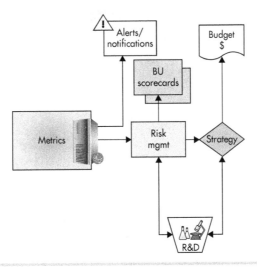

Figure 1-3 Information reporting and processing stage

and risk management functional components in the areas that have been looked into. Staying aware of newly developed technologies and approaches to information security keeps the information security program ahead of the game and can help to make the most out of limited resources, especially if there's a new way to do something differently that is more effective than the way it has been done in the past.

Information Security Outcomes

The information security outcomes stage, shown in Figure 1-4, is where the information gathered, processed, and reported is taken and used to create results throughout the organization to promote secure behaviors that ensure the information security assets of the organization are properly protected. Information security outcomes take place in two major areas: culture and technology.

Culture   The information security team has many different ways to impact an organization's security culture. This includes developing and publishing information security policies and standards so that employees and customers have requirements to guide them as they go about their day-to-day business.

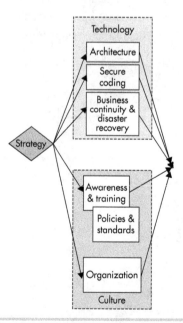

\formation security outcomes stage

In Actual Practice

Any information security program has the ability to influence the culture of the organization, no matter where the information security team is located on the company organizational chart. This can be achieved via an effective security metrics and communications program, which is discussed further in Chapter 9.

Providing training to employees to teach them what they need to know about information security will also affect the company culture. This training can be done for specific roles that may need to know greater detail about their information security–related responsibilities (developers need to know about secure coding practices, system administrators need to know about patching and secure builds, and so forth), or for all employees to educate them on topics such as phishing and social engineering.

Finally, how information security is structured within an organization and how it relates to other business functional components or management organizationally will play a role in its impact on culture. An information security program may be more effective if it's located higher up on the food chain and has the ability to influence the culture and the decisions of upper and executive management than if it is buried within a specific information technology or operations organization.

Technology   The complement to information security culture is information security built right into an organization's technology. This is where the information gathered, processed, and reported can be built into the processes that create the organization's product and incorporated into the organization's work.

Developers who create code for the organization's website (internal for employees or external for customers) will produce better and more secure code if they are provided information security training on secure coding practices. Architects who design the organization's products and consult with experts on the information security team will be aware of existing and potential vulnerabilities that may occur depending on how they design the product. If the information security program is involved early in the design and development cycle, a bigger impact can be made to influence the products and systems used and created by the organization.

Business Continuity and Disaster Recovery   Finally, the business continuity and disaster recovery functional components ensure that in the case of an event, business continues to run and critical applications and processes are available as much as they need to be.

The predictive security model is a continuous cycle, and all of the components are always running. As explained in the "Information Processing and Reporting" section, security metrics are critical for information security management to be able to make the best decisions for achieving the best outcomes and ultimately to create and maintain the most effective information security program possible.

Benefits of a Security Metrics Program

Why spend the time, money, and resources on a security metrics program anyway? This section will review the benefits of such a program.

A Lesson for Security Metrics from the Traffic Safety Industry

Starting and maintaining an security metrics program provides three main benefits—visibility, education, and improvement. These benefits can be derived from using metrics not only in the information security industry, but in any industry. Figure 1-5, an example from the traffic safety industry, illustrates the impact of metrics that can be used to help promote seatbelt usage, thereby saving lives.

In 1908, the affordability of Henry Ford's Model T opened car travel to middle-class Americans. That is the year in which automobiles became popular in the United States.

Country	Seatbelt Usage	Traffic Fatality Rates
United States	75%	15 per 100,000
Great Britain	90%	6 per 100,000
Germany	90%	9 per 100,000

5   Traffic safety industry metrics (Source: Centers for Disease Control and Prevention nal Highway Traffic Safety Administration)

In his 1922 autobiography *My Life and Work,* Ford recalled saying the following about his game-changing vehicle:

> I will build a car for the great multitude. It will be large enough for the family, but small enough for the individual to run and care for. It will be constructed of the best materials, by the best men to be hired, after the simplest designs that modern engineering can devise. But it will be so low in price that no man making a good salary will be unable to own one—and enjoy with his family the blessing of hours of pleasure in God's great open spaces.[1]

When cars first became popular, few people worried about automobile safety. Consumers were so excited about being able to travel and the dramatic improvements and changes it made in their lifestyles that safety concerns were an afterthought. In the late 1960s, a few experts recognized the safety issues and pushed for consumer awareness and government legislation. These efforts paid off. Over time, seatbelts have become so culturally embedded that, for most people, putting on a seatbelt is now practically a reflex. The use of metrics to encourage the use of seatbelts was key to achieving this objective, as described next.

Seatbelts originally were not intended as a means of providing safety in an emergency accident scenario. Rather, they were built into automobiles and airplanes for the purpose of keeping the passenger inside the vehicle. The automobile industry in the 1960s did not want to focus much attention on seatbelts because they did not want the public to fear driving. Traffic-related government funding was invested mostly in studying disposal of scrapped cars, and only a very small percentage was dedicated to highway safety.

In Actual Practice

Have you ever experienced a situation where a proposed awareness and training campaign highlighting information security risks to customers has been turned down due to concern that customers will be scared to use a product or will associate the product with security issues? (This is a situation that many information security professionals may relate to.) Information security metrics can, in fact, help rather than hinder in this type of situation, as will be further discussed in this section regarding the benefit of education. Security metrics provide a common language for key stakeholders and sponsors, which, in turn, provides for better information security awareness and education throughout an organization.

Collecting, tracking, and reporting metrics, as well as communicating them properly to key stakeholders and sponsors, changed the opinion of both the public and the government about traffic safety. In 1966, the Highway Safety Act and the National Traffic and Motor Vehicle Safety Act were passed, creating the National Highway Safety Bureau (the present-day National Highway Traffic Safety Administration, or NHTSA) and mandating seatbelt installation. Metrics enabled improvement in the areas of traffic safety funding and driver behavior. Here are a few metrics published by the National Highway Traffic Safety Administration that were key to developing this important legislation:

- Seatbelts reduce a person's chances of dying in a crash by 45 percent (NHTSA).

- Seatbelts reduce a person's chances of being injured in a crash by 50 percent (NHTSA).

- Seatbelts prevent total ejections from a car during a crash; 75 percent of occupants who are totally ejected during a crash are killed (NHTSA).

- The odds of serious injury for people not wearing seatbelts are four to five times greater than for people who are belted (various independent studies).

- The average inpatient charge for an unbelted driver is over 60 percent greater than the charge for a belted driver.

Here is a metric that shows the impact of the legislation which followed: Between 1975 and 2000, seatbelts saved over 135,000 lives; if all vehicle occupants had used seatbelts, over 9,000 additional lives could have been saved in 2000 alone (NHTSA).

However, even after installation of seatbelts in all vehicles was mandated, not all people were using them. Misinformation about the risks of wearing seatbelts was more widely available than studies promoting seatbelt use, and people believed that seatbelts would prevent passengers from escaping a vehicle in water or fire, or even that it would be safer to be ejected from a vehicle in the event of a crash. In response, between 1985 and 1995, mandatory seatbelt use laws were enacted in many states. Metrics show clearly that increased seatbelt use has decreased traffic fatalities over the years (see Figure 1-6).

Note

The numbers in Figure 1-6 also show that mandating *availability* of seatbelts was not enough. Mandating the *use* of seatbelts was required to actually decrease traffic fatalities. Keep this in mind when designing information security metrics, to ensure that the metrics actually accomplish what you intend. Of course, mandating use also requires appropriate enforcement.

	1981	**1997**
USA seatbelt use*	11%	68%
Motor vehicle fatality rate**	21.49 per 100k population	15.69 per 100k population
Motor vehicle fatality rate**	3.2 per 100M vehicle miles	1.6 per 100M vehicle miles

* Centers for Disease Control and Prevention
** NHTSA

Figure 1-6   Fatality rates and seatbelt use (Source: Centers for Disease Control and Prevention and National Highway Traffic Safety Administration)

Under the Clinton administration, the "Presidential Initiative for Increasing Seat Belt Use Nationwide" set goals of 85 percent usage by 2000 and 90 percent usage by 2005. This is a great example of defining objectives and goals for use in tracking a metric, which will be further discussed in Chapter 7.

Measurement Provides Visibility

One major advantage of deploying a security metrics program is that it provides visibility into the information security program. The first step to improving the outcomes of an information security program is obtaining visibility. Sometimes it makes sense to use metrics to gain insight into the current state of the information security program even before its objectives and goals are defined.

Measurement Educates and Provides a Common Language

Another huge benefit of measuring security is that it establishes a *lexicon,* or common language and set of terms, that can be understood throughout an organization, beyond just the information security team. Without an information security lexicon and communications strategy, many employees of a company or members of an organization might not even be aware that the information security team is protecting the company's or organization's information assets from malicious attacks.

IMHO

An effective information security program must inform and educate many key stakeholders outside of the direct information security team. It is the responsibility of the CISO and the information security team to be the experts and inform others as necessary. These stakeholders do not need to know every little detail of what is taking place security-wise in an organization, but they do need to know some things. A good security metrics program will highlight key information for various folks in the organization and tell them what they need to know and do with regard to information security.

Measurement Enables Improvement

The purpose of security metrics and measuring items related to information security is to improve the maturity and effectiveness of the overall information security program. The first step to starting security metrics and improving the information security program is to identify a target (or a few targets) for improvement. Security metrics may be used to fix a security process that is broken, to focus limited resources on protecting the most valuable assets, or to ensure that basic security processes are in place and working well.

Process optimization, a common objective in security metrics, involves taking steps to adjust a process in order to maximize or minimize a particular outcome. To achieve a desired outcome, it first must be defined. The use of the terms "maximize" and "minimize" indicates that something must be measured, and that there is a desired general direction that is different from the initial starting point, or baseline. Measurement must initially take place to determine the baseline, the current status of the item being measured. Measurements must then occur periodically to compare the current status of the item to its baseline status. These recurring measurements may take place weekly, monthly, quarterly, or annually. At the time of each measurement, the current measurement is compared to the baseline and also compared to the desired outcome. Discussions take place between key stakeholders to review progress and generate new ideas for closing the gap between the current measurement and the desired outcome.

Note

Process optimization in the context of information security differs from process optimization in other areas, such as chemical engineering or equipment optimization, in that a security metrics program may not necessarily seek to completely maximize or minimize a particular parameter. Completely maximizing or minimizing a particular security-related item may require too much money or too many resources (often both), and in the end the work effort required may not be worth it. Because of the reality of limited resources, achieving perfection in one area is usually accompanied by not dedicating enough resources to another area. Information security covers a broad range of functional components and responsibilities, and balancing and prioritizing work efforts is a must.

Because information security is by nature an area that deals with uncertainty, a *risk tolerance* must be defined. Risk tolerance refers to how much risk an organization is willing to take on and accept as part of its business model. A more risk-tolerant organization is willing to accept more risk, whereas a more risk-averse organization is willing to accept less risk. Defining a risk tolerance is not a clear-cut exercise. Trade-offs exist for any level of risk tolerance and may include greater or lower investment for a greater or lower risk, resulting in a greater or lower reward.

An organization's risk tolerance will influence the desired outcomes, goals, and objectives that are appropriate for the organization's overall approach to information security. In developing a security metrics program, it is very important to know and

In Actual Practice

Defining an organization's risk tolerance is not solely the responsibility of the information security team. More often, the information security program is a consumer of the information about an organization's risk tolerance. The risk tolerance may be defined by a chief risk officer, if there is one, or by a chief financial officer or another executive responsible for managing the organization's overall financial assets and risk. It is important for a CISO to find out who in the organization defines the risk tolerance, and to set up proper communication channels with the person responsible. In the case where a risk tolerance definition does not exist, the CISO may be able to start these conversations by presenting information security–related risk issues and expertise for an appropriate role to evaluate and make a determination.

understand the company's risk tolerance. This will guide decisions regarding the amount of resources to invest in information security as well as the level of perfection and optimization to be targeted and achieved by the security metrics program. Some level of fraud and loss due to unauthorized use may be acceptable. It is to the advantage of an information security program to understand and appreciate an organization's risk tolerance so that it can align with the organization's overall objectives and provide value in line with the overall business plan.

Measurement is simply the scientific process that involves obtaining size, length, rate, and the quantity of a particular item. Measurement in of itself is not particularly useful; however, if measurements are used properly in the context of well-defined targets for improvement, well-defined outcomes, and well-defined timelines, and are communicated effectively to sponsors and stakeholders, they can add tremendous value to an information security program.

The overall objective of security metrics is to track and assess metrics to ensure that the information security program is effectively meeting the security needs of the organization and managing risk. Both business strategies and information security risks are constantly changing, and security metrics enable an information security program to evolve and stay ahead of the game.

Components that support this overall objective fall into three major categories:

- Management of the information security program
- Justification for investment in the information security program
- Driving change in the organization

Management of the Information Security Program

Organizations struggle to make cost-effective security investment decisions; information security professionals lack widely accepted and unambiguous metrics for decision support.[2]

—Center for Internet Security

A security metrics program provides the information security team with information for better decision making at both strategic and operational levels. An effective program should influence the strategy such that decisions informed by the data from the security metrics program are different from what they would be without the data. Operationally, an effective program guides day-to-day decision making and optimizes the performance of existing technologies and processes.

Budget Note

What's the difference between the terms cost-effective and cost-benefit? Cost-benefit implies that for a given decision, one particular option has both a cost and a benefit. The decision of whether to choose the option is made after analyzing whether its benefit outweighs its cost. If so, the option is chosen. Otherwise, it is not (perhaps in favor of another option). In comparison, cost-effective, according to Merriam-Webster, means economical in terms of tangible benefits produced by money spent. We talk often in information security about cost-benefit analysis, but the most accurate representation of the situation we commonly find ourselves in is how to be as cost-effective as possible.

IMHO

An ineffective security metrics program can be identified by looking to see if the management team acts any differently based on having the metrics data. If security metrics data is consistently ignored or not taken into consideration, then the team may want to reconsider what data is being collected and tracked.

Security metrics that show the level of maturity in different areas of an information security program are used to prioritize initiatives and drive strategic roadmaps and the associated resourcing and budget. In information security, there is always more work to be done than there are people and dollars to do the work. There are also many different mitigating controls that can be implemented for any given risk, and information security leadership is responsible for choosing the controls that will be implemented and maintained. Security metrics are used for justification purposes when information security leaders are asked to make tough decisions and choose between implementing one control or another.

Not only are there many different mitigating controls to choose from when managing risk, but many information security professionals feel very strongly about which of the many mitigating controls to choose. Ultimately, many of these differences in opinion are subjective and based on different experiences in the past or differences in formal security training. For example, different approaches to identity management may utilize different technologies and methodologies when associating a user's identity to an account. Security metrics can be used to support a technology or methodology decision in an objective manner. In fact, experimentation and testing cannot be done without metrics.

Documenting the rationale for business decisions is easier to do when the decisions are informed by metrics. Decisions supported by metrics that are carefully designed in alignment with an information security team's objectives and priorities will "stick" and enable the team to drive change throughout the organization.

Justification for Investment in the Information Security Program

As in every line of business, every year the CISO, as head of the information security department, must make a case to upper management for funding of the information security program. Having an effective security metrics program in place can support this necessary endeavor. Security metrics can be used to show the changing maturity of an information security program over time. Metrics and reporting can also be used to display the results and outcomes of past investments, for use in determining future investments.

Driving Change in the Organization

Driving change in an organization is a key functional component of an information security program and is largely supported by security metrics. Reporting provides visibility of the quantity, severity, and importance of security issues to issue owners so they can perform remediation.

Using metrics to drive change has been shown to be effective in the area of auditing. Often, what is counted and tracked gets fixed. Organizations that must undergo annual audits such as Sarbanes Oxley (SOX) or the Payment Card Industry Data Security Standards (PCI DSS) will test a specific set of controls and track each issue until the issues are remediated. Change seems to happen very quickly when an external auditor points out a security issue, especially if there are penalties to the organization for noncompliance.

Even outside of regulatory compliance audits, security metrics support ownership and accountability for security issues by informing business unit owners of their security status. Reporting that occurs on a regular basis should be sent to business unit leaders, and the security team and the business unit leaders should communicate so that the business unit leaders understand the reports and know what they are responsible for doing to remediate security issues.

Sometimes it is a challenge for the information security team to drive change because the business unit responsible for remediation has not prioritized the information security–related "fix-it" type of work. Every business line will have its own specific issues to manage (information security related and otherwise) and priorities for each. In this case, security metrics reporting provided to the manager of the business unit leader can be effective, especially if the number of issues, severity of issues, importance of issues, and urgency of remediation are clearly communicated by the information security team. This particular situation is further addressed in Chapter 9.

Why Are Security Metrics So Hard to Do?

In security metrics, measurement may or may not be quantitative. Often, qualitative "measurements" are just as valuable, if not more, depending on what target has been defined for improvement and the definition of the desired outcome. For example, understanding that a particular company's or organization's culture is not particularly conducive to following rules and regulations (such as security policy) but that the culture does follow after the leadership of a few key individuals may be enormously useful in effectively conducting information security awareness initiatives. In some cases, quantitative data simply does not exist. In others, the gathering of completely accurate or completely comprehensive quantitative data may be impossible or not worth the work effort required. This can be discouraging at first, but do not let it prevent you from doing what needs to be done in order to build security metrics into your information security program. Just because something is hard to do does not mean you should not do it. This book and others are available to help you.

Information security is not, and may never be, an exact or hard science. Security measurements cannot be compared to measurements in the natural or physical sciences because of two continuously changing variables—technology and attackers. For example, as Moore's law describes, the number of transistors that can be put onto an integrated circuit doubles approximately every two years. Processes and technologies to store, transfer, and protect information and information systems grow and change accordingly. At the same time, hackers, fraudsters, and attackers are continuously updating and trying out new methodologies to steal information for unauthorized use.

Information security can be thought of as a war or a game between two competing entities: the "good guys," otherwise known as the information security team (as well as sponsors and stakeholders in an organization), and the "bad guys," otherwise known as hackers, fraudsters, attackers, information stealers, and information abusers. However, the "game" of information security is unlike any other. There are no rules and regulations governing the actions of the "bad guys," whereas the "good guys" are constrained by not only rules and regulations, but also corporate bureaucracy, schedules, and limited resources.

We've Covered

The purpose of an information security program

- The purpose of an information security program is to protect information and information systems from unauthorized access, use, disclosure, modification, or destruction.

The three benefits of an security metrics program

- Measurement provides visibility.

- Measurement educates and provides a common language for understanding the information security program.

- Measurement improves. It improves an information security program in three key ways: it enables the best possible management of the information security program, it enables investment planning and decision making, and it drives necessary change throughout the organization.

The inherent challenges of creating a security metrics program

- Information security is not, and may never be, an exact or hard science.

Endnotes

1. Security Benchmarks, CIS Consensus Security Metrics v1.1.0, November 2010, http://benchmarks.cisecurity.org/en-us/?route=downloads.show.single.metrics.110.

CHAPTER 2

Why Security Metrics Are Needed Now

We'll Cover

- Today's constantly changing technology and threat landscape
- Current profiles of hackers, fraudsters, and cybercriminals
- Recent breach information
- How security work is performed today
- The value of security best practices and controls and standards frameworks

This chapter discusses the importance of an effective security metrics program in today's constantly changing technology and threat landscape. It begins by reporting on the fast-changing evolution and sophistication of the threat and discussing the fact that security work is never finished. Next, the chapter discusses malware and attributes of today's malware that make it a particularly challenging threat. The implications of cloud computing for the information security professional are then addressed, followed by information about today's hackers, fraudsters, and cybercriminals and how the profile of an attacker has changed over time. I then report on recent breaches that compromised large numbers of records and caused large monetary losses, to show that the impact of security-related incidents is greater than ever.

The second half of the chapter analyzes how security work is performed today and discusses the value of security best practices and controls and standards frameworks. I discuss the value of best practices and standards frameworks as a starting point for an information security metrics program.

Security Work Is Never Finished: Technology Changes and Moore's Law

Since the total workload for information security professionals is proportional to the cumulative sum of all attack vectors yet invented, but the total work factor for the attack side is proportional to the cost of creating a new attack tool, the professionalization of the attack class punctures the existing security equilibrium by converting the security battlefield from a moderately symmetric one to a highly asymmetric one where the advantage is structurally more favorable to the attackers.[1]

—Daniel E. Geer, Jr., Sc. D., *Economics and Strategies of Data Security*

Managing information security is not like building a car, a house, or a website—it's a job that's never finished. It requires ongoing funding, continuous support, and constant evolution because the attacks never cease and are constantly evolving. Big factors in the world of security today include rapidly evolving technology change (consistent with Moore's law); a huge increase in malware, more sophisticated attackers and attacks; changing attack vectors; cloud computing and deperimeterization, meaning organizational assets must be protected outside of traditional boundaries, increasing the severity of incidents.

Technology is constantly changing as well, roughly at an exponential rate. This trend is known as Moore's law, named after Gordon E. Moore, who first described it in *Electronics Magazine* in an article titled "Cramming more components onto integrated circuits" (April 19, 1965). The article stated the following:

> The complexity for minimum component costs has increased at a rate of roughly a factor of two per year... Certainly over the short term this rate can be expected to continue, if not to increase. Over the longer term, the rate of increase is a bit more uncertain, although there is no reason to believe it will not remain nearly constant for at least 10 years. That means by 1975, the number of components per integrated circuit for minimum cost will be 65,000. I believe that such a large circuit can be built on a single wafer.[2]

Moore's predicted rate of exponential growth has proven to be fairly accurate since 1965 when applied to memory storage and processing power, so it is a good descriptor for the rate of technology change, especially over the past few decades. From mainframes to personal computers to iPhones, today's veteran information security professionals have seen dramatic changes in the technical landscape of how organizations and companies manage data. This rapid rate of change has resulted in amazing new technologies, but computer hackers, fraudsters, and cybercriminals have kept pace, with corresponding increasingly sophisticated threats and tools in their toolkits. This section presents a few statistics on the emerging threats from 2009.

Verizon Business 2009 Data Breach Investigations Report

Verizon "is a leading provider of global IT, security, and communication solutions for enterprises and government agencies around the world" and has "one of the world's most connected IP networks.... The Verizon Business RISK team is dedicated to informing Verizon Business clients and driving other security products and services through extensive risk intelligence operations" (www.verizonbusiness.com). In 2009, the RISK team published its *2009 Data Breach Investigations Report (DBIR)*, which included an analysis of 90 confirmed breaches in their 2008 caseload, encompassing 285 million compromised records. All results are based on firsthand evidence collected during data breach investigations conducted by Verizon Business from 2004 to 2008. The following is an excerpt from the 2009 report:

> One of the telltale findings from the previous DBIR was that more than half of breaches were caused by rather unsophisticated attacks. Within a few percentage points, our 2008 cases reveal a very similar statistic. The proportion of breaches requiring no special skills or resources (*None*) rose while low difficulty attacks fell to offset that gain. Attacks of moderate difficulty increased a few points and the percentage of highly difficult attacks remained the same. These subtle shifts are likely inconsequential and give little reason to believe that attack paradigms changed in 2008. On the whole, it would appear that criminals are still not required to work very hard to breach corporate information systems and 2008 was just a year like any other. Appearances, however, can be deceiving. While it may be true that the majority of breaches are not the result of highly skillful attacks, an alternate view of the data suggests that the really high-value targets require extensive effort. These relatively few highly difficult attacks compromised 95 percent of the 285 million records across our caseload—a truly stunning statistic and one that is part of a larger story.[3]

The latest report can be viewed online at http://www.verizonbusiness.com/resources/reports/rp_data-breachinvestigations-report-2011_en_xg.pdf.

Symantec Global Internet Security Threat Report

Founded in 1982 by "visionary computer scientists, Symantec Corporation provides security, storage, and systems management solutions to help individual consumers, small businesses, and large international organizations secure and manage their information." Symantec's research and analysis division, Symantec Security Response, "conducts ongoing, in-depth research and analysis of current trends impacting users on the Internet" and publishes an annual *Global Internet Security Threat Report* that is available to the public (www.symantec.com). This section highlights findings in the 2008 report (published April, 2009), which discusses a significant uptick in the amount of malicious code, attributed to an increase in the organization and professionalization of cybercriminals.

Note

Keep in mind that all trend analysis is data dependent. Continuous measurement in a consistent manner is required for reliable trend data.

From the 2009 report:

A significant spike in new malicious code threats occurred during 2008. Symantec created 1,656,227 new malicious code signatures during this time period. This is a 165 percent increase over 2007, when 624,267 new malicious code signatures were added. This means that of all the malicious code signatures created by Symantec, more than 60 percent of that total was created in 2008. The explosive growth can be attributed to the professionalism of malicious code development, supporting the demand for goods and services that facilitate online fraud.

Malicious code that exposes confidential information is a valued asset in the underground economy. Advertisements seeking malicious code authors are often looking for a one-time development of specific code to create new variants of existing threats, rather than developing entirely new threats.

Variants of existing malicious code can be developed more easily and can therefore be posted for sale on the underground market much more quickly. This is evidenced by the flourishing profitability of confidential information sales, as discussed further in the Symantec *Report on the Underground Economy, November 2008*.[4]

Figure 2-1 displays the number of new threats per year since 2002. A dramatic increase can be observed from 2006 to 2007 (a 345 percent increase, from 140,690 to 624,297) and from 2007 to 2008 (a 165 percent increase, from 624,267 to 1,656,227).

The latest report can be viewed online at http://www.symantec.com/business/threatreport/.

Ernst & Young's 12th Annual Global Information Security Survey

Ernst & Young (www.ey.com) is a global leader in assurance, tax, transaction, and advisory services. Their Technology and Security Risk Services division helps customers protect IT assets against external viruses, cyberterrorism, malicious attacks, and internal security threats; advises on software application controls integrity; improves IT processes; and addresses regulatory compliance on IT applications. They also conduct and publish an annual survey that looks at how organizations are addressing today's changing environment.

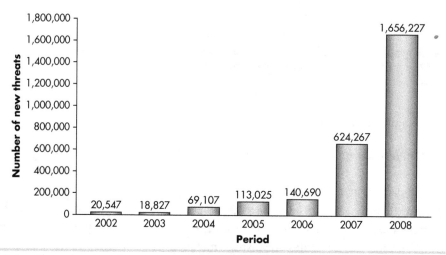

Figure 2-1   Chart showing the increase in the number of new threats from 2002 to 2008

E&Y's *12th Annual Global Information Security Survey*, published in November 2009, reports the following:

> [T]he current economic environment is fueling an increase in the number of threats organizations are facing. The increase is driven not only from external sources—our survey found that 41% of respondents noted an increase in external attacks—but also from within the organization: 25% of respondents witnessed an increase in internal attacks, and 13% reported an increase in internally perpetrated fraud.[5]

The latest survey can be viewed at http://www.ey.com/Publication/vwLUAssets/ Global_information_security_survey_2010_advisory/$FILE/GISS%20report_final.pdf.

More on the Increasing Sophistication of Attacks

This section takes a closer look at some of the elements of technology change in the landscape in which information security professionals operate today: malware and botnets.

Malware

Malware advancements have kept pace with the advancement of security tools and technologies. Just as security technology has matured in the areas of professional-grade management consoles and user interfaces, so, too, has malware creation, customization, and distribution software matured into a service economy. Protections such as administrative passwords and encryption for important communication channels are being leveraged by both the bad guys and the good guys. Malware creators use tools and subscription services from antivirus and other security software vendors to track and report on detection of the malware that they have created. They can use this information to manage their malware release schedules. Some high-end malware kits even come with 24×7 support from the sellers and money-back guarantees for malware caught by antivirus products.

The effectiveness of antivirus software against malware has diminished in recent years, due to a variety of factors, including the reliance on signature-based antivirus software, which simply cannot keep up with the speed at which new malware creators release their programs (which are written to evade detection by this type of software). Malware creators looking to stay ahead of the antivirus and security software curve will create many different variants of the malware, and release them in a timed fashion so that they stay one step ahead as antivirus vendors write and release signatures for the malware. The opposition is attacking not only the antivirus technology itself, but also the fundamental business model of the entire antivirus industry. This renders antivirus and other security software essentially defenseless against the malware variants, as even the most up-to-date antivirus software will not be able to detect or remove the malware variants.

New technologies and product vendors are continuing to pop up in the antimalware space, but at the time of writing, there do not seem to be any big breakthroughs in this area.

Commercial Build-It-Yourself Malware Kits

There is an extensive underground community in which cybercriminals collaborate and sell or exchange malware in their specialized areas of expertise. A type of product commonly hawked in this market is the build-it-yourself malware kit. The seller does not necessarily directly benefit financially from the results of executing the malware on a victim's machine, but typically makes money by selling the kit to other hackers and fraudsters. The hackers who purchase these kits use them to obtain user credentials and financial information, which they can then either use to benefit themselves or sell to other fraudsters. These kits are sold for hundreds of dollars at the low end and thousands of dollars for the most advanced versions. The high-end versions are highly customizable to suit different interests and motivations of hackers. This customization also contributes to the difficulty of identifying and removing the malware using traditional antivirus software.

Botnets

A malicious botnet is a network of compromised computers that is used to transmit information, send spam, or launch denial-of-service (DoS) attacks. Essentially, a botnet is a supercomputer created by and managed by a hacker, fraudster, or cybercriminal.

LINGO
Bot is short for "robot"; the term originally described a function to handle repetitive tasks. **Malicious botnets** are also known as *zombie armies*.

Note

There are also good botnets. A good botnet is a large number of individual machines voluntarily under the control of one user or organization. For example, SETI@home is a scientific experiment that uses Internet-connected computers in the search for extraterrestrial intelligence (SETI). Anyone can participate by running a free program that downloads and analyzes radio telescope data.

A hacker who is creating a malicious botnet compromises machines that do not have proper security controls in place (such as antivirus or a firewall), typically via malware or phishing attacks. *Botnet agents* are typically deployed by malware onto compromised machines. Each individual agent reports to an overall command-and-control (CNC) structure, a server, or set of servers that receives remote transmissions from each individual botnet. At the time of writing, malicious botnets have been discovered that comprise millions of compromised machines.

LINGO
Phishing attacks use e-mail or malicious websites to trick users into revealing account information, personal information, or financial data.

Botnet Attack Types

Botnets can be used to launch a variety of malicious attacks:

- A denial-of-service attack typically involves a botnet using a service so much that the server's bandwidth is exhausted and legitimate users cannot access the service.
- Botnet agents can be used to harvest e-mail addresses and send spam e-mails in very large volumes.
- By using malware to install keyloggers on a victim machine, botnet agents can compromise credentials, even when encryption has been deployed, by capturing the keystrokes of a user on the machine.
- Key logging and phishing perpetrated by a botnet can be used to perform identity theft.
- Botnets can be used to falsely inflate the rate of pay-per-click systems (in which ad sales generate revenue based on the number of clicks received), using compromised zombie machines to click rather than legitimate users.

Zeus

Zeus is one example of particularly prolific malware at the time of writing. It targets financial institutions and their customers by stealing user credentials at the time of login. These are then sent in real time to a CNC server. Variants of Zeus replace real browser renderings of financial websites with malicious sites intended to steal personal information (credit card numbers, PINs, and more). Machines infected with Zeus become part of a larger botnet, which can also be used to launch DoS attacks.

The most alarming fact about the Zeus virus is that most antivirus products can't detect it, even if the antivirus signature file is completely up to date. Zeus attacks are being launched at financial institutions internationally, including in the United States, Germany, South Korea, and the UK. Zeus has been blamed for millions of dollars in bank account losses.

New Developments in Information Security

Information security best practice used to be focused on a concept called *protecting the perimeter,* or more specifically, *protecting the network perimeter*. Simply put, this theoretical view of which resources must be protected assumes that all important information resources belonging to an organization or company are stored primarily on a corporate network that lies inside a network perimeter. This is shown in Figure 2-2.

Protecting the network perimeter used to be straightforward. As long as all the information assets that were important and valuable to an organization or company were inside the network perimeter, hardening (applying security controls and configurations to) the network perimeter was all that was required to ensure the confidentiality, integrity, and availability of the information resources.

Today's world is much more complex, requiring information security professionals and the research community to think differently and to do things very differently. We must take into account the fact that most organizations and companies do not manage only information resources on a network that resides inside a perimeter that can be hardened. Mobile devices, including laptops and smart phones, have now become corporate assets that are constantly outside of the traditional perimeter.

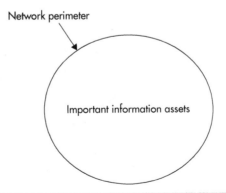

Figure 2-2   Protecting the perimeter concept

Many organizations and companies now feature customer-facing websites that transfer, store, and manage customer data, including personally identifiable information. These external-facing websites—in addition to applications on the corporate network that transfer, store, and manage employee and customer data—need to be protected. Thus, application security plays a larger role in today's information security world, meaning network security is no longer the only focus.

Companies have further perforated the network perimeter concept by working closely with external vendors and partners, outsourcing and offshoring business functions in ways that move customer, employee, and private data all over the world. Cloud computing elevates the task of managing the security of a vendor or partner to a whole new level.

This section provides brief updates in each of these changing and growing areas.

The Increasing Importance of Application Security

Companies and organizations must become increasingly aware of and practiced in the area of application security as they manage both internal corporate applications and external customer-facing applications to obtain, transfer, store, and manage private, customer, and employee information. Two organizations in particular have risen to the task of forming communities that promote education and information in this area: the Open Web Application Security Project, founded in 2001, and the Web Application Security Consortium, founded in 2004.

Open Web Application Security Project

As stated on the Open Web Application Security Project (OWASP) home page (www .owasp.org/), it is "a 501c3 not-for-profit worldwide charitable organization focused on improving the security of application software. Our mission is to make application security visible, so that people and organizations can make informed decisions about true application security risks. Everyone is free to participate in OWASP and all of our materials are available under a free and open software license."[6]

OWASP Foundation has over 70 Local Chapters and all the meetings are free to attend.

Web Application Security Consortium

The Web Application Security Consortium introduces itself as follows (www.webappsec.org/):

> The Web Application Security Consortium (WASC) is 501c3 non profit made up of an international group of experts, industry practitioners, and organizational representatives who produce open source and widely agreed upon best-practice security standards for the World Wide Web.

As an active community, WASC facilitates the exchange of ideas and organizes several industry projects. WASC consistently releases technical information, contributed articles, security guidelines, and other useful documentation. Businesses, educational institutions, governments, application developers, security professionals, and software vendors all over the world utilize our materials to assist with the challenges presented by web application security.

Volunteering to participate in WASC related activities is free and open to all.[7]

Web Application Vulnerability Statistics   WASC has published an alarming set of statistics based on a compilation of web application security assessment projects conducted in 2008. Here are a few highlights from the results (available at http://projects .webappsec.org/w/page/13246989/Web-Application-Security-Statistics[8]):

- More than 13% of all reviewed sites can be compromised completely automatically.

- About 49% of web applications contain vulnerabilities of high risk level (Urgent and Critical) detected during automatic scanning.

- Detailed manual and automated assessment by white box method allows detection of these high risk level vulnerabilities with probability up to 80–96%.

- The probability to detect vulnerabilities with risk level more than medium (PCI DSS compliance level) is more than 86% by any method.

- Detailed analysis shows that 99% of web applications are not compliant with PCI DSS standards.

These statics show that application security, as a relatively new area of focus for the information security community, is still in an immature state and has room to grow.

Note
This particular set of metrics references compliance with the Payment Card Industry Data Security Standards. Keep in mind when considering PCI DSS that PCI compliance has not stopped 100 percent of attacks.

The Cloud
Cloud computing allows end users and businesses to run and use services for which the details of the technology infrastructure are abstracted away and managed by the organization providing the cloud service. Large online companies are providing cloud services to their users. Some of these include Google, Salesforce, Amazon, Microsoft, and Yahoo!.

The on-demand cloud computing model is changing how businesses run their technology infrastructures, and dramatically changing the environment in which many information security professionals and researchers conduct their practice. At the time of writing, security best practices for cloud computing are not well known, well defined, or widely distributed.

Security experts formed the nonprofit Cloud Security Alliance (https://cloudsecurityalliance.org/) in 2008, whose mission statement is, "To promote the use of best practices for providing security assurance within Cloud Computing, and provide education on the uses of Cloud Computing to help secure all other forms of computing."[10] The objectives of the group are as follows:

LINGO
The National Institute of Standards and Technology (NIST) defines "**cloud computing** as a model for enabling convenient, on-demand network access to a shared pool of configurable computing resources (e.g., networks, servers, storage, applications, and services)" (http://csrc.nist.gov/groups/SNS/cloud-computing/).[9]

- Promote a common level of understanding between the consumers and providers of cloud computing regarding the necessary security requirements and attestation of assurance.

- Promote independent research into best practices for cloud computing security.

- Launch awareness campaigns and educational programs on the appropriate uses of cloud computing and cloud security solutions.

- Create consensus lists of issues and guidance for cloud security assurance.

Chapter 17 covers security metrics for cloud computing.

Targeted Attacks

In 2010, Google reported to the public that the company had detected an extremely targeted attack on their corporate infrastructure, resulting in intellectual property theft. This attack originated in China and appeared to target e-mail accounts of Chinese human rights activists. Through further investigation, Google discovered that the accounts of several European and Chinese advocates of human rights in China had been accessed by third parties (not as part of the reported attack but more likely through social engineering schemes such as phishing and malware). The attack led Google to review the feasibility of its business operations in China.

This is one example of targeted attacks on a specific group or enterprise. Targeted attacks such as these are becoming increasingly common, as criminals and hackers further leverage computer and Internet technology to achieve their objectives.

The Impact of Social Networking

Social networking has exploded as an Internet phenomenon, and websites such as Facebook, Twitter, and FourSquare are some of the most popular websites on the Internet. These websites allow for virtual interaction between friends and colleagues and sharing of personal information. Users share everything from where they're currently enjoying a meal, to what their plans are for the night, to pictures of their kids and pets. Friendships and relationships are being created and strengthened around the globe, and user-generated content is ubiquitous. These types of online interactions and the websites that support them are growing enormously in terms of the number of users and each user's daily activity use. It's changing the way that we do business, interact, play games, and much more.

Social networks are completely redefining privacy as we know it. Consumers and online social networking sites are still defining who can see what information. This includes sharing information with accepted contacts on a site as well as marketers and every other business that values this type of demographic and "interest" information. Sites typically offer some type of granular controls that are dictated by the user. These controls continue to evolve as users and legislatures demand more privacy for individual consumers.

The nature of these types of websites also means that many different companies and websites are coming together in one place and interacting with each other. Trusted and untrusted sites can appear to be coming from the same place, so a new level of user awareness is required to stay ahead of social engineering attacks. Phishing and malware are taking advantage of established trust levels among connected users on these sites.

Profile of a Hacker

One reason that information security is so challenging and constantly evolving is that the work of information security professionals and researchers is not limited to uncovering vulnerabilities and insecure configurations, but also includes working against fraud agents. The inherent problem that makes the information security field so interesting is that fraud agents, hackers, and cybercriminals are real people. Though areas of information security can

LINGO
Hackers are also known as crackers, attackers, script kiddies, and cybercriminals.

be very technical, it is actually much more a social science than a "hard" science. The human agent component is what makes this field very different from sciences such as mathematics, physics, and biology.

The "Old" Profile of a Hacker

The popular stereotype for a computer hacker is a nerdy, introverted, American teenager who is generally not impressed by authority figures. Commonly male, his interest in hacking is merely out of curiosity and primarily for intellectual and creative pursuits. This person may gain small personal value from hacking attacks, but generally he is not malicious in nature or intending to cause significant financial damage. In the past, some computer hackers have even been feted by the media for the cleverness of their schemes.

Kevin Mitnick is a great example of this type of hacker. Early in life, he had an interest in using social engineering to learn about and manipulate technology systems. In the mid-1970s, at age 12, Mitnick learned how to bypass the Los Angeles bus ticket system. While still a teenager, he later learned how to evade long-distance telephone charges and access speaker systems of fast food restaurants by manipulating the technology systems of the telephones and radio equipment. He went on to steal software code from several technology companies, for which he was arrested by the FBI and spent five years in prison. Mitnick never profited from this activity or intentionally destroyed information or computer systems. He hacked networks for the purpose of finding more security vulnerabilities to further his intellectual pursuits and curiosities.

Today's Hacker

The typical hacker today is very different from the Kevin Mitnick–type of hacker. Today's hacker is typically from a country or background where cybercrime pays far more than making a fair and honest living. A high percentage of professional fraudsters are located in Eastern European countries and China. Although the standard of living in these countries is not high, obtaining knowledge and proficiency in computer technology is relatively inexpensive and easy. Financial gain is a primary objective of today's hacker, and he is more than likely partnering with other criminals in organizations involved in additional fraud, theft, pornography, drug and human trafficking, and terrorism. Cybercriminal organizations are well educated and well informed, and actively recruit young people with advanced computer skills. Hacking schools are advertised in locations where young potential future cybercriminals can take advantage of the learning resources.

Organized cybercriminals today have become so business-savvy that they have in place standard business practices, complete with counterfeit product research and supply chains. Organizations are typically hierarchical and highly compartmentalized, with specific roles and responsibilities. Different actors playing different roles in a project or ongoing fraudulent program might never even know or come into contact with each other. Activities are coordinated by a separate individual or set of individuals.

Computer and Internet security attacks today are easier than ever, as ready-made attack toolkits are bought, sold, and traded between cybercrime organizations. Markets for counterfeit items and stolen financial accounts exist. Cybercriminals have even extorted money from financial institutions merely by *threatening* to attack customer-facing websites with DoS attacks. Some criminals have chosen to pursue cybercrime rather than more traditional rackets, such as drug trafficking, because they believe it is easier to make a profit and harder to get caught.

Real Crimes

Today's cybercriminals are involved in serious crimes beyond just stealing and selling information. Terrorist groups and criminal organizations are using cybercrime to finance their other criminal activities, from human trafficking to drug trafficking. Easier and more convenient to carry than cash, stolen credit cards and debit cards are often used to finance both day-to-day operational activities and purchases of weapons and other larger-ticket items. Stolen credit card numbers, Social Security numbers, and online banking accounts are being sold both for profit and to obscure the patterns of moving money.

Very specific, targeted malware focuses attacks on specific entities for specific purposes. Sometimes fraudsters go after the big money by extorting legitimate institutions whose business includes managing large, customer-facing websites (online banks, e-commerce websites, and other transactional websites). These cybercriminals control huge botnets and threaten their victims with distributed denial-of-service (DDoS) attacks and information-stealing hacks. They might take down part of their victim's website or another, smaller website for the purposes of demonstrating their abilities. Critical infrastructure and the government entities and corporations managing critical infrastructure are also at risk.

Smart hackers know that it's wise to stay below the radar; in fact, amateurs, often referred to as "script kiddies," will make a big deal out of their fraudulent activities and are more easily caught. The smart ones who know how to take a little at a time and remain undetected by monitoring or filtering security controls are the ones who end up with a steady cash flow. Deals to sell and move illegal drugs are being done in web forums and at Internet cafes to avoid detection. Skype and other Voice over IP (VoIP) chat rooms are being used to conduct fraud because of the secure and encrypted communication mechanisms. Alternative payment mechanisms and hacks on transactional websites are also being used to move money under the radar.

One highly publicized example of real crimes committed by a computer hacker involves a Turkish fraudster with the online identity Cha0, who in 2008 advertised and sold ATM skimmers in a criminal marketplace forum on the Internet called DarkMarket. Cha0 claimed in his online advertisements that his skimmers would capture both magnetic stripes as well as PIN numbers from ATM machines, and make his customers rich. Another hacker with the online identity Kier provided Turkish media and law enforcement with information on Cha0 and was reportedly abducted and beaten by Cha0. Cha0 released pictures of Kier online showing Kier only in his undergarments and holding a sign warning other hackers not to do as Kier had done.

Resources, Not Restraints

Cybercriminals do not face the same boundaries that information security professionals and researchers face. They are not required to comply with standards, rules, or regulations, and they do not need to justify budgets to executive management the way that information security professionals must do on an annual basis. They do not need to worry about users' privacy. They are not bound by legacy systems that may have been put in place long before they were in charge of them. Cybercriminals are not limited in their resources, and their pursuits are not affected by bureaucracy. They have effective ways of working with each other and sharing information, whereas the information security industry is still developing effective organizational structures and processes to share information among the community. Criminals involved in different types of illegal activity seek each other out and form alliances to strengthen their forces.

Real Money

In the earlier example of Kevin Mitnick, as a profile of what used to be considered a typical computer hacker, the companies that suffered data loss didn't lose large sums of money. Today, companies that experience data breaches are losing millions of dollars. Additionally, significant breaches are occurring more often. Recent data breaches have cost real companies real money—in the tens and hundreds of millions of dollars. Examples in the past ten years of companies losing millions of dollars due to security breaches include ChoicePoint (2004), TJX (2007), Heartland (2008), and Sony (2011).

This book provides recommendations on how to use metrics to tighten security practices to avoid breaches and associated monetary impacts. Nothing can be guaranteed, especially in a war against intelligent, powerful, and organized groups, but as information security professionals, we have to do the best we can with the resources we have available, and that means using metrics. As technology evolves, so too must the information security industry. This book proposes that information security metrics is the way to keep up with the pace of change.

Reactive security alone will not work anymore. Information security programs should include a good combination of both reactive and proactive security controls, and the mix that works for one company or organization may be very different from what works for another. This should be determined by the company's risk tolerance as well as its business context and strategies. Metrics take information security out of the dark ages and into something that is predictable, manageable, defensible, and business-friendly. It helps to keep pace with the constant change, which is inevitable, and, hopefully, stay ahead of the curve.

Today's "Security Best Practices" Are Not Good Enough

In today's information security world, strategies, plans, and controls are primarily based on best practices. How do these best practices come about? An expert who's been working in the field for a long time and has years of experience comes up with an idea and calls it a "best practice," or, alternatively, a consultant or analyst conducts a study or a survey to see what everyone in the field is doing regarding a particular issue and then, taking what the majority of people are doing, calls that a "security best practice." Sometimes folks who like to think about security even come up with a "best practice" without testing it or observing it in practice. Oftentimes security researchers and consultants advise practitioners on these best practices. Then these folks publish their findings in a report and present at conferences and recommend that everyone put their idea into practice. When practitioners begin to put these ideas and recommendations into practice, they sometimes run into real challenges and discover that "best practice in theory" is not the same as "best practice in reality." As you'll discover later in the chapter when I discuss some breach attribute data, most "best practices" are, in fact, not in use or even being practiced! One of the reasons that security metrics programs are needed now is that they are based in reality and have the objective of making what is really being practiced better, rather than attempting to put an idea into place that often falls short due to a disconnect between theory and reality.

Here are a few examples of documented best practices in information security:

- Guide to general server security
- Guide to Bluetooth security
- Guide to enterprise password management
- Guide to information security testing and assessment
- Guide to securing external devices for telework and remote access
- Guide to building secure applications

…etc. The list goes on and on.

IMHO

I believe that the term "best practice" is technically misused in the security community. A best practice should refer to an approach or methodology that is understood to be more effective at delivering a particular outcome than any other technique when applied in a particular situation. Best practices are supposed to be outcome driven and ideally are based on the approach that requires the least amount of effort for the best results. They are also supposed to be based on practices that have been tested and proven by many people. In security, best practice is a term that's often used to refer to something that's really a minimum security requirement, a baseline upon which to improve, which is a misleading use of the term.

In today's information security world, many best practices refer to ideas and recommendations that have not been fully implemented or put into practice. The value of implementing a best practice is generally only measured by the fact that something is in place rather than not being in place, rather than being determined by measured results or outcomes. Implementing a security metrics program enables an organization to truly implement best practices.

A Good Starting Point for Strategy

Don't get me wrong—many security best practices out there today are based on very good ideas. There are, however, a few best practices that suffer from deficiencies and need to be improved. This book proposes that best practices can be largely improved by

Budget Note

Another element that today's "security best practices" approach does not take into consideration is the limited budget and resources that are available to security organizations. Attempting to implement a laundry list of ideas and recommendations often ends when the money dries up. An effective security metrics program ensures that the highest priorities and biggest impact items are being funded as well as optimizes and makes the most out of existing security processes and technologies.

incorporating a formal security metrics practice into your overall information security program. Let's begin by examining some of these deficiencies and identifying areas for improvement.

Areas for Improvement

Here are my thoughts on areas where security metrics programs could fundamentally change how we think about, manage, and implement the work that we do as security professionals.

Best practices in security change and go out of date very quickly.   For example, a security best practice often promoted to protect corporate laptops and applications containing sensitive, confidential, or personal information is to "lock a user out of the system for 15 minutes after 3 attempts to log in with an incorrect password." The theory is that if someone was trying to maliciously break into an account, he or she might try different guesses (likely automated) at a password until finding the correct one. This brute-force technique is often referred to as a *dictionary attack.* Locking this attacker out after a few incorrect attempts would create enough of an obstacle that he or she might stop and go and try to crack a different account without this control in place, thereby acting as a deterrent. Things have changed, however. Today, if organizations have this control in place, then they are vulnerable to a denial of service (DoS) type of attack in which a hacker might choose to log into accounts multiple times using incorrect passwords intentionally to prevent legitimate users from being able to log in.

In information security, one size does not fit all.   Every organization has different needs for different controls at different times based on its current business and technology

Budget Note

If the actual result of implementing a best practice does not match or come close to a desired outcome, then a security practitioner has to make a decision: Either identify what's wrong with the control and fix the best practice to achieve the desired outcome, or drop this particular control and allocate precious resources and budget elsewhere to implement a control that will actually have the desired impact. Stopping and refocusing security work after an evaluation determines a control to be ineffective is an important part of making the most of a limited security budget.

environment. Best practices today are often written with the assumption that every organization should be doing the same thing at the same time. But a bank has different security needs and has to implement different security controls than a healthcare provider whose needs differ from those of a retailer whose needs differ from a waste management company. The most effective security controls are aligned with your specific business's strategy and objectives.

Best practices are not always outcomes-based and generally don't provide guidance on how important one control is relative to another. Many best practice recommendations are out there. The exercise of compiling and trying to implement all controls is typically futile due to an organization's limited budget and resources. Without tying best practices to outcomes (a primary objective of a security metrics program), how are you supposed to know what's making an impact versus controls that aren't making any difference at all? Two important factors that are *not* generally part of today's security best practices are the measurement of the results or impacts (outcomes-based evaluation of a control's effectiveness) and prioritization to ensure that the controls and processes that "move the needle" are where limited security resources are focused.

> **LINGO**
> **Move the needle,** a term commonly used in business, means to make a noticeable difference.

Controls and Standards

Often a best practice turns into a control or a standard after time and maturation. A standards body composed of experts in the field may be created specifically with the intent to formalize a standards framework and revise and maintain it over time, for example, the Payment Card Industry (PCI), National Institute of Standards and Technology, and International Organization for Standardization. An organization may implement these controls to comply with the standards and may check them periodically during an internal or an external audit. Ideally, this check is used to determine the control's effectiveness, but oftentimes this exercise results in the less useful and simpler exercise of checking a box to ensure that the control is being performed.

A security metrics program is built with the objective of achieving specific outcomes and is used to measure effectiveness, something that is not always done using today's typical methodology of controls and standards audits.

IMHO

Controls and standards, like best practices, do not always proceed with outcomes or effectiveness in mind. A box-checking mentality can lead to and even promote a lack of honesty within an organization as it examines its information security program. The importance of honesty when performing metrics analysis will be discussed further in Chapter 3, but here I'd like to ask these questions: How often do security and related teams such as system administrators answer questions from auditors (whether internal or external) with complete honesty? How many organizations and companies can say they've never stretched the truth during an audit? What happens as a result of this box-checking, "just get it done" type of mentality is that it almost promotes a "blinders-on" examination that purposefully points in the direction of compliance versus focusing on those areas that may need more attention—and which present the highest risk. What is documented, presented to executive management for sign-off, and can frequently direct, if not heavily influence, a company's information security strategy for the next year or so may not actually highlight the areas needing the most focus for the purpose of managing risk and thus may not lead to desired outcomes.

The next sections describe examples of standards bodies that are currently used to assess and guide information security programs today. The International Organization for Standardization and Payment Card Industry Security Standards Council are only two out of the many that are out there and are presented here to provide a flavor of the standard controls frameworks in this area. I encourage you to explore and examine additional frameworks and standards sets to see which ones make the most sense for your company or organization.

International Organization for Standardization (ISO)

The International Organization for Standardization develops and publishes the *International Standards for Business, Government, and Society*. These standards cover a variety of areas including automotive, education, energy, food safety, healthcare, local government, medical devices, petroleum and gas, risk, ship recycling, supply chain security, and, of course, the area of interest to readers of this book—information security.

Many security organization leverage ISO standards for managing their security programs; many information security consulting firms perform evaluations and benchmarking using ISO standards; and many security technology products and tools include ISO as an assessment guide. ISO, in conjunction with the International Electrotechnical Commission (IEC), publishes a new standard (or an updated version of an existing standard) in the area of information security every two years or so. Individually and taken as a group, these standards do a good job of covering the general basics of information security best practices.

These standards were originally based on BS 7799, a British standard that was published in 1995. Over the last decade and a half, this standard has been revised, widely used, and has evolved into the standards outlined in Table 2-1.

Table 2-1 details a few of the information security standards with a very high-level overview of the information that they cover. For a complete list, please visit www.iso.org.

Payment Card Industry Data Security Standards (PCI DSS)

PCI DSS grew out of five different data protection programs run by Visa, MasterCard, America Express, Discover, and JCB. These were each intended to protect card issuers by ensuring that merchants meet a minimum level of security when storing, processing, and transmitting cardholder data. The PCI Security Standards Council was formed and published PCI DSS in 2004. Today, the PCI Security Standards Council continues to develop, disseminate, and implement security standards for account data protection.

PCI DSS consists of twelve requirements for information data protection in the following areas:

- Building and maintaining a secure network
- Protecting cardholder data
- Maintaining a vulnerability management program
- Implementing strong access control measures
- Regularly monitoring and testing networks
- Maintaining an information security policy

Standard Number	Publication Date	Topics
ISO/IEC 27002	2005	Information technology/security techniques/code of practice for information security management
ISO/IEC 27001	2005	Information technology/security techniques/information security management systems/requirements
ISO/IEC 27006	2007	Information technology/security techniques/requirements for bodies providing audit and certification of information security management systems
ISO/IEC 27005	2008	Information technology/security techniques/information security risk management
ISO/IEC 27000	2009	Information technology/security techniques/information security management systems/overview and vocabulary

Table 2-1 ISO Information Security Standards

IMHO

ISO and PCI DSS are only two examples of a great many sets of guidelines that have been standardized for information security. The development and distribution of these standards has, overall, been very useful for the information security industry and has pushed the overall industry into a greater state of maturity. My concern is about information security professionals who believe that if their organization follows the guidelines put forth in these standards, their job is "done" and they have nothing further to worry about. As I describe further in this chapter, I believe that best practices and standards ought to be a starting point upon which a metrics-driven program is built, one that continually optimizes a company's information security program.

Process Improvement Models

Process improvement models are related to best practices and standards. Two that I would like to reference here include Six Sigma and the Capabilities Maturity Model. Six Sigma was developed in the 1980s by Motorola and is intended to identify and remove the causes of defects and errors. It's used widely in manufacturing, in particular, but is applicable to many different industries and certainly to information security processes such as vulnerability and patch management.

The Capabilities Maturity Model is a process improvement model developed by Carnegie Mellon University and funded by the Department of Defense. It began in the field of software development but can also be applied to other business processes. Metrics are absolutely fundamental to driving change, growth, and maturity through formal process improvement. In Chapter 6, I will also discuss the use of metrics through the process of risk assessments.

Applying Metrics to Best Practices

Standards and controls are built based on years of practical security experience in real businesses—but our experiences constantly change and evolve. Today, every security practitioner needs to know how to optimize his or her own unique program. This book proposes that not only are best practices, standards, controls, and audits an excellent starting point, but also that they are just that—a starting point. To get to an outcomes-oriented, most effective program for a unique business and technology situation, the application of information security metrics to these best practices, standards, and controls is critical.

Your Plan

A security metrics program should ask the following questions in order to optimize the use of best practices implemented within the organization. In Chapter 4, I will explore each of these questions in much greater detail, but here I'd like to show that best practices are a good starting point for a metrics program and that the application of security metrics can, indeed, make "best practices" the "best" that they can be.

- How relevant to the organization's business model and business strategy is this best practice?
- What is the objective of implementing this particular control/best practice?
- What is the desired outcome of implementing this particular control/best practice?
- Are all the relevant stakeholders aware of and properly performing their role with regard to the implementation of this best practice?
- What's the actual result of implementing this best practice, and how does that compare to the desired outcome?

We've Covered

Today's constantly changing technology and threat landscape

- Today's challenges include rapid technology changes and, with the move to cloud computing, organizational assets that have to be protected outside of traditional organizational boundaries.
- We are seeing a huge increase in malware, along with changing attack vectors, and more severe incidents.

Current profiles of hackers, fraudsters, and cybercriminals

- Today's hacker is not a teenager coding hacks in his mom's basement for the sake of bragging to his friends. These are true cybercriminals with financial gain in mind.

Recent breach information

- Breach reports and statistics from companies such as Verizon, Symantec, and Ernst &Young detail emerging threats.

How security work is done today

- Best practices in security change and go out of date very quickly.
- In information security, one size doesn't fit all.
- Best practices are not always outcomes-based and generally don't provide guidance on how important one control is relative to another.

The value of security best practices and controls and standards frameworks

- Standards and controls are built based on years of practical security experience in real businesses—but this is something which is constantly changing. Today, every security practitioner needs to know how to optimize his or her own unique program.

Endnotes

1. Daniel E. Geer, Jr., Sc. D., *Economics and Strategies of Data Security* (Waltham, MA: Verdasys, 2008), 30–31.

2. Gordon E. Moore, "Cramming more components onto integrated circuits," *Electronics Magazine* (April 19, 1965), 4.

3. Verizon, *2009 Data Breach Investigations Report (DBIR),* www.verizonbusiness.com/resources/security/reports/2009_databreach_rp.pdf.

4. Symantec Security Response, *Global Internet Security Threat Report,* April 2009, http://eval.symantec.com/mktginfo/enterprise/white_papers/b-whitepaper_internet_security_threat_report_xiii_04-2008.en-us.pdf.

5. Ernst & Young, *12th Annual Global Information Security Survey,* November 2009, www.ey.com/Publication/vwLUAssets/12th_annual_GISS_pub/$FILE/12th_annual_GISS_AU0383.pdf.

6. Open Web Application Security Project (OWASP), www.owasp.org.

7. Web Application Security Consortium, www.webappsec.org.

8. Web Application Security Consortium, Web Application Security Statistics, 2008, http://projects.webappsec.org/w/page/13246989/Web-Application-Security-Statistics.

9. National Institute of Standards and Technology (NIST), http://csrc.nist.gov/groups/SNS/cloud-computing/.

10. Cloud Security Alliance, https://cloudsecurityalliance.org/.

PART II

Essential Components of an Effective Security Metrics Practitioner

CHAPTER 3

Analytics

We'll Cover

● A definition of analytics as the combination of metrics and interpretation

● A description of what analytics can do

● How to identify tools that can generate analytics yet do not require the user to have extensive training or sophistication in the underlying mathematics

● Examples of the use of analytics, along with explicit evidence of how interpretation enriches metrics

"What are Analytics—an overused word and an underused resource."[1]

Ironically, this quote is from a healthcare management publication. Analytics are used far more successfully in healthcare than in many other disciplines, including information security. Evidently, despite the existence of epidemiology—the formal study of how to use quantitative analysis in medicine—the author of this statement thinks the healthcare industry is not using analytics to their fullest potential.

A recent publication from Microsoft Research called *The Fourth Paradigm*[2] identifies a fundamental shift in the advancement of science that is due to a relatively recent phenomenon: the amount of data collected is outstripping the resources available to validate, analyze, visualize, and communicate the information contained in it. This has not always been the case. Until recently, scientific theory outstripped the available data to validate or calibrate it. Through various data storage technologies that became ubiquitous in the 1990s, "remembering" has become easier than "forgetting" for the digital inhabitants connected to the Internet and internal corporate networks.[3] There is new, broad appreciation of the art and science of analytics as the discipline that can rescue piles of neglected data from incoherence and deliver insight to those willing to see it. My personal favorite evidence of this is the IBM commercials that speak of a "smarter planet" and the sexy analysts who are working on it.

This chapter is intended to be a first step for you to start using analytics as an integral component of your security metrics program, thereby transforming the data that you already have into valuable new insight. The chapter starts with a general description of analytics, and then discusses what you can do with them and how you can do it. Finally, the chapter provides some concrete examples of the use of analytics in real life.

What Are Security Analytics?

In their most general context, analytics are associated with investigating data for its quantitative properties, such as counts, percentages, ranks, relationships, or trends. The term *analytics* can refer to the *process* used to obtain results, as in "I performed *analytics* on this data," or to the *results* themselves, as in "My investigation resulted in the following *analytics*."

The most valuable analytics pass the "who cares?" test, meaning that there is a direct association between the result provided and a decision or action to be taken. Of course, any "who cares?" test is, by definition, subjective. "Who cares?" is definitely, like beauty, in the eye of the beholder. This fact is typically expressed by saying that analytics are *context sensitive*.

IMHO

Analytics are the juice that makes metrics useful. Without analytics, metrics are a set of numbers that can potentially be misinterpreted and, worse, used as the basis for incorrect action. One of the most popular statistics books ever published (with over half a million copies sold) is *How to Lie with Statistics,* by Darrell Huff (1954). This book provides numerous examples of how metrics without analytics can be used to support incorrect conclusions or even intentionally mislead. Analytics can save raw metrics from this type of misuse.

"Who Cares?" Test

Looking at the table in the following "In Actual Practice" sidebar, it is reasonable to ask: What is the difference between a metric and an analytic result? The answer is not crisp and certainly is not universally accepted. However, for the purposes of this book, I will be very explicit:

Analytic result = metric values + interpretation

Most of this book is dedicated to a discussion of the metrics component of this equation. This chapter is dedicated to the interpretation component.

Interpretation deals with many issues, such as the following:

- What the metric is telling us
- How to graphically visualize metrics as an aid to communication
- How the metrics compare with goals

In Actual Practice

Here are some examples of security analytics that would likely pass the "who cares?" test in almost any context:

Analytic Result	Who Cares and Why
Percentage of critical applications for which a risk analysis was performed within policy guidelines is 90 percent, which is up significantly from last quarter.	Executives: A leading indicator of potential external audit problems Managers: Allocation of internal audit resources
Percentage of new user accounts provisioned within the service level agreement (SLA) is 75 percent, which is significantly short of our goal of 95 percent.	Managers: Impact of credential granting on operations
The ranking of business units with respect to the number of negative PCI audit findings is USA worst with 23 and EMEA best with only 1.	Executives: Exposes differences in ability of business units to comply and is a leading indicator of possible penalties or fines Managers: Indicator of where their business unit stands and where they might go for help if they are not a leader in the ranking
Trend in firewall configuration changes per month is increasing at a rate of 10 percent per month.	Managers: Indicator of security exceptions being granted and implemented Operations: Indicator of workload trend—do we need to add or delete staff dedicated to firewall configuration management?
Values for security incident response before and after the installation of an SIEM solution differed by 30 minutes.	Executives: Answers the question as to whether the SIEM solution was worth the investment Managers: To set new (hopefully, more ambitious) goals for security incident response

Think of some metrics of your own that you could add to this table along with a rationale to justify why each passes the "who cares?" test.

- How the metric is changing over time, and how past metric values might be used to forecast the future
- Which factors are most influential in driving desired or undesired outcomes
- Whether a strategy exists for optimizing desired results
- What level of confidence we have in the conclusions that we are deriving

- Formulation of what-if scenarios
- What can the metric results explicitly rule out
- Possible explanations of the results, especially if they were not expected
- What actions the results suggest, plus a rationale
- Possible avenues for further investigation, including suggestions for changing current data collection techniques and a discussion of benefits that would result

Interpretation adds significant value to metrics. Analytics aren't possible without metrics. However, too often metrics are presented with incomplete or, worse, misleading interpretation. These are not analytics, but rather the worst kind of practices that lend credence to statements like Mark Twain's often quoted "There are lies, damn lies, and statistics."

It is not impossible for a metric, without any interpretation, to pass the "who cares?" test. This happens when the interpretation is self-evident. Often, the result is so obvious that the metric is just a nice factoid to confirm what everyone already knew.

Tip

To perform a quick "who cares?" test on a metric, find someone in your company who you think should most care about the metric. Ask that person how they would use the metric if you could compute it regularly for them. If they can't give you an answer, then you probably can conclude that the metric didn't pass the test.

Visualization

Many of the standard visualization methods, such as pie charts, bar charts, and line graphs, can and do present self-evident metrics efficiently. These methods are familiar to the widest possible audience, can easily be generated with simple, common, cheap tools such as spreadsheets, and can capture obvious patterns.

What You See May Not Be What You Get

However, let's look at a counter-example. Consider the bar graph shown in Figure 3-1 (generated with a spreadsheet), which shows the average number of days required to remediate a security incident for two business units, BU A and BU B. The metric being graphed is mean time to remedy (MTTR) a security incident. MTTR is calculated by taking the average length of time (in days) it took to remediate each security incident in a sample set. Figure 3-1 shows that BU A takes 100 days on average and BU B takes 75 days on average to remedy a security event.

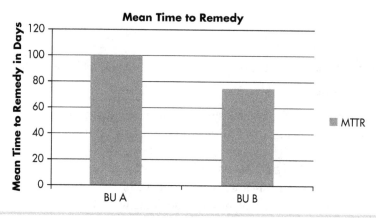

Figure 3-1 Metric that is not an analytic

IMHO

Figure 3-1 is an example of how a lack of analytics can lead to an inaccurate conclusion. It is one of my personal pet peeves to see bar graphs that fail to expose the information needed to give the real picture. If a bar graph provides an accurate impression, then by all means use it. But check first to make sure that you cannot be accused through your selective display (which is what a bar graph is) of lying with statistics.

Based on Figure 3-1, it is tempting to conclude that BU A's performance is much worse than BU B's. But there is a huge risk that this bar graph is not telling the whole story. Using the one metric, MTTR, can be very misleading. Metrics that characterize variation in days to remedy, or analysis that identifies and eliminates outliers prior to calculation of summary metrics (like MTTR), may lead us to a different and more accurate conclusion. Consider the two raw data sets shown in Table 3-1 and Table 3-2, each of which could have produced the bar graph in Figure 3-1.

Tables 3-1 and 3-2 show the number of days to remediate six security incidents, I-1 through I-6. The column labeled MTTR is the average of the six values. The column labeled stdev(TTR) shows a statistic called the *standard deviation* of the six values. The standard deviation is a common metric from parametric statistics that is used to measure the variability in a set of values—the higher the standard deviation, the more variation in the values. In general, a low standard deviation indicates consistency and predictability.

In Data Set 1, shown in Table 3-1, BU A is generally doing much better than BU B, with the one exception of incident I-3, an outlier that must have been very complicated

Data Set 1	I-1	I-2	I-3	I-4	I-5	I-6	MTTR	stdev(TTR)
BU A	10	10	550	10	10	10	100	220.5
BU B	75	75	75	75	75	75	75	0

Table 3-1   Effect of an Outlier

Data Set 2	I-1	I-2	I-3	I-4	I-5	I-6	MTTR	stdev(TTR)
BU A	101	103	102	99	98	97	100	2.4
BU B	64	64	65	80	87	90	75	12.1

Table 3-2   Effect of Variation

(taking 550 days to remediate). BU B is extremely consistent (stdev(TTR) = 0, no variability). It would be safe to predict that BU B will handle the next security incident in 75 days, or certainly within 70–80 days.

In Data Set 2, shown in Table 3-2, BU A is performing very consistently—remediating incidents reliably in 97 to 101 days. BU B is not so consistent: the first three incidents were handled expeditiously, but the subsequent issues took longer and longer to remediate. Is this a trend? If we had to predict, what would we say about BU B's performance in remediating future incidents? The data in Table 3-2 gives us no reason to be optimistic.

Multiple Metrics for a More Complete Picture

The bar graph in Figure 3-1 depicts information from just one metric, MTTR. As Tables 3-1 and 3-2 demonstrate, this clearly is not enough data to draw conclusions about the performance of the business units. Is there a way to simultaneously present metrics that capture both the average and the variability of a metric? Indeed there is. It is called a whisker plot. Figure 3-2 shows a whisker plot for Data Set 2.

As you can see, there is one "whisker" for each business unit. Looking at the whisker for BU A, there are five values (or metrics) depicted:

- The minimum of all observed values
- The value that marks the upper boundary for the lowest quartile of observations
- The median value for all observations
- The value that marks the upper boundary for the third quartile of observations
- The maximum observed value

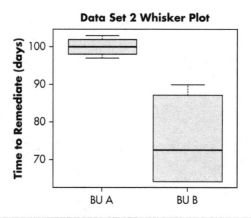

Figure 3-2   Whisker plot showing Data Set 2 distributions

Note

Because observations (such as security incidents I-1 through I-6 in the example) typically can't be divided nicely into four equally sized quartiles, statisticians consistently apply rules to define and visualize quartiles in box plots.[4] Also, note that for BU B, the minimum observed value is equal to the upper bound for the third quartile. This is why the BU B whisker does not show a separate horizontal line for the minimum value.

The visualization in Figure 3-2 does capture both a central value (the median) and the variability (the gap between the first and third quartiles) for a set of values. From this diagram, you can see that the variability of BU A's performance is much less than that of BU B's. You can also see that BU A took longer than BU B to remediate the six incidents in the analyzed data set. Also, notice that the median for BU B divides the gray whisker box into unequal parts—the top part is larger than the bottom part. Since each of these subareas of the whole gray area contains one quarter of the observations, this means that the observations that were higher than the median value were more variable than those that were lower than the median. This indicates a skew in the values of the observations for BU B toward higher values of time

LINGO
Quartiles divide all the observations into four equal groups, which hold the lowest one-fourth of all observed values (first quartile), the highest one-fourth of all observed values (fourth quartile), and the two middle fourths, one-fourth above and one-fourth below the median value (or the value that divides the set of observations into two equal halves).

to remediate. Note that the observations for BU A are distributed evenly below and above the median and in a narrower range.

The whisker plot does not capture anything about time or trends. The fact that BU B's MTTR times have been increasing steadily is not visible in this type of plot.

Bundling Interpretation and Metrics

The discussion in the previous section illustrates that analytics are a key way to deliver metrics bundled with interpretation. This is particularly true when one metric is not enough to give an accurate characterization. A common theme in analytics is to find ways to combine metrics—in both visualization and narrative description as well as just numbers. The previous section presented an example where analytics combined a measure of central tendency (the mean or median) and a measure of variability (the standard deviation, or the size of the middle two quartiles about the median—called the *interquartile range,* or IQR, by statisticians). In some of the examples presented later in this chapter, we will look at analytics that combine several metrics to recognize trends, test hypotheses, and estimate the level of confidence associated with various statements that are derived from metrics.

Do I Need a PhD in Math?

Perhaps you have concluded from the discussion thus far that analytics is a highly specialized discipline with many prerequisites—*skills* such as data management and related automation tools, and *knowledge* of various disciplines from applied mathematics such as statistics and operations research. To a certain degree, this is true. But this fact has not impeded widespread use of analytics in marketing, finance, healthcare, baseball, and even online dating. In fact, early adopters of analytics have been rewarded with often significant and (appropriately) measurable advantages over their competitors. This section provides some examples of how you can use analytics without first gaining the skills and knowledge commonly assumed to be prerequisites for using analytics. It also describes what analytics can do and have actually done.

Tip

The best way to recognize effective use of analytics is to look at examples. The second half of this chapter provides several examples. Look also on the Web at MetricsCenter, www.metricscenter.net, and other websites that provide demonstrations of quantitative analysis software.

Your Plan

Here is a checklist that you can use to find a tool that will help you incorporate analytics into your metrics program:

❏ *Identify commercially available software.* Ideally, the software should be targeted at security metrics, but it doesn't have to be. There are many packages that incorporate sophisticated analytics that are designed to visualize any type of data. You should evaluate as many packages as you can to find the one most appropriate for your needs. Some good candidates are identified in Chapter 12.

❏ *Develop a spreadsheet that lists your requirements.* These requirements should address both strategic issues (for example, whether you want all metrics to be computed in the cloud, whether you want to benchmark your performance against others, and so on) and features for data collection, metric computation with analytics, and visualization of results. Many example requirements are identified in Chapter 12.

❏ *Perform hands-on evaluation of at least three different packages.* See how easy or difficult it is for each package to ingest your data, try to compute some metrics, and try to visualize results.

❏ *Fill out your requirements spreadsheet to compare the packages.* This will help you decide which product is best suited to your specific needs.

Leverage Analytic Patterns Developed by Others

One of the reasons that analytics have become so widely used in other disciplines is that certain highly useful and broadly applicable patterns have emerged. Once identified, these patterns can be implemented in software as part of vertically specialized products or general-purpose tools such SAS, SPSS, Spotfire, and Mathematica.

An example of a vertically specialized analytics product is Google Analytics, which is intended for web masters. They use it to quantitatively analyze the effectiveness of websites—a discipline called *web analytics*. Google Analytics provides predefined snippets of JavaScript that the web master embeds in the pages of a target website. These snippets gather data that the Google Analytics service collects and analyzes. The results are periodically (once per day) fed back to users via standard web pages. Within some limits, users can customize displays and dashboards of metrics about their websites. Users cannot modify which data is collected or which metrics are computed. Despite these limitations, Google Analytics delivers an excellent set of analytics that is useful to a very broad audience and for hundreds of thousands of websites of a wide range of shapes, sizes, and complexity. Many Google Analytics users have no formal training in statistics, software development, or marketing. Despite this, they rely on web analytics to drive many decisions about website content and performance.

Cool the PhD: You Can Leverage Patterns Without It !

In contrast to the users, the developers of Google Analytics had to know a lot about web technology, marketing, and quantitative analysis. They used this knowledge to recognize patterns of investigation that any website owner would want to pursue. These patterns include the following:

- **Lines of investigation**   What are the key questions, and along what sort of dimensions should the answers be sliced? For example, every web master wants to know how many visitors have visited their site, which pages they visited, how long they spent at the site, and whether they returned. Moreover, they want these values aggregated based on categorical criteria such as type of browser, visitor location, and traffic sources.

- **Data**   Which data is required to get answers, and where can it be obtained? For example, individual page hits, client information, time between clicks, source IP address, and referring site IP address are all data elements that must be captured. Sources for these data elements include such places as HTTP headers and cookies.

- **Metrics**   Which metrics should be derived from this data? Counts and percentages are simple metrics. A more creative metric is *bounce rate*. This metric is computed for each page. It reflects what percentage of visitors leave the site after visiting the page.

- **Models**   Which models should be used to enrich and interpret metric results? In the previous section, you saw an example of a very simple model for describing the distribution of a metric. Mean, standard deviation, and variance are all quantities (metrics, actually) that use simple calculations defined in parametric statistics. Quartiles and medians are metrics from nonparametric statistics. But, happily, users of Google Analytics don't need to know any of this. Google automates the calculation and hides everything but guidance on interpretation.

- **Visualization**   Which graphs and charts should be used to best convey the information derived and to answer all the key questions? Google provides a highly interactive interface to display metrics, aggregated along a fixed set of user-selectable dimensions. Web masters can zoom from less granular aggregation to more granular aggregation, and can see click patterns from graphics overlaid on top of their own web pages.

So, experts with the right skills and knowledge can extract patterns of analysis and serve up an automated capability that is simultaneously sophisticated and consumable by users who just want answers to questions. Google Analytics is free. There are other packages (not free) that incorporate even more sophisticated analytics that can quantify trends, forecast, and provide levels of confidence—all functions that a free package such as Google's does not do now, but certainly may do some day.

Use the Trend Analysis Pattern

Let's look at a specific example of how an automated package, such as Google Analytics, can deliver sophisticated analytics to users who do not have a background in math or statistics. *Trend analysis* identifies patterns in the value of a metric as it changes over time. The most common type of trend analysis answers questions such as the following:

- Are values of a metric staying the same over time?
- Are values of a metric decreasing over time?
- Are values of a metric increasing over time?

In Actual Practice

The most common model used to answer questions such as whether the values of a metric are increasing, decreasing, or staying the same over time is *linear regression*. This is a model from statistics that finds the "best fit" line through the points on a two-dimensional graph, where the x value is the time that the observation was made, and the y value is the observed value of the metric at time x. The best fit line is described by the equation

$$y = mx + b$$

where m is the slope of the line and b is the y-intercept.

Briefly, let's look at how the slope m of a line and the y-intercept b of a line are defined. The *slope of a line* is a value that represents how fast the y values are rising or falling as the x values of the line increase. A line consists of a series of points, each having an x and y coordinate. Each point on the line can be represented as a pair of values (x,y), where x is the horizontal displacement from zero and y is the vertical displacement from zero. Values for x and y can be positive or negative. They can

(continued)

be whole numbers or not. For the set of (x,y) values that forms a line, the slope is computed as the change in y divided by the change in x for any two points on the line. The following is a formal definition:

Slope of line = $(y_2 - y_1) / (x_2 - x_1)$, where (x_1,y_1) and (x_2,y_2) are any two points on the line

The *intercept of a line* identifies the point where the line crosses the vertical y-axis. An intercept is typically expressed as a single value, b, but can also be expressed as the point (0,b). Does every line touch the y-axis? Actually, no. Any line that is parallel to the y-axis—namely, any vertical line—will not touch the y-axis. What is the slope of a vertical line? If you look at the preceding equation for the slope of a line, you will be able to derive the answer. Since all of the x values are the same for a vertical line, the denominator of the equation for the slope has the value 0. You might say that the slope of a vertical line is infinity or, alternatively, that it is undefined, as is its intercept.

The linear regression model, in addition to finding values for m and b, provides metrics that characterize how well the line fits the actual data. This "goodness of fit" metric is based on *residuals,* namely the difference between actual observed values and the values "predicted" by the line—the higher the residuals, the worse the fit. The residuals can be viewed as errors in the line's predicted values. Whenever you have a bunch of numbers (in this case, residuals), you can fit them to a *probability distribution* that associates a probability with each observed value. This distribution has a mean and a standard deviation. If you add in an assumption about the shape of the distribution (for example, that it is normal), you then have a function that can associate any possible observed residual with a probability.

There is a famous theorem in statistics called the *central limit theorem* that (to net things out) can be used to justify an assumption that the residuals have a normal distribution. Now, based on the central limit theorem, we can estimate the probability that, given what we observed, the values of the metric stay the same over time (in other words, that the slope m of the line is zero). For this probability, we can set a threshold that must be met for us to conclude that the slope is, indeed, zero. A commonly used threshold is 95 percent, called a .95 confidence level. This means that if the linear regression model tells us the probability that the slope is zero is *less* than 0.05, then (and only then) will we be confident enough to state that the slope is not zero and that the trend is up or down.

The primary value of using a linear regression model is to identify trends in the value of a metric over time. With a good fit, linear models can be used to make projections.

Budget Note

In a metrics project, you need to be sure to budget for the entire lifecycle of each metric, from the initial design through the presentation of results and the ongoing update of those results over time. The following list provides tasks that your budget should include (examples of which are provided in the examples that follow):

- **Question**   Identify the question you wish to answer.
- **Metrics**   Define the metrics that will provide insight into your question.
- **Data sources**   Locate the data sources that can be used to compute the metrics and determine what, if any, processing is required prior to using the data.
- **Models**   Identify any models from statistics or other quantitative disciplines that you will be using. Specifically discuss any assumptions that these models may require.
- **Tools**   Determine which tools you will need to obtain data, perform computations, and report results.
- **Results**   Design how you will present the results, including what level of detail you will include and what additional annotation will be required.
- **Visualization**   Determine whether the presentation will be textual or graphical, how interactive it will be, and whether it will be hardcopy or web based.

If you haven't yet read the "In Actual Practice" sidebar, the model used to answer the preceding questions is the linear regression model. This model will produce (among other things) two key metrics:

- **slope**   An estimate of the slope of the line that goes through our observed values of the metric over time
- **p-value**   An estimate of the probability that the slope of the line is zero—or, put another way, an estimate of the probability that the value of the metric does not change with time

Based on these key values, you can decide which of the preceding three questions is true with some known level of confidence.

First, you must decide what level of confidence is required. The most common value is 95 percent. Assuming this is the confidence level needed, then:

- If the p-value is greater than 0.05, you can conclude that the metric does not change value with time.

- If the p-value is less than 0.05 and the slope > 0, you can conclude that the metric increases with time.

- If the p-value is less than 0.05 and the slope is < 0, you can conclude that the metric decreases with time.

All of these conclusions have an associated confidence level of 95 percent.

This set of steps is extremely easy to automate and deliver as a package to end users who want to detect trends yet also want to remain blissfully ignorant of all the underlying mathematics.

Examples of Applying Analytic Patterns

The next few sections provide several examples that show how to apply analytic patterns. Example 1 provides an example of applying trend analysis to security vulnerability data. Example 2 shows how to use hypothesis testing to help make data-driven decisions. Example 3 presents an analysis that compares trends for internal and external breaches over time. Example 4 illustrates the importance of selecting a data set that is truly representative of the context that you wish to analyze. And Example 5 provides a case study that uses a combination of analysis patterns to tell a story regarding the state of software security.

Note that all of the following examples use data from real-world applications of security metrics. The data sets fall into two categories: real data from public data sources and data from Veracode (www.veracode.com), a private application risk management company that offers a cloud-based service to review software for the purposes of identifying and managing security risk.

Example 1: Trend Analysis—Microsoft Vulnerabilities

In this example, we apply the trend analysis pattern. This pattern is designed to show how specific metrics change over time. We will use trend analysis to investigate the following question:

Question   Is the number of vulnerabilities in software released by Microsoft increasing or decreasing over time?

Metric   The first decision is to identify which metric to use. We will use the count of discovered vulnerabilities. Let's name it **vulnCount**. To investigate a trend, we examine the value of **vulnCount** over time.

Data Source   The second decision is to identify an appropriate source from which we can either directly or indirectly obtain **vulnCount** values for Microsoft. As it happens, there is an excellent, well-funded, highly regarded source for this data: the National Vulnerabilities Database (NVD). The NVD (http://nvd.nist.gov) is the official U.S. government repository of vulnerability data. Government agencies use the NVD to automate management of many IT security functions, as well as proof of compliance of commercial software products with various federal regulations such as the Federal Information Security Management Act (FISMA). One component of the NVD is a repository of known vulnerabilities. Each vulnerability in this repository has data elements that provide the date when the vulnerability was discovered, and identification of the manufacturer, product, and version (among other things).

Model   Our third decision is to identify the appropriate model to use. For a trend analysis, linear regression is usually the best place to start. This model requires a time series of points (x,y), where x is time and y is the value of a metric at time x. For this example, y is the value of **vulnCount** at time x.

We need to decide the granularity for time x. It could be one day, one week, one month, one quarter, or any of numerous other possibilities. If we select one quarter as the appropriate granularity, then the (x,y) points would be computed as follows:

x = the name of a quarter in the form YYYY-Q, where YYYY is a four-digit year and Q is either 1, 2, 3, or 4

y = **vulnCount**, computed as the count of all vulnerabilities discovered during quarter x

What is the best granularity? The answer depends primarily on a few important characteristics of the data source. In particular, if updates to the NVD are timed to be current on a quarterly basis, then the best granularity would be quarterly. Sometimes this information is readily obtainable. Sometimes it's not. If it's not, then we can experiment by aggregating counts by various time periods and look for patterns. For example, suppose that when we looked at the NVD **vulnCount** by week and by month, we noticed lots of zero values, indicating that updates to the NVD might not be made consistently on a weekly or monthly basis. To be safe, we'll select quarters, since we know we have years of data, giving us 18 observations (starting from 2006-1 through 2010-2).

We are ready to proceed with our analysis. The NVD holds millions of records, covering thousands of vendors, products, and versions. Manual analysis is clearly not feasible. This brings us to our last decision.

Tool   What automation can we use to perform the analysis? This is a meaty topic to which I have dedicated an entire chapter (see Chapter 12). For the time being, I will simply mention that, at the highest level, you can select a general-purpose tool or a vertically specialized tool. Some of the differences were alluded to earlier in this chapter and will be explored more completely in Chapter 12.

Let's skip to the good part—the results.

Results and Visualization   We get the values (as of the end of August 2010) shown in Table 3-3.

It is more revealing to show the data in Table 3-3 via a scatter plot, as in Figure 3-3.

Quarter	vulnCount
2006-1	3475
2006-2	6600
2006-3	9450
2006-4	7925
2007-1	4417
2007-2	3825
2007-3	4361
2007-4	4432
2008-1	3475
2008-2	6600
2008-3	9450
2008-4	7925
2009-1	4417
2009-2	3825
2009-3	4361
2009-4	4432
2010-1	3475
2010-2	6600

Table 3-3   Quarterly Microsoft vulnCount from the NVD

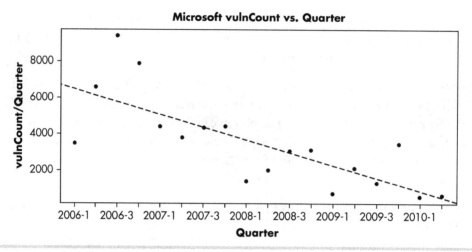

Figure 3-3   Microsoft vulnCount trend by quarter

I added a dashed line to show the best fit trend line through the points, using a linear regression model. The regression model returns the following values:

- Slope of the line m = −353 vulnerabilities/quarter
- y intercept b = 6848 vulnerabilities
- p-value = .0003

Based on the p-value and slope, we can say with over 99 percent certainty that the trend for software released by Microsoft is a decreasing vulnerability count over time, based on data from the NVD.

Note

This is just Microsoft's data, aggregated across all of its hundreds of products and versions. You can create similar plots for any vendor, make comparisons, and apply the analysis shown here to a much broader scope. To do this, follow the steps provided in this example but replace Microsoft's vulnerability data with that of the company that you want to analyze.

Example 2: Hypothesis Testing

Hypothesis testing is a technique from statistics that is used to help make decisions based on data, sometimes referred to as *data-driven decision making*. The decision can be stated in the form of a question: Is X true? To answer the question, one collects data.

The data may be obtained from a *controlled experiment* or from making *observations*. In a controlled experiment, the analyst tries to set up a formally contrived set of conditions in which data are collected. The conditions typically define two or more groups that are as identical as possible with the exception of one or more controlled values, sometimes called *treatments.*

For example, drug trials often define two groups of randomly selected people of the same age, height, weight, and so on, with one group taking a drug and the other getting a placebo. The hypothesis might be: Does drug X help men lose weight? The analyst then collects data about the two groups to measure the effects of the treatment by comparing key characteristics (metrics) associated with the two groups. Another way to test a hypothesis is to simply collect data by making observations. Some data elements (called *independent variables*) collected from the observations are used to define subgroups; other data elements (called *dependent variables*) are collected to compare or investigate differences between the subgroups. In this example, we use data about security data breaches collected via observations. Based on the data we collect, we can divide the security breaches into groups based upon whether the breach was perpetrated by insiders (employees) or by outsiders (independent variable). The dependent variable that we observed is breach severity. Our hypothesis can be stated as the following question.

Question   Are insider data breaches more severe than external data breaches?

Metric   We will use the total number of people affected by the data breach as our primary measure of breach severity. Let's call this metric **affected**.

Data Source   An excellent source of data about breaches that affect consumers is the DatalossDB, compiled by the Open Security Foundation (OSF, www .opensecurityfoundation.org). Starting in July 2003, California's SB 1386 and similar subsequent legislation in almost all the states mandated the reporting of data breaches that disclose personally identifiable information about individuals. As a result, there is publicly available, though often very unstructured, information about data breaches. This publicly available breach data is typically derived from reports that are submitted by the target of the breach to the authorities, as mandated by legislation. Many breaches get covered by the press. The OSF's DatalossDB project was established to find this information from scanning press articles and, in many cases, submitting Freedom of Information Act requests to States Attorney's offices. Once obtained, the data is transformed by OSF volunteers into structured records and stored in a database. The database is freely available to anyone who wants to analyze it. You can find out more details about how the OSF performs its analysis as well as the results of this analysis at http://datalossdb.org.

The structure of the OSF data breach database is simple—one record for each breach. For this analysis, we are interested in two properties:

- **source**   Possible values are inside-malicious, inside-accidental, inside, outside, and unknown

- **affected**   An integer that gives a count of the number of individuals affected by the breach

From inspection of the values for the **affected** property, we see a huge range that is as low as zero to an all-time high of 130,000,000 (the famous Heartland breach in January 2009, described in Chapter 2). When values span such a large range, it is often useful to use a logarithmic scale instance of the more familiar linear scale. This is what we will do. So, we'll invent a new metric called **logAffected** that is computed as the $\log_{10}$ affected.

Don't panic. Logs are really not too complicated. First, a definition. The log to the base 10, or $\log_{10}$, of a value x is the exponent to which you would have to raise 10 to obtain x. Here are some examples:

$\text{Log}_{10}\ 10 = 1$ because $10^1 = 1$
$\text{Log}_{10}\ 100 = 2$ because $10^2 = 100$
$\text{Log}_{10}\ 1000 = 3$ because $10^3 = 1000$
$\text{Log}_{10}\ 1000000 = 6$ because $10^6 = 1000000$

Things get dicey when you want the log of a number that is not a power of 10. But you don't need to know about that for purposes of this example. The big concept here is that we are applying to the values of the metric **affected** a scaling factor that transforms a huge interval that ranges from 0 to 130,000,000 to an interval that ranges from 0 to 9. Why 9? Well, $\log_{10}$ 100,000,000 is equal to 8. Since the top value of **affected**, 130,000,000, is greater than 100,000,000, the $\log_{10}$ 130000000 is higher than 8. But it is less than 9 because 130,000,000 is less than 10^9, or 1,000,000,000.

So, from our inspection of the data, we now have two metrics: **affected** and **logAffected**. We are looking at five sets of breaches, one set for each value of the categorical property: **source** (inside-malicious, inside-accidental, inside, outside, and unknown).

In addition to using the logarithm to transform the **affected** property into a new **logAffected** property, a second transformation on the property called **source** is desirable, based on our knowledge of the data. Our analytic objective is to determine whether inside breaches are worse than outside breaches. At least for the present, we don't care whether

In Actual Practice

I know how we geeks like math problems, so indulge me in these:

- What is the $\log_{10} 10{,}000$?
- What is the largest integer that is less than $\log_{10} 10{,}325$?
- What is the smallest integer that is greater than $\log_{10} 10{,}325$?

You can look at the answers now, located at the end of the chapter, if you like.[5]

So why are logarithms useful in quantitative analysis? In the example of investigating the distribution of **totalAffected** individuals associated with breach events, mapping that number of affected individuals to the log of the number of individuals has two benefits. First, visualizing the distribution of the log values shows something very close to a normal distribution. Looking at just the raw values gives us no such insight because the raw values span such a broad range (from near zero to tens of millions). The second benefit is that we can use the normal distribution to apply a wide range of statistics that provides additional values such as levels of confidence and margins of error.

the inside breach was accidental or malicious. So, we create a new property of a breach called **inOut**, defined as follows:

- **inOut** = "in" if **source** = inside-malicious, inside-accidental, or inside
- **inOut** = "out" if **source** = outside

We throw out all breaches for which **source** = unknown.

Model   Analysis of variance (ANOVA) is a common model for determining if two or more groups are different with respect to some metric. Like regression analysis, using the ANOVA model is a pattern for analysis. You apply the model and you get two estimates for each group:

- Estimate for the group mean
- Estimate for the probability that the group mean is the same as the mean for the reference group

The reference group is one of the groups being analyzed. It really doesn't matter which group is the reference. The model just picks one group and then uses it as a reference against which the other groups are compared.

A special case of ANOVA applies when there are only two groups. In this case, the Student's *t*-test is equivalent to an ANOVA with only two groups. The ANOVA model handles the more general case of greater than two groups. In this example there are two groups: Inside breaches and Outside breaches.

Note

There are some important considerations when applying either a Student's *t*-test or ANOVA. First, you have to be sure that each observation belongs to exactly one group. Second, if you have any reason to believe that the standard deviations (or variation) of the observations for the groups will be different, then ANOVA is not the right model.

Looking at the analysis that we want to perform, it is not necessarily clear that a breach has to be strictly either inside or outside. The perpetrators might be a team consisting of both employees and professional criminals. Based on the information at the OSF website, we don't have any visibility regarding how breaches were classified.

We also have a potential problem with using an assumption of equal standard deviations. We really don't know; on the surface, it is hard to come up with a compelling argument that the severity of inside breaches will vary more or less than that for outside breaches.

So what do we do? We make a note of the preceding facts and press on.

Tool Again, refer to Chapter 12 for a discussion of tools.

Results and Visualization The results of a Student's *t*-test can be graphically captured via a whisker plot with notches, as shown in Figure 3-4.

The whisker plot in Figure 3-2 does not have overlapping notches. The notches graphically depict a 95 percent confidence interval about the median of a distribution of values. In this case, we can see the two distributions for inside and outside breaches, side by side. If the notches overlap, then we conclude that there is no statistically significant difference between the two groups. If the notches do not overlap, then we conclude that, with 95 percent confidence, there is a difference. Since the notches do not overlap in Figure 3-4, the two groups of breaches (inside and outside) have different means at a level of at least 95 percent confidence. Outside breaches impact more individuals than do inside breaches. Table 3-4 gives actual metric values generated from the model. The interpretation is as follows:

- We can state with over 99 percent confidence that outside breaches affect more individuals than do inside breaches.

- The impact of an outside breach is generally four times that of an inside breach.

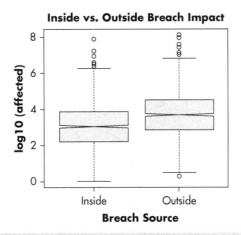

Figure 3-4   Comparing inside and outside breaches

Example 3: Trend Comparison

Using the same observed data that we used in the preceding example, we can obtain information about three trends over time: overall breach frequency, insider breach frequency, and outsider breach frequency. This example provides an analytic pattern for first deriving and then comparing these trends. Specifically, we will assess the following questions.

Questions

● What is the trend in breach frequency? Is it increasing, decreasing, or staying the same?

● How does this trend compare for inside versus outside breaches?

   Given that these questions are about trends, the pattern for using linear regression is a good candidate for deriving analytics to answer these questions. The difference between

Metrics	Inside	Outside
Estimate of mean for **logAffected**	3.07	3.67
Estimate of mean for **affected**	$10^{3.07} = 1175$	$10^{3.67} = 4677$
p-value = the probability that the means for the two groups are equal	$2.2 \times 10^{-16} \ll .001$	

Table 3-4   Metrics for Inside vs. Outside Breaches

the preceding example and this example is that, rather than looking for one trend, we will look at three trends by applying the pattern to each of three groups of breaches:

- All breaches
- All inside breaches
- All outside breaches

Metric   Quarterly **breachCount** aggregated along the values of one dimension: breach source whose members are inside and outside.

Data Source   The DatalossDB is again used as the data source. An important decision exists regarding which quarters of data should be used. The first data breach disclosure law became operative in July 2003 (2003–2). Over the following four years, additional states passed laws. There were at least two important consequences of these laws:

- More data breaches were reported due to the requirements imposed by the legislation.
- Media coverage of incidents increased due to public interest.

The graph in Figure 3-5 depicts a distinct increase in the number of reported data breaches as states following California's lead began passing similar laws. From 2003 to 2007, the vast majority of states adopted disclosure laws that include a provision that requires companies to disclose a data breach if any affected individual is a resident of that

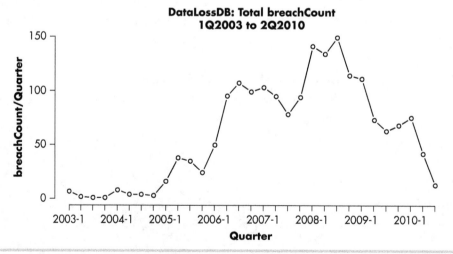

Figure 3-5   breachCount since 1Q2003

state. So, even if a company located in a state without a disclosure law experiences a data breach, it must disclose the breach in each state with an applicable disclosure law if any affected individual resided in that state. Under these circumstances, very few breaches can escape the disclosure requirement. Figure 3-5 reflects both this result and the increasing media interest during this period.

The period from just before July 2003 through the next several quarters (say, to 1Q2006) can be viewed as the period in which states were passing laws and existing laws were beginning to have an impact. The period from 1Q2006 through 3Q2008 is when the impact of the laws became apparent. But, as you can see in Figure 3-5, the graph depicts a third period, namely the period after the peak in 3Q2008. What explains the apparently precipitous drop in breach disclosures after 3Q2008? Could it be operational improvements driven by public awareness? A more sobering interpretation is that the media, an important information source for the DatalossDB curators, has lost interest, thereby vastly reducing media exposure and making it much more difficult for breaches to find their way into the DatalossDB.

So, we need to make a decision: which period or periods should be included in our trend analysis? As long as we document both the decision and its rationale, we are providing a complete picture to the audience for our analysis. Let's use data starting from 1Q2006 and continuing up to and including that last complete quarter at the current time, 2Q2010. Our rationale is that this is a representative sample of quarters for the purposes of our analysis of the current trend in data breach frequency. If anything, our frequency estimates will be pessimistic, due to the apparent steep decline of breaches since 3Q2008.

Model   Linear regression will be used to characterize the change in **breachCount** over time, in quarters, since 1Q2006.

Tool   See Chapter 12 for a discussion of the tool possibilities.

Results and Visualization   The results are listed in Table 3-5 and shown in Figure 3-6.

Metrics	Inside	Outside	Total
Estimate of slope	−.25	−2.0	−2.3
Estimate of mean for intercept	31.4	81.2	112.6
p-values	0.65	0.06	.11

Table 3-5   Metrics for breachCount Trend

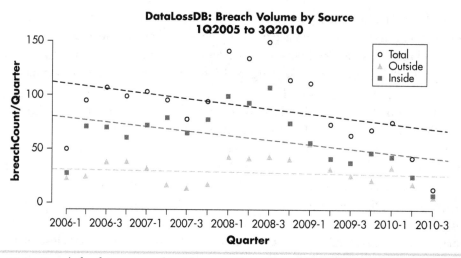

Figure 3-6 Trends for frequency of inside, outside, and total breachCount

From the preceding results, our key findings are as follows:

- The lines fit so badly (p-values all greater than .05) that we really can't say the **breachCount** is not flat over time.

- The data and the p-value of .65 for inside **breachCount** suggest that inside breach frequency is constant over time and the apparent negative slopes for total and outside breaches are due to a declining trend for outside **breachCount**.

Example 4: Data Sample Effect

In the preceding example, if we had not limited our samples to breaches since 1Q2006 but instead used all breaches in the DatalossDB, the graph and metric results would have been quite different, as shown in Table 3-6 and Figure 3-7.

Metrics	Inside	Outside	Total
Estimate of slope	1.1	2.0	3.2
Estimate of mean for intercept	−0.43	.66	.23
p-values	0.0001	0.0012	0.0002

Table 3-6 Metrics for breachCount Trend: 1Q2003–2Q2010

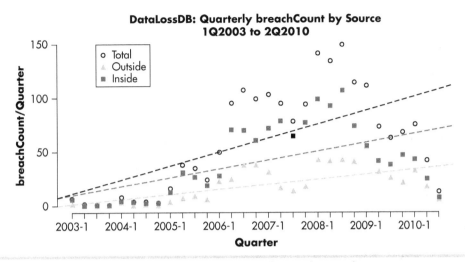

Figure 3-7   Trend in breachCount based on all breaches in the DatalossDB

The p-values for all three slopes in this analysis come out to less than .0001, indicating over 99 percent confidence that, for the period shown, the slope of all three lines is positive.

This illustrates how important it is to know the context in which you are evaluating data. In this case, an event in 2003 was important enough to drastically influence our analysis.

Looking at all the analysis that we performed in this example, we have provided information about both the current state of breaches, in terms of their impact, as well as the trend, in terms of frequency of occurrence:

- Inside breaches affect fewer individuals than do outside breaches (99 percent confidence).

- The frequency of outside breaches is not increasing quarter over quarter (94 percent confidence).

- The frequency of inside breaches is not increasing quarter over quarter (89 percent confidence).

Example 5: Telling a Story

A very powerful use of metrics is to combine several related results that provide insight or tell a story. This example deals with the trend in application software security to demand a third-party security review from suppliers prior to deployment of an application.

Questions   As with the previous examples, we begin with questions—this time a set of related questions:

- Are companies concerned about the security of purchased software?
- For which types of software are consumers most likely to request a review by a third party?
- Which types of applications are most likely to be reviewed?
- How many reviewed applications get a passing grade?
- If an application does not pass, how long does it take to fix it?

Metrics   To address the preceding questions, we introduce the following metrics:

- **appCount**   A count of applications that were requested to be reviewed by a third party. **appCount** will be aggregated along four dimensions: RequestorIndustry, VendorType, AppType, 1stScanVeracodePass.
- **appTTA**   The average length of time for an application to achieve an A rating from a third-party reviewer.
- **appBTA**   The average number of reviews before an application achieves an A rating from a third-party reviewer.

Data Source   The source of data for computing these metrics is a unique dataset compiled by Veracode, the world's leading independent provider of third-party application reviews. Veracode (www.veracode.com) provides a unique, cloud-based service that permits a *consumer* to submit or have a *provider* submit applications in binary form for review by Veracode. A *consumer* can be a company that purchased software for internal use from a provider or it can be a company that is performing due diligence on a software provider for purposes such as acquisition or some type of business partnership. A *provider* is a company that develops software for use or sale by others. A Veracode *review* attempts to discover security-related flaws in an application and then reports the findings, along with other related information, to the submitter. In addition to the security review service, Veracode has invested heavily in building an anonymized repository of review results. For each review performed, the anonymized Veracode repository holds the following information:

- **Application Requestor Industry**   This field has the following values:

RequestorIndustry	Description
Fin	Financial and related industries (for example, Banking and Insurance)
SW	Software
Other	All other industries

As you can see, the granularity for classification of requestors is limited to only three possible values: Fin, SW, and Other. This reflects the current state of the Veracode data. The important lesson here is that Veracode has started performing analytics and implementing the discipline necessary to support finer granularity as its dataset grows.

- **Vendor Type**   This field has the following values:

VendorType	Description
Cloud+Deployed	Provider of services that are delivered in a cloud or private cloud format
Integration	Provider of professional services plus software to integrate heterogeneous applications
ISV	Classic independent software vendor
Cloud	Cloud services provider
Deployed	Deployed private cloud services provider
Consulting	Professional services provider

- **Application Function**   This field has the following values:

AppFunction	Description
Operations	Day-to-day business activity, including business process management, product development, information management, IT management, and nonfinancial governance applications
Customer	Customer service activity, including customer relationship management, content management, and web-facing services
LearningGrowth	Employee-oriented activities such as HR, training, and human capital management
Financial	Traditional accounting and finance functions as well as an important and growing class of applications that provide mobile access for banking and other finance-related tasks

The categories are derived from the Balanced Scorecard (BSC) model, a widely used model for strategic planning and management.[6]

- **1stScanVeracodePass**   This field has the following values:

1stScanVeracodePass	Description
Pass	The application achieved a passing grade based on discovered flaws
Fail	The application achieved a failing grade based on discovered flaws

Model We use two models: linear regression, for discovering trends, and analysis of variance, for identifying significant differences between groups of third-party application review requests.

Tool See Chapter 12 for more information about the available tools.

Results and Visualization Results and visualization are provided in the following sections.

Are Companies Concerned About the Security of Purchased Software?

First, let's look at the trend of third-party review requests, namely the **appCount** metric, over time. Figure 3-8 shows just the trend line without any annotation on the y-axis. This illustrates a technique that can be used to support a conclusion without revealing information that is not public. In this case, the information that is not to be shared is the precise volume of requests submitted to Veracode. This is proprietary information that is not needed to make the point—namely, that the number of requests for third-party reviews is rapidly increasing.

The p-value for the line is 0.003, so we can state with over 99 percent confidence that demand for third-party reviews is increasing. Without the benefit of a scale on the y-axis, the steepness of the slope cannot be determined. This is certainly a key piece of information, but it is not required to establish our first finding—that the trend is up.

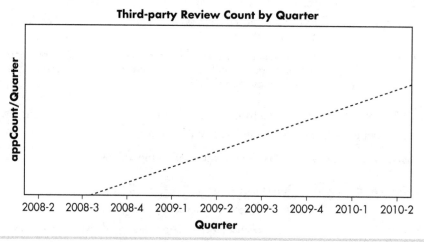

Figure 3-8 Trend: appCount per quarter

This is hard evidence that companies that purchase software from third-party suppliers are indeed concerned about the security of those applications. They are acting upon these concerns by requesting third-party reviews.

For Which Types of Software Are Consumers Most Likely to Request a Review?

Consumers are acting upon their concerns about software security by requesting third-party reviews. Consumers can obtain a third-party review from Veracode by asking their software provider to submit the software, or they can request permission from the provider to submit the software themselves. The data collected by Veracode includes an industry category property (called **RequestorIndustry**) for each third-party request.

To determine what types of consumers are most likely to make these requests, we look at how the requests aggregated along the **RequestorIndustry** dimension, as shown in Figure 3-9.

The SW industry accounts for over half of the requests. Some of these requests may be initiated by software vendors that are concerned about application security. Some of these requests may be the result of a customer-imposed requirement. With the data that we currently have, it is not possible to determine the motivation underlying the requests. As a result, requests attributed to industries other than SW may be underrepresented in Figure 3-9.

Figure 3-9 also shows that the Fin segment's requests outnumber requests from all companies in the Other category. This suggests additional lines of investigation. What proportion does the Fin segment represent across all of Veracode's reviews? Is it higher or lower than the 27.8 percent reflected in Figure 3-9? Is the difference significant? Instead of covering these questions here, I refer you to the full version of Veracode's latest "State of Software Security Report," available at the Veracode website.

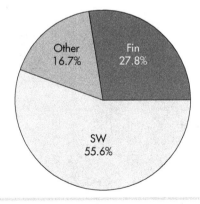

Figure 3-9   Proportion of third-party reviews by RequestorIndustry

Which Types of Applications Are Most Likely to Be Reviewed?

This question relates to the target applications that were reviewed. It addresses both which types of vendors and which types of applications were most frequently reviewed.

Figure 3-10 shows that applications from vendors that provide cloud-based services (either externally or internally deployed) account for almost 60 percent of third-party requests. This suggests that new lines of investigation should be initiated to investigate the interaction between cloud-based services and the sensitivity of consumers to application security. From this data, it appears that customers have the highest concern about the security of applications running in the cloud.

Figure 3-11 shows that operations accounts for almost half of all third-party review requests. Finance is second.

How Many Reviewed Applications Get a Passing Grade?

Veracode has a scoring system that translates the detailed results of a review into a pass/fail grade. The pass/fail grade assigned after the first review of the application is an attribute called **1stScanVeracodePass**, which is assigned to each application after its first review. The value of **1stScanVeracodePass** is TRUE if the application passes and FALSE if it does not.

By simply counting the applications with **1stScanVeracodePass** equal to TRUE and equal to FALSE, we get the results listed in Table 3-7.

So, the likelihood that an application will pass on the first attempt is less than 20 percent. This indicates consumers are definitely well served by requesting third-party reviews.

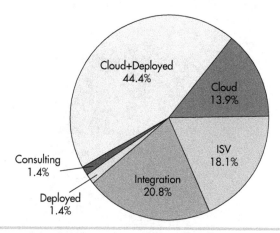

Figure 3-10 Proportion of third-party reviews by VendorType

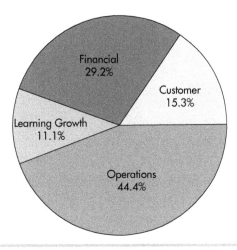

Figure 3-11   Proportion of third-party reviews by application function

How Long Does It Take to Fix a Failed Application?

For the applications that fail the first review, the Veracode service provides detailed information on discovered flaws as well as guidance on how to pass future testing. We introduce two metrics to quantify "what it takes" to pass:

- **appTTA**   The total time between initial submission and reception of a passing grade
- **appBTA**   The number of reviews (of successive builds of the app) performed up to and including the reception of a passing grade

These values are assigned to each reviewed application. As you might expect, there is some attrition for which we must account. There will be some applications that never achieve a passing grade—for whatever reason. To compute **appTTA** and **appBTA**, we restrict our sample to applications that have valid values for **appBTA**, namely one or more follow-up reviews. The resulting metrics describe the distributions for **appBTA** and **appTTA**, as listed in Table 3-8.

1stScanVeracodePass	Percent
FALSE	81%
TRUE	19%

Table 3-7   Review Results after First Scan of Third-Party Application

1stScanVeracodePass	Min.	1st Quart.	Median	Mean	3rd Quart.	Max.
appBTA	1	1	1	1.2	2.0	4
appTTA (days)	0.00	0.00	0.00	19.64	11.00	211

Table 3-8   appBTA and appTTA Distribution Metrics

For 75 percent of the reviewed applications, an 11-day effort was required to remove enough flaws to achieve a passing grade. No application took more than four builds and associated reviews to achieve a passing grade, and there was at least one outlier that took over 200 days in this dataset.

Summary of Findings (The Story)

The preceding metrics tell a story about current trends in application software security. Following is a summary of our findings:

- Increasingly, consumers of applications are asking their vendors to submit their software for a security review by a third party.

- The most likely requestors are financial companies and the software companies themselves.

- The most likely vendors to be asked for reviews sell services, as external or internally deployed cloud apps that perform operational and finance functions.

- Only one in five applications submitted for review receives a passing grade the first time.

- 75 percent of applications that did not receive a passing grade the first time took less than 11 days and two builds to achieve one.

- All applications took less than four builds to achieve a passing grade.

These types of metrics are the most valuable because they are placed into a business context and suggest a particular course of action. In this case, the suggested action for consumers is to request a third-party review of application security. The hard facts are that most applications will fail the initial review, but their vendors will not take long to transform them to meet an acceptable level of security. For vendors, these facts suggest that they should be more proactive about reviewing the security of the software that they sell.

We've Covered

A definition of analytics as the combination of metrics and interpretation

- Metrics are the numbers.
- Analytics include statistical inferences based on the numbers, interpretation within a business context, insights, and suggested action.

A description of what analytics can do

- Analytics can avoid lying with statistics.
- Analytics can ensure passing the "who cares?" test.
- Analytics map metrics to the business.

How to identify tools that can generate analytics yet do not require the user to have extensive training or sophistication in the underlying mathematics

- Examples include Google Analytics and Spotfire.
- These tools implement patterns recognized by experts and baked into software so that you don't need a PhD to do sophisticated analysis.

Examples of the use of analytics, along with explicit evidence of how interpretation enriches metrics

- Examples included analysis of security breach data, vulnerability data, and application software security data.

Endnotes

1. Timothy C. D'Auria, "What are Analytics? An overused word, an underused resource," *Managed Healthcare Executive*, Oct. 1, 2008, http://managedhealthcareexecutive .modernmedicine.com/mhe/article/articleDetail.jsp?id=557640.

2. Tony Hey, Stewart Tansley, and Kristin Tolle, eds., *The Fourth Paradigm: Data-Intensive Scientific Discovery* (Seattle, WA: Microsoft Research, 2009), http://research .microsoft.com/en-us/collaboration/fourthparadigm/.

3. Viktor Mayer-Schonberger, *Delete: The Virtue of Forgetting in the Digital Age* (Princeton, NJ: Princeton University Press, 2010).

4. Wikipedia, "Box plot," http://en.wikipedia.org/wiki/Box_plot.

5. Answers: 4, 4, 5.

6. The BSC model was originally developed in the 1990s by Drs. Robert Kaplan (Harvard Business School) and David Norton. BSC is a performance measurement framework to enrich traditional financial performance measures with strategic, nonfinancial performance measures, thereby giving a more balanced view of organizational performance. For additional information, see www.balancedscorecard.org.

CHAPTER 4

Commitment to Project Management

We'll Cover

- The value of discipline, commitment, and project management

- A project management methodology and framework

- How to get the most value out of limited resources for an information security program

Chapter 2 discussed the difference between security best practices and security work that is outcomes (or results) based. With limited resources and a limited budget, security practitioners are interested in getting the most value for their money and focusing on work that makes an impact. Developing a security metrics program and incorporating it into the overall information security program can ensure that security work is outcomes-focused instead of a haphazard effort that throws resources and dollars into a black hole of hazy security "best practices" work.

This chapter discusses the value of discipline, commitment, and project management to an information security program. It outlines how to leverage a specific project management methodology and framework to create a security metrics program and get the most value out of limited resources for an information security program. Starting with clearly defined success criteria and metrics for a project ensures that information security management knows what work is being done and how the team resources and dollars are being spent. It is not easy to qualify or quantify the impact of security efforts, but implementing and sticking to a tried-and-true project management methodology can provide visibility into the security work that is being done and show impact and progress.

Information Security Culture

In my experience, security professionals are very intelligent and passionate people who are fascinated by new technologies and a constantly changing threat landscape. They typically are idealistic and hard working and strive for perfection. They can be relied upon to respond to security incidents promptly and to do whatever needs to be done in a crisis situation. They will take calculated risks and put short-term solutions in place where needed to prevent further damage.

Information security professionals are often creative innovators, as they need to think very quickly and handle many different issues going on simultaneously during an emergency. Security practitioners are often rewarded by executive management (and even direct security management) for their heroics and expertise when something goes wrong and they are able to fix it. In such an environment, where crisis-mode heroics are often rewarded highly, day-to-day responsibilities can seem mundane and unimportant by comparison.

Part of the culture that accompanies responsibility for responding to and managing incidents is a tendency to be in "fire-fighting" mode most of the time. This requires self-discipline, because in the midst of a crisis, it is easy to panic and request technology and resource allocations quickly without thinking about ongoing maintenance and sustainability once the immediate need has passed.

Like any subject matter experts, security practitioners characteristically have a great deal of confidence and pride in their work. They often have broader and more technical knowledge than many other roles in operations and information technology, and believe strongly in their own approach to solving problems. When it comes to day-to-day work, security professionals prefer to rely on tried-and-true practices. When they find a reliable methodology for doing something, they like to stick to it.

Improvement of the information security program—one of the major goals and benefits of implementing a security metrics program—requires honesty from the team as they evaluate and strive to uncover the true current status of different components of the program. Seeking the truth instead of trying to make the data fit what you expect is not always easy, and being critical of your own work can be difficult. Focusing on security compliance, which tends to lead security practitioners into the habit of trying to please external auditors, can be a detriment to the program when applied to internally driven metrics and other improvement-focused projects. The most effective approach is to be willing to discover and learn something new, without allowing politics or the need to be right to get in the way.

The fact that sacred cows are part of information security culture is a result of both a lack of formal and standardized education for security professionals and a cultural fixation on security best practices.

> **LINGO**
> The information security industry also has a lot of **sacred cows**. This is an idiom for a practice that is implemented simply because it is "how it's always been done," without regard for its usefulness or whether it can help achieve a target goal or outcome.

Information security professionals tend to come from a wide variety of backgrounds—economics, IT, computer science, banking, bioengineering, and others. Unlike other professionals, such as attorneys, doctors, CPAs, architects, and engineers, you do not have to meet certain academic requirements and pass a certification exam to practice as an information security professional. Each information security professional progresses along their own path to intermediate and advanced levels of expertise throughout their career.

However, a variety of different certifications do exist that enable you to demonstrate you have achieved a recognized level of competency in the field, such as the CISSP, CAP, CISM, SCPM, CIPP/G, GIAC, CISA, and SSCP. Related certifications common to the information security practice include PMP, ITIL, and COBIT. Employers often seek candidates who hold at least one of these certifications.

Many security professionals transition to information security from a related field and learn the practice on the job. Often, junior-level information security practitioners learn from their management, who learned from their management at previous jobs, and so on. Consequently, one group at a company may insist on doing a procedure in exactly one particular way—with little regard for business need, alignment with business strategy, or changes in technology—simply because that is how they learned it the first time. This is different from understanding why something is done the way that it is or basing a procedure on a desired outcome or result. When a security practice fails to ensure a higher level of security than what was in place without it, it is unnecessary and a waste of resources. Additionally, if no one knows whether the implementation of a security measure has made a difference, either because no one is paying attention or because no one has adopted that measure, there is room for improvement. Implementing a security metrics program can provide insight into which practices are making an impact versus which practices are sacred cows instilled in security managers' minds.

Tip
Identifying and removing sacred cows from a security organization's day-to-day practice can eliminate the wasteful use of precious and limited resources and can help alleviate budgetary constraints.

IMHO
The fact that no formal education or career path is required for the information security professional today can be valuable, because people bring a diversity of experience to the job when they transition from a different industry to the information security industry. Because the threats and risks we are facing as an industry are constantly evolving, having people from different backgrounds offering different solutions can be advantageous (by avoiding groupthink).

Project Management

With good project management, what is planned gets done. A security metrics project should be like any other project, with a specifically defined goal, objective, or justification. Keeping in mind that developing a security metrics program is all about achieving desired outcomes and results, defining success criteria for a security metrics project is also important. Defining metrics to measure the success of a metrics project may sound odd at first, but without metrics, how will you know whether the project has been successful? Incorporating project management and planning into the culture of an information security organization can hasten maturity of the team culture. A more formal education process can eliminate the sacred cow phenomenon and establish a unified methodology for planning and execution.

IMHO

Just because a project is "done" is no longer good enough. Even applying the term "done" to security projects is often not descriptive enough. "Done" doesn't tell you the state of the project. For example, many security projects involve installing a new technology. Just because you purchased the technology does not necessarily mean the project is done. Just because you implement the technology does not necessarily mean the project is done. When you have purchased and implemented the technology and devoted resources to actively maintaining the technology and following a process that has been defined to make it work, then you've reached a legitimate completion state. Success criteria must be defined up front.

Even when success criteria have been met, most security projects can be thought of as paused rather than complete, under the assumption that the threat is still mutating and further work will be required in the future.

Defining success criteria up front can ensure that a desired outcome is specified even before work begins. Then, at the completion of the project, everyone knows whether or not the project has been successful. One benefit of incorporating project management into a security metrics program (or, more generally, into a security program) is that it ensures that management knows what work is being done. Qualifying and quantifying security efforts is not easy to do, but implementing good project management methodologies is a step in the right direction.

Additional benefits of incorporating project management include the practical and responsible use of security budgets through good planning, the ability to request budget increases by showing resources are being used effectively in an on-time and on-budget project, and the ability to set expectations of management by giving them a clear picture of how they will benefit from the project.

The next several subsections go through the individual details of a recommended project management methodology. This methodology is not specifically tied to any formal project management framework, but is instead designed with security in mind. It is not intended to be simply a form to fill out; rather, it is intended to be a lightweight management tool that helps you to think properly and comprehensively about a project before deploying it. Each section ends with one or more questions that are intended to assist you in developing a project plan against which to manage as the project is deployed. The example used is specific to a security metrics project, but this methodology can (and should) be applied to any type of information security project. An example showing the use of this methodology is provided at the end of this section.

Brief Objective Statement

The first thing to do when thinking about a project and starting to put together a project plan is to identify the project objective. Every project should add value to the business and should have a justification for implementation.

Questions

- What is the purpose of this project?
- What will change as a result of this project?
- What goal does this project seek to accomplish?

Type of Change

All projects can be categorized as either a new project or a project that changes something that already exists. Project types include, for example, putting a new process in place or enhancing an existing process; creating a new development or product or improving an existing development or product; and deploying a new technology or improving an existing technology.

Questions

- Will this project enhance or improve something that already exists?
- Is this project a completely new development?

Proposed Start Date and End Date

Every project should have a start date and an end date. Projects run by information security programs typically have a start date but don't necessarily have a defined end date. For example, a project might start as a "build" type of project, where something completely new is being developed or put in place, and then, once the build phase is finished, move into a manage and sustain mode. In this situation, the project might be seen as never-ending. A better solution is to consider this to be one build project with a defined end date, followed by one "run the business" activity.

In Actual Practice

Information security has a lot of "run the business" type activities, including incident response, which must have the flexibility and adaptability of running outside of a typical project management methodology and project plan, and these activities will be covered later in this chapter in "Run-the-Business Activities."

Because no one can foresee the future, even the best project and business managers can only estimate how long a given project is going to take. There are many factors that impact project time estimates. Most of these involve dependencies between cross-functional groups when many different types of resources are required. One objective of having a project plan in place and defining resource allocations up front is to ensure that the risks and delays inherent to any project are minimized.

Questions

- When will the project start?
- When is the project expected to be finished?

Roles and Responsibilities

Defining roles and responsibilities is an activity that should be performed during the planning phase of any project. It is important to know who is doing what so that, as the project is being executed, there is no confusion as to who is responsible for making which decisions. It also helps the project manager (or management overseeing the project) determine who to consult to resolve issues that come up. Clear roles and responsibilities help prevent both duplication of effort (when multiple resources or teams are doing the same work but in separate silos disconnected from each other) and gaps (when required work is not being performed because each

LINGO
RASCI refers to a project management methodology for assigning roles in projects that involve many people and teams. Each letter in RASCI stands for a different type of role—Responsible, Approver, Supporter, Consultant, and Informed—and each role has corresponding responsibilities.

of multiple resources or teams believes that someone else is taking care of it). This section presents one methodology for defining roles and responsibilities, called the RASCI model.

Note

I first learned about the RASCI model when I worked at eBay. The company was using it to organize roles and responsibilities for projects. I believe the model was originally developed in the 1970s and formally written about by Erling S. Andersen, Krostoffer V. Grude, and Tor Haug in the mid-1980s in their book *Goal Directed Project Management.* Their basic model has continued to be developed and refined for over two decades.

Responsible

The *R* in RASCI stands for Responsible. The R is the owner of the project. Whereas there may be multiple A's, S's, C's, and I's, there should be only one R.

Questions

- Who is responsible for managing the project and ensuring that it is completed?
- Who is accountable for the project?
- Who is responsible for managing and resolving any issues related to the project?
- Who will management approach first to ask questions about the project?
- Who is responsible if something goes wrong with the project?

Approver

The *A* in RASCI stands for Approver and is the person from whom the R needs to get ultimate approval for the project requirements and its results. There may be multiple A's to whom the R is responsible. For example, if a chief information security officer (CISO) is deploying a project that supports multiple independent business units, each of the business unit leaders may be an A in this model.

Questions

- Who is responsible for approving the project?
- Who has a sense of the bigger picture to which this project is contributing and can provide feedback to the R regarding how this project aligns with higher-level objectives?

Supporter

The *S* in RASCI stands for Supporter. The S's are the people and the teams that help the R get the project done. There may be multiple S's who play different roles in supporting the R. Generally a project will have more S's than A's, C's, and I's.

For example, in a technology deployment project, the vendor team that is selling the project may be a Supporter to the person or group Responsible for managing the project. If the technology is being deployed in a site or corporate network, then teams from the operations infrastructure group and the information technology group may be involved in supporting the project.

Questions

- Who performs the tasks necessary to make the project happen?

- Who is responsible for managing the systems, people, or processes affected by the project?

Consultant

The *C* in RASCI stands for Consultant. There may be multiple C's supporting any one project, and they may provide consulting services for different aspects or areas of the project. Instead of directly supporting the project, the C may play an advisory role to the R or to the S's. The C is not directly responsible for the project or any particular component of the project, but acts as a subject matter expert (SME) when expertise is required in an area that does not belong to the R or to the S's. Consultants can be, but are not always, contracted from outside the organization, and they often are paid a premium for their specialized services.

Examples of consultants in the area of information security projects include consultants who specialize in a particular threat area, consultants who provide language- or culture-specific advice in the case of a regionally specific incident or investigation, and consultants who are experts in the area of upcoming relevant regulation or know about changes to compliance standards or frameworks that the organization is required to follow.

Questions

- Whose specialized expertise is required to fulfill project requirements?

- Who has specific subject matter knowledge that is not available within the core team of the Responsible owner or the group of project Supporters?

Informed

The *I* in RASCI stands for Informed. There may be many people or groups who should be Informed about the project, so that they know about the potential impact to their own projects or daily work, even if they do not provide input or approval. Often the Informed teams are customers or receivers of the benefits of the project (conversely, they may be teams that are adversely affected by the project). For example, following the completion of a project to revamp information security policies and standards, all employees of an organization need to be informed about the changes so they have proper guidance on secure behaviors.

Question

● Which people and groups outside of the core project team will be affected by this project?

Milestones and Critical Success Factors

When defining the roles of each person responsible for the project, it is essential to include the owner of milestones and critical success factors. In many cases, this is the function of the R and the A team members.

IMHO

Communication to Informed groups can be very important at the start of the project, during the execution phase, and especially after the completion phase (depending on the extent to which the Informed group will be affected). In the case of deploying a new technology that employees or customers must get accustomed to using, or changing a technology or a process that they are used to using, effective communication will be key to minimizing delay in using the new technology or process.

Project Name

It is important to have a single, consistent project name that folks can refer to across the board. Project names are useful for mapping related vendors, purchase orders, contracts, and status tracking and reports to the correct project. A lot of the paperwork and documentation required to allocate and move funds and purchase and ship materials will refer to a project by its name.

A good project name should be simple and descriptive. This will ensure that all of the different teams involved in the project (external vendors, finance, procurement, legal, HR, and different groups outside of the information security team), even those who are less familiar with the intimate details of the project, can identify the project and distinguish it from other projects. This becomes especially important when someone who is peripheral to the project but is involved in an approval flow needs to match the project name from one system to another.

Sometimes organizations have standard project-naming formats that tie the project to a particular timeline, such as including in the name the week, quarter, or year in which the project is being performed. This is more common in engineering organizations, where many projects have a similar type of format and similar expectations involved;

for example, a project might be named 2011Q2_Project1234. In other cases, a project may need to have a name that intentionally masks what the project is about. For example, if an organization is planning to close one of its regional offices and wants to keep that information a secret, then it might use a generic project name that is understood only by project members.

Question

- What is the name of the project?

Problem Statement

Every project should have a clear problem statement that defines the issue or problem that the project is intended to solve. Some projects may have multiple problem statements, or one large problem statement that has many substatements. The more specific a problem statement or a set of problem statements is, the more useful it can be for later defining project requirements. For example, "This organization's customer-facing website has 2500 instances of cross-site scripting vulnerabilities, 50 of which are located on transactional pages of the site" is a more descriptive and therefore more useful problem statement than "The website is vulnerable to attack."

Questions

- What problem or issue is the project intended to solve?
- What is the current status of the project target?

Solution Statement

As a complement to the problem statement, every project should include a specific, descriptive solution statement that outlines how the project will solve the problem. The solution statement should be equal to the problem statement in detail and specificity. For example, "Design and develop an input and output checking framework and implement it on the organization's customer-facing website, starting with the transactional areas and finishing with the remaining areas, to remediate 2500 cross-site scripting vulnerabilities" is a much more useful solution statement than "Secure the website."

Note

In this particular example, the assumption is that the 2500 vulnerabilities are known but have not been discovered (and remain unexploited) by hackers and fraudsters. Presumably, if any of the vulnerabilities is being actively exploited and the company or organization knows about it, the remediation is happening as part of a more immediate response effort rather than as part of a longer-term strategic project as described here.

Ideally, each problem statement in a set of problem statements should have at least one solution statement. However, this is not always the case. Sometimes a project that is intended to tackle a complex problem set with many problem statements has solutions for only some of the problems. This is perfectly acceptable; perhaps other projects will deploy solutions for the remaining problems, the priority of the remaining problems is too low to address them at this time, or the organization's cost-benefit analysis shows that some of the problems aren't worth addressing at all.

Even if not all of the problem statements are addressed, matching up front the ones that do have solution statements as part of this project is a good way to provide insight and visibility into what the project is actually intended to solve. This also prevents potential confusion by ensuring that no one will misunderstand the intent of the project and incorrectly believe that the project will solve more than it is intended to solve.

Question

- How does this project solve one or more of the problem statements in the problem statement set for this project?

Team Priority or Principle Supported

Determining the team priority or principle supported by the project helps to answer the question "why are we doing this project?" and ensures that a limited budget and limited resources will be allocated appropriately to organization and business priorities. It requires the management of an information security program to go through the exercise of defining priorities or principles for the team. Priorities typically are defined for a particular time interval, such as a half year or full year, whereas principles are more foundational to a program and typically are addressed in the information security team's mission statement and charter.

If the information security management team finds that no team priority or principle is supported by the project, they should consider these options: drop the project; revise the project so that it supports a team priority or principle; or reevaluate the priorities and principles to determine whether the environment has changed and the project does support a team priority or principle.

Question

- What team priority or principle is supported by this project?

IMHO

There is nothing wrong with changing priorities, and in the complex field of information security, this happens quite frequently. What is important is to recognize when a potential change to priorities has come up and to address it by having a discussion to reconsider and possibly change priorities. This is much easier to do, and can be done more effectively, at the start of a project rather than in the middle or, in the worst case, at the end of the project.

Project Scope

Defining a project scope up front also forces a prioritization exercise, as in most cases a project will not be comprehensive and cover every possible use case. Typically, focus areas are chosen based on business needs or priorities. Parameters such as time, budget, and resource availability often are factors in how far the scope of the project reaches.

As an example of defining the scope of a project, consider an organization that has offices in many different regions around the globe. It is preparing to deploy a new process with an associated technology, but the budget is sufficient to cover only a few of the regions in which offices are located. The scope for this project will identify which regions will be covered by this project, and which will not.

LINGO

The **scope** of a project indicates project coverage, typically by identifying the different regions, different networks, and/or different groups of people the project encompasses.

Questions

- Does this project comprehensively address everything in this area?

- If not, which areas are addressed and which are not?

Project Description

This can be a high-level overview or a detailed description, depending on what works best for the culture and the needs of the team. The project description provides additional details about the project that may not already be addressed, enabling project members who want to know more about the project to find more information on what the project entails.

A project description may be very similar to a solution statement but provide additional details about how a project will solve the problem.

Change Details and Impacts

As previously addressed in the section "Type of Change," there are usually two types of projects: completely new projects and projects that make a change to something that already exists. A statement of change details and impacts typically isn't necessary for new projects, whereas one is almost always required for projects that make a change to something that already exists.

Descriptions of change details and impacts are typically very technical and may describe interfaces between the current project and other affected systems. It is important to define and document each process, technology, and team that will be affected and describe how it will be affected.

Questions

- Which existing processes, technologies, and teams will be affected by this project?

- What changes to existing processes and technologies need to occur in order for this project to be successful?

- How are existing processes and technologies affected by this project?

Risks of Not Implementing This Project

As with problem and solution statements, a statement of the risks of not implementing the project is most useful when it is specific. For example, "If this network vulnerability project is not implemented, user accounts will continue to be compromised at the unacceptable rate of 100 per day" is more informative than "If we do not take on this project, then the network will not be secure."

A risk description often resembles a problem statement and is another way of describing or defining the problem.

Question

- What will happen if this project is not implemented?

Dependencies or Risks

Any project that depends on resources from multiple teams, budget approval, vendors or external partners providing services, and so forth, will have inherent dependencies or risks. If one of these items changes or is delayed, then the project depending on it will also be affected.

In Actual Practice

For information security especially, identifying the risks of not implementing the project is important not only because managing risk is a major objective of the information security program, but also because it informs and educates others in the organization about the threats that the information security team is addressing. Many people are oblivious to the work that we as security professionals do every day, so putting in writing what might seem obvious to us can help enlighten the organization. Contemplating a project in terms of the risk that remains if the project is not implemented is simply another way to think about justification and objectives. For folks who struggle to define objectives and justification, addressing this question can be one way to do it.

Dependencies arise when projects are complex and involve multiple components, especially in terms of resources. If resources are occupied by multiple projects simultaneously, they may not be able to dedicate as much work effort as is needed for any single project to complete in the shortest timeframe possible. Planned resource allocations and project plan timelines that account for realistic resource work efforts can mitigate and decrease the risks involved in resource dependencies, as can addressing potential project risks up front. One example of a resource dependency is an information security project that involves a technology deployment onto the corporate network. This requires IT resources and is dependent on the availability of those resources.

When the budget has not been approved for a project, funding is a clear dependency. The project typically will not start until the budget has been approved. A budget dependency also arises when a project is partially complete and funding is frozen. Multiple funding sources can complicate a project further.

A third type of dependency may be if a project depends on an existing process flow and a new process is put into place. Those participating in the existing process will have to learn the new process to participate in it and ensure a successful transition.

Risks may occur whenever a dependency exists. I recommend identifying dependencies at the start of project planning so that you can incorporate appropriate time buffers into the project plan and meet with resource and budget owners to obtain commitment.

Questions

- Which resources or teams are required for project support?
- Have the managers of these teams been made aware of the project expectations?
- Have adequate and appropriate resources been committed to the project?
- What type of funding is required?
- Will multiple funding sources be needed?
- Have cost estimates been performed and has funding been approved and secured?
- Which existing process flows does this project depend on?
- What are the risks of these process flows changing during the project?
- What happens if funding runs out?
- Is there a plan for what to do with partial results?

Metrics/Success Measures

This book is about improving information security programs by using metrics to identify, implement, and report on project outcomes and results that make an impact. Information security is not a success simply because a program is in place; similarly, information security project success should not be determined simply by project completion. Every information security project, metrics-related or otherwise, should have success criteria. It is important to define success criteria for a project so that when the project ends, it is clear if success was achieved.

Ideally, an information security project will affect higher-level business or organizational metrics or quantifiably reduce the organization's risk profile. For example, if an information security project affects a company by driving a desirable metric up a few percentage points or an undesirable metric down a few percentage points, then the value to the organization is clear. The best success measures tie directly to metrics.

Questions

- At the time of project completion, what will indicate that the project has been successful?
- How will you know when to stop?
- What metrics does this project support?
- How will the metrics change as a result of this project?
- What will change as a result of this project being implemented, and by how much?

Major Deliverables and Deadlines

Defining deliverables and deadlines (also called timelines and milestones) is critical to putting together a project plan. Especially for projects with many dependencies, defined deliverables and deadlines can assist with setting expectations and obtaining buy-in and commitment. These may be hard to set in stone, but an estimate is better than nothing.

> **LINGO**
> A **deliverable** is the specific result that shows something has been accomplished. Examples of deliverables include reports, process diagrams, or a decision outcome.

A "do it until it is done" mentality can result in very ineffective use of time and resources. Projects that lack specifically defined deliverables and timelines are subject to more delays, as projects with defined deliverables and deadlines often take priority over and take resources away from projects without. As the project progresses, project plans should always be updated to reflect more accurate timelines.

Note

Some security work, such as reviewing IDS logs, falls into the category of run-the-business, maintenance-type work. Unlike project work, which has specific deliverables and timelines defined, this type of security work may never, in fact, be complete, but rather is an activity that takes place on some regular (or random, as determined by the approach decided upon by the activity owner) basis.

Questions

- What are the major deliverables of this project?
- What are the major milestones that must be met to complete this project?
- How long will it take to reach each of these milestones?

Required Budget

It is important to understand the budget impact of a project prior to starting it so that budget approval can be requested and obtained. The clearer and more complete the estimate is, the more easily the budget Approver can say "Yes, there is enough room in the budget for this project, and I will reserve it for this project." At first, the budget required will always be an estimate. This estimate requires careful preparation. If the estimate is too high, the budget may not be approved; if the estimate is too low, the budget may run out before the project is complete.

Milestones can be tied to incentives for those performing the work, which may include the internal team, the external vendor, or both. Milestones may be interdependent, requiring successful completion of one milestone before the project can proceed to the next phase or to the ultimate deliverables. In many cases, it is critical to achieve milestones according to plan to ensure that projects are done on time, on budget, and to the specifications of the project team.

In order to receive the proper budget, project outcomes and benefits must be clearly communicated up front. Many times, showing how this project helps management achieve overarching business goals, strategy, or cost reduction will allow for the appropriate allocation of budget.

Most projects involve more than one type of funding. Typical funding types include consulting (operating expenses, or opex), maintenance contracts and software licenses, capital expenses (capex), and other expenses (travel, sponsorships, memberships, etc.). For an information security professional who is putting together a project budget justification, it can be useful to understand the unique attributes of each of these types of funding and how they differ.

Consulting dollars are used for consulting engagements, where a subject matter expert or resource intended for staff augmentation works for an organization for a set length of time and an agreed upon amount. Typically, consulting engagements are billed hourly, with an estimate of how much the project will cost provided up front. If the consultant exhausts the estimated fees before the engagement is completed, the consultant's contract might be renegotiated to provide additional money. Finance departments generally track consulting dollars by the quarter in which the work is performed.

The budget for maintenance contracts and software licenses typically is spread over the period for which the maintenance contract or license is active (usually 12 months). For example, a $12,000 annual license will be tracked by the finance department as $1,000 per month out of an organization's budget. They are typically renewed on an annual basis.

Capital expenses typically refers to hardware and software purchases, but can also be used as a category for paying development resources who are involved in building a new software product. Depending on how long the capital expense is expected to provide value, the finance department will track the expense and pay it out over the duration of its expected value. For example, if a server's expected duration of value is three years, then the funds for a purchase of a server in the first quarter of 2012 will be tracked in 2012, 2013, and 2014, and the initial expense for that quarter will be only 1/12 of the full cost.

Examples of other expenses include travel expenses (such as hotel and food costs for work-related travel), sponsorships, and memberships. Annual memberships are tracked by the finance department in a similar fashion to maintenance contracts and software licenses (over 12 months). Sponsorships may be tracked over 12 months or, in the case of sponsoring a single event, only for the quarter in which the event occurs.

Budget requests are not as simple as saying "This project will cost $200,000." The budget approver will ask, "How will the $200,000 be spent?" Information security projects that require third-party vendors and products typically involve a combination of hardware purchases (capital expense), maintenance contracts, and software licenses, and consulting to install and customize the product. Travel may be required for team members or for consultants, and those expenses will also need to be built into the cost up front.

Questions

- How much money is required in the budget to support this project?

- Will external consulting be required? If so, how much will it cost?

- Will hardware or software need to be purchased? If so, how much will it cost?

- What maintenance contracts and software licenses will be required?

- What kind of travel and other expenses will be required?

- What kind of training is required for in-house resources who may be responsible for running or maintaining these systems in the future?

Information Security Resources Required

Information security projects typically require resources from different functions of the team. For example, a risk assessment project may require policy resources as well as testing or monitoring resources. You should identify the roles required and estimate how much time will be needed from each role. To go a step further, you can identify specific names. For example, perhaps a project to remediate a set of previously exploited vulnerabilities requires the consulting expertise of someone on the investigations team who has details about what happened when the vulnerabilities were exploited in the past. This role might be required for eight hours, and Caroline Wong might be the name of the specific resource requested.

Identifying these resources up front will allow you to consult the manager of each resource to book and commit the resource's time to the project.

Questions

- What type of expertise is required from the information security team for this project?
- What type of role possesses this skill set and expertise?
- Approximately how much time will be required from this resource or set of resources?
- Can specific resources be identified by name?

Other Resources Required

Resources outside of the information security team may also be required for a project to be successful. Typical groups from which these resources will come include vendor partners and internal departments such as information technology, operations infrastructure, legal, human resources, and privacy. Security projects that are intended to provide new services to a group occasionally require resources from the customer group to assist with developing requirements and reviewing plans. These may include customer service or other customer-focused groups.

Questions

- What type of expertise is required from outside the information security team for this project?
- What type of role possesses this skill set and expertise?
- Approximately how much time will be required from this resource or set of resources?
- Can specific resources be identified by name?

Tip
It may be useful in some cases to present to the Approver a list of potential other resources required so that the Approver can provide their input on who must be involved versus who is optional.

Example Application of the Project Management Methodology

Table 4-1 presents an example of an information security metrics project that uses the project management methodology described in this chapter. This example includes the questions and a brief summary of what is required for each section of the plan.

Brief Objective Statement

What is the purpose of this project? What will change as a result of this project? What goal does this project seek to accomplish?	The purpose of this project is to create automated reporting of incident response metrics. Currently, these metrics are gathered manually and in an ad hoc manner, with no reporting, search capability, or visibility into the work that the incident response team performs. After the project, the process will be automated, with tools available to search, organize, and view the metrics. The goal of this project is to provide to management insight and visibility into incident response work.

Type of Change

Will this project enhance or improve something that already exists? Is this project a completely new development?	This project is largely a new development. Currently, some incident response metrics are gathered manually and in an ad hoc manner, but they are not centralized or organized formally.

Proposed Start Date and End Date

When will the project start? When is the project expected to be finished?	This project will start at the beginning of Q1, 2012, and is expected to be finished at the end of Q3, 2012.

Roles and Responsibilities

Responsible

Who is responsible for managing the project and ensuring that it is completed? Who is accountable for the project? Who is responsible for managing and resolving any issues related to the project? Who will management approach first to ask questions about the project? Who is responsible if something goes wrong with the project?	The incident response team

Approver

Who is responsible for approving the project? Who has a sense of the bigger picture to which this project is contributing and can provide feedback to the R regarding how this project aligns with higher-level objectives?	The chief information security officer

Table 4-1   Project Management Methodology Example

Roles and Responsibilities

Supporter

Who performs the tasks necessary to make the project happen?	The information security metrics team External vendors providing monitoring and alerts to the incident response team
Who is responsible for managing the systems, people, or processes affected by the project?	

Consultant

Whose specialized expertise is required to fulfill project requirements?	The information security risk management team
Who has specific subject matter knowledge that is not available within the core team of the Responsible owner or the group of project Supporters?	

Informed

Which people and groups outside of the core project team will be affected by this project?	Enterprise Risk Management Committee Other executives (presidents, CFOs, etc.)

Project Name

What is the name of this project?	Incident Response Metrics

Problem Statement

What problem or issue is the project intended to solve?	The project is intended to address the lack of clear and organized incident response metrics reporting. The organization currently has no visibility into how much time is spent on incident response metrics, which areas have the most and least number of incidents, the severity level of incidents, or the priority level of incidents.
What is the current status of the project target?	

Solution Statement

How does this project solve one or more of the problem statements in the problem statement set for this project?	This project will leverage a new incident response case-tracking technology and the centralized information security metrics reporting technology to gather incident response metrics information and automatically create a useful and searchable reporting database.

Table 4-1 Project Management Methodology Example (*Continued*)

Team Priority or Principle Supported

What team priority or principle is supported by this project?	Information security metrics visibility

Project Scope

Does this project comprehensively address everything in this area? If not, which areas are addressed and which are not?	This project will cover all incidents, including incidents occurring on the corporate network as well as production networks.

Project Description

	This project will leverage a new incident response case-tracking technology and the centralized information security metrics reporting technology to gather incident response metrics information and automatically create useful and searchable reporting. This reporting will enable decision making and changes to overall security strategy and resource allocation based on better visibility into the data.

Change Details and Impacts

Which existing processes, technologies, and teams will be affected by this project? What changes to existing processes and technologies need to occur in order for this project to be successful? How are existing processes and technologies affected by this project?	The incident response team will need to create new processes for gathering and tracking incident data. Existing manual processes will be replaced by automatic processes enabled by the technology.

Risks of Not Implementing This Project

What will happen if this project is not implemented?	If this project is not implemented, the organization will continue to lack visibility in the area of incident response. Without this information, it will be hard to know how many resources to dedicate to the team and impossible to optimize the effectiveness of responding to and closing out incident cases.

Table 4-1   Project Management Methodology Example (*Continued*)

Dependencies or Risks	
Which resources or teams are required for project support?	This project is dependent on the external vendor who is deploying the product solution. It will be affected by how much time and resources the vendor can dedicate to this project and how responsive the vendor is to requests. This project is also largely dependent on a willingness and commitment from the incident response team to provide work effort in this area. Because the incident response team is also responsible for responding to day-to-day incidents, their time availability is always an unknown, as direct incident response will likely take priority over this project. If funding runs out, a change order will need to be proposed and reviewed. This should include a description of the benefits achieved with partial results and what has not been achieved yet.
Have the managers of these teams been made aware of the project expectations?	
Have adequate and appropriate resources been committed to the project?	
What type of funding is required?	
Will multiple funding sources be needed?	
Have cost estimates been performed and has funding been approved and secured?	
Which existing process flows does this project depend on?	
What are the risks of these process flows changing during the project?	
What happens if funding runs out?	
Is there a plan for what to do with partial results?	

Metrics/Success Measures	
At the time of project completion, what will indicate that the project has been successful?	This project will be successful if the metrics that are defined by the information risk management team are available in a clear reporting format and are continually kept up to date. It will be successful if the new incident response processes required to support getting the data into the system are operational by the end of the project timeframe.
How will you know when to stop?	
What metrics does this project support?	
How will the metrics change as a result of this project?	
What will change as a result of this project being implemented, and by how much?	

Major Deliverables and Deadlines	
What are the major deliverables of this project?	Information security risk management team defines the metrics desired for visibility and metrics requirements; end of Q1, 2012.
What are the major steps milestones that must be met to complete this project?	New incident response team processes defined; end of Q2, 2012. External vendor incident response case-tracking product deployment; end of Q2, 2012.
How long will it take to reach each of these milestones?	New incident response team processes operational and continually providing data into the new system; end of Q3, 2012.

Table 4-1 Project Management Methodology Example (*Continued*)

Required Budget

How much money is required in the budget to support this project?	The budget requires $237,000, broken down as follows: $150,000 in consulting will be needed in Q1 and Q2, 2012, for the vendor product installation and customization. $20,000 in hardware will be required and purchased in Q2, 2012. $50,000 in annual maintenance will be required, starting in Q3, 2012. $15,000 in travel will be required to pay for vendor resource travel from out of state. $2,000 in training is also required for the vendor to train in-house resources on how to operate and maintain the systems in the future.
Will external consulting be required? If so, how much will it cost?	
Will hardware or software need to be purchased? If so, how much will it cost?	
What maintenance or license renewals will be required?	
What kind of travel and other expenses will be required?	
What kind of training is required for in-house resources who may be responsible for running or maintaining these systems in the future?	

Information Security Resources Required

What type of expertise is required from the information security team for this project?	Incident response team: all resources for ten hours per week for three quarters
What type of role possesses this skill set and expertise?	Information risk management team: one resource for three hours per week for one quarter
Approximately how much time will be required from this resource or set of resources?	Metrics team: One resource for six hours per week for one quarter
Can specific resources be identified by name?	

Other Resources Required

What type of expertise is required from outside the information security team for this project?	Information technology team: three resources for ten hours per week for two quarters to deploy case-tracking technology on the corporate network
What type of role possesses this skill set and expertise?	
Approximately how much time will be required from this resource or set of resources?	
Can specific resources be identified by name?	

Table 4-1   Project Management Methodology Example (*Continued*)

Following the project management methodology in Table 4-1 takes time and an appropriate skill set and knowledge base. A management-level perspective on the big picture and impact to the overall organization may be required to best specify project requirements, roles, and responsibilities.

In Actual Practice

At this point it should be clear that one of the additional benefits of following the project management methodology is that it ensures project requirements are specified and documented. This prevents the "single point of failure" issue, where only one of the project team members knows everything about the project and that information is not documented. If that person leaves the organization, changes roles, or is unable to work because of personal reasons, other project members may struggle to piece together information. This can result in a longer time to bring new project members on board, project delays, and misunderstandings about the original project intent and expected outcomes.

It is also much easier to move different resources on and off of the project when project requirements, roles, and responsibilities are clearly documented. Changing resources midway through the project is more common in longer and more complex projects. The more complex a project, the more value is added by documenting and sharing this information within the project team.

Run-the-Business Activities

As mentioned at the beginning of this chapter, information security organizations constantly struggle to balance strategic, proactive planning with responding in a timely manner to unforeseen incidents and serving a variety of customers. It is easy to lose focus on strategic planning and get caught up in reactive fire-fighting mode, not only because of the critical nature of incidents, but also because of the personal acknowledgment and rewards for providing value in this area. However, I strongly believe that the only way to truly advance and improve an information security program is to focus an appropriate amount of resources on outcomes-based planning to ensure that goals are specified and met.

One approach to beginning to plan run-the-business versus project-based activities is to begin keeping track of how much time is consumed by a team on run-the-business tasks. You can use any ticketing system (JIRA is one example) to keep track of incoming requests/ incidents. By simply beginning to track certain types of data for run-the-business tasks, you can begin to develop a better understanding of how much overall time is consumed on run-the-business activities (and, therefore, the amount of team the security team is not available for project work). Preliminary data to track to accomplish this goal includes the following: date and time of request, date and time of request completion, and number of hours to complete. You can build more sophisticated reports if you want to keep track of data types such as business unit of requestor.

There are different ways to allocate information security resources for both strategic build projects and run-the-business, maintenance tasks. Based on the information you get from this type of data gathering, it will be up to each CSO/CISO to determine how many resources to allocate each to project work, metrics work, detection work, and response work.

We've Covered

The Value of discipline, commitment, and project management

- Balancing discipline, commitment, and project management with the "fire-fighting" nature of information security culture can have a positive impact on program effectiveness and improvement.

A project management methodology and framework

- Using a project management methodology that incorporates specific objectives, problem and solution statements, roles and responsibilities, success criteria and metrics, and resource allocations can add a proactive, strategic planning arm to information security programs, which are typically more focused on reactive, tactical work. This chapter provided an example of a specific project management methodology and framework.

How to get the most value out of limited resources for an information security program

- Resource allocation and prioritization, two important factors in project management, can help you to get the most value out of limited resources for an information security program.

PART III

Decide What to Measure

CHAPTER 5

Identify Core Competencies, Information Security Work, and Resourcing Options

We'll Cover

- Identifying information security core competencies

- Analyzing core competencies for metrics

- Determining what should be measured and for what purpose

- Resourcing information security work

- Outsourcing and offshoring

This chapter discusses the core competencies of an information security program, including how to identify them, how to apply metrics to them, and how to allocate resources to them. This chapter begins with a discussion of the primary groups in an organization that perform information security functions (the information security team, technology groups, and corporate functions). I also introduce a worksheet of information security core competencies that you can use for evaluating your own organization to see where you are in terms of performing each of these competencies. Next I present a model for evaluating the different types of work required in an effective information security program and provide recommendations for how to best leverage the various types of staffing resources. This discussion of core competencies lays the groundwork for Chapter 6, in which we discuss in detail various methods for how to identify a target for a metrics project.

Evaluating Security Core Competencies for Metrics Projects

One of the biggest challenges of kicking off an information security metrics program is figuring out where to begin. A security metrics program consists of metrics projects, and each metrics project must have a target area of focus. This is the area into which you will want to gain visibility for the purposes of communicating a status or driving change. There are many potential areas to choose from when determining a target for a metrics project, and one way to go about figuring out where to begin is to evaluate the various core competencies of an information security program.

As an example, consider technology asset inventory and management. How much information security work relies on or uses a technology asset inventory? How many companies manage their technology assets well? For those that do not (most), should the information security team step in and perform or manage some of the technology asset inventory work? Going through a core competencies definition exercise will assist in determining whether technology asset inventory and management work is an information security core competency (and should be addressed as such) or is a core competency of another department. Should the information security team handle the work simply because it uses technology assets, even though the work is a core competency of another corporate function that is truly responsible for doing the work? For example, if the security team is interested in understanding what percentage of corporate laptops and desktops have up-to-date antivirus software, the security team would ask the IT teams who are responsible for managing the corporate systems. The security team shouldn't take over operational responsibility for managing these systems to ensure that the percentage of machines with antivirus increases, rather the security team should come to an agreement with the IT teams regarding service level agreements (SLAs) for the timeframe in which IT must update systems when a signature update is available.

> **LINGO**
> **Core competencies** are the fundamental strengths of a program that add value to the organization. They are the primary functions of a program.

An information security program affects and interacts with many other groups throughout the organization, and in some cases the information security team has shared responsibility or distinct responsibility to perform work in a particular area. The following groups in an organization perform information security program functions or related functions:

- **Information security team**   The functions of the information security team may be performed in-house, outsourced, or offshored, depending on the type of function (as discussed in the next section).

- **Technology groups**   These include the operations infrastructure, information technology, and product development teams.

- **Corporate functions**   This category includes the HR, legal, audit, privacy, and risk management departments.

Who does what in an organization will certainly differ by industry and by individual organization, and may also change over time, but the core competencies worksheet shown in Figure 5-1 should be a good tool to help any organization determine who is responsible

	Information Security			Technology			Corporate Functions					Other
	In-House	Outsource	Offshore	Operations Infrastructure	Information Technology	Product Development	Human Resources	Legal	Audit	Privacy	Risk Mgmt	
Security Architecture												
Security Metrics												
Risk Management												
Security Awareness												
Personnel Security												
Vulnerability Management												
Security Policies												
Patch / Configuration Management												
Identity Management												
Security Monitoring												
Audit & Compliance												
Security Development												
Third-party Security												
Information Classification												
Asset Managemen												
Business Continuity & Disaster Recovery												
Incident Response												
Physical Security												
Secure Builds												
Network Security												
Product Security												
Legal & Privacy												
Encryption												

Figure 5-1 Core competencies worksheet

for the various functions related to information security. For each function listed down the left side that applies to your organization, you would put a check mark into the box corresponding to the group that is primarily responsible for performing that function. This exercise will indicate which functions the information security team and program should focus on (its core competencies) and which functions belong to other groups in the organization.

Sometimes a group performs certain information security–related functions only because another group is neglecting its duties. For example, the performing group may need an output of a function that another group is neglecting, so they will perform the work that needs to be done to get that output. Using a specific example from Figure 5-1, suppose the information security team performs the Backup, Recovery, & Archiving function simply because they set the policies and standards in this area and neither the operations infrastructure team nor the information technology team has taken responsibility for the function. The more appropriate roles might be for the information security team to set the policies and standards and perform audits to ensure that the policies and standards are being followed, and for the operations infrastructure or information technology team to perform the actual backup, recovery, and archiving work. Security work involves planning for failure and deciding which failures are tolerable.

IMHO

I recommend performing a core competencies exercise twice—once for how your organization actually functions, and a second time for how it ought to function. This may give you even better insight into which functions the information security metrics program should focus on.

Spectrum of Information Security Work

The types of work that information security involves covers a wide spectrum, from well-established, mature work to novel, cutting-edge work. The types of work can be broadly categorized based on whether they are intended to sustain, establish, or build information security projects, processes, and technologies:

- **Sustain**   Routine, task-oriented work
- **Establish**   Work that is intended to establish formal processes and documentation for unstructured or informal information security practices
- **Build**   Cutting-edge, innovative work where new features are being built

This section reviews each of these categories in depth and discusses which types of metrics are best suited for each category. It also briefly discusses which resourcing model—offshore, outsource, or in-house—is the best fit for each category. All three categories of work, as well as the resourcing models and typical metrics that support each, are shown in Figure 5-2.

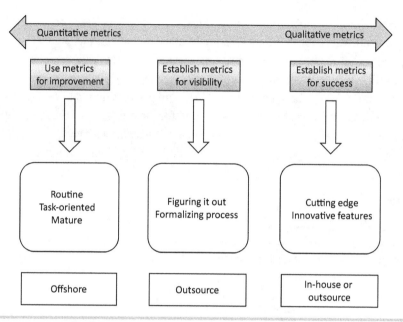

Figure 5-2 Spectrum of information security work

Sustain

This refers to the type of information security work that is performed to sustain ongoing security operations. It involves projects, processes, and technologies that are mature and well documented, and that the information security team has already mastered, either because the team has done them routinely for years or because the work is straightforward and task-oriented. This type of work is well defined and easy to transition from one resource to another, provided that the resources have the right skill set and expertise. Sometimes this type of work is very technical and requires specialized knowledge or formal training.

Examples

One example of routine, task-oriented work in the information security arena is the review of firewall rule change requests. The procedure for reviewing these requests is something for which a playbook can be written to describe the policy and standards to which firewall rule changes for a particular company or organization must adhere. In reality, the playbook will likely be complex, but at a high level, if the firewall rule change request complies with the policy and standards, then it can be implemented; otherwise, a policy exception can be submitted. Implementation of these types of requests may also fall into the category of routine, task-oriented work. This is a case where specialized technical

In Actual Practice

Why wouldn't an organization's internal information security host-hardening standards simply match the CIS-recommended secure configurations? The answer is that the decision depends largely on what works for a particular information security organization. One organization may choose to adopt the CIS standard as its own and document policy exceptions for noncompliance. Another organization may have strong business reasons for not complying with a particular CIS recommendation, and thus will choose to modify the standard to better reflect business reality. The latter organization will likely have fewer policy exceptions. In both cases, the same objective can be achieved—deviations from the CIS standard are known and documented. The difference is only whether the documentation occurs in the standard or in exceptions to the standard.

skills are required, including knowledge of working with firewall security products and general computer science expertise.

Other examples of routine, task-oriented work include updating an internal information security standard to reflect changes to a compliance regulation, or performing an annual comparison of internal information security host-hardening standards with Center for Internet Security (CIS)-recommended secure configurations. Performing technical vulnerability scans or remediation may also fit into this category.

Resourcing

If a playbook can be written to describe the decision-making points and actions required to perform routine, task-oriented work, then any resource with the required skill set should be able to do the work with relatively little transition time. A playbook also allows for this type of work to be performed fairly independently, without requiring real-time input from others or depending on others' time constraints. In the policy comparison and update example, the work is fairly time independent, as it may simply need to be performed on an annual basis. However, in the firewall rule change example, this type of work is best performed as a 24×7 operation, so that requests can be answered and implemented immediately to enable speedy technical implementation of strategic business needs. Often this type of work is done on a recurring basis, as a run-the-business activity rather than as a project.

These attributes (relative independence from working with the core information security team, relative independence from strict timelines in some cases but the need for

24×7 support in others) make routine, task-oriented work a great fit for the offshoring resource model. As long as resources can be identified who have the right background and skill set, it does not matter where in the world they are located.

Refer to the left-hand side of Figure 5-2 for where sustaining work fits into an overall metrics and resourcing program.

Tip
Of course, this model requires some metrics to ensure that what should happen does happen.

Later in the chapter, the section "Leveraging the Outsourcing and Offshoring Models" discusses the benefits of offshoring information security work as well as common concerns and risks with offshoring security work and how to mitigate both.

Metrics
Metrics for routine, task-oriented types of information security work are typically the most straightforward and quantitative. Defining metrics for work that is clearly defined and well understood is much easier than defining metrics for new, cutting-edge work. These metrics normally are also easier to collect, analyze, and report. Typically, the goal of these types of metrics is improvement, although visibility may also be a desired outcome. For example, the process of reviewing and implementing firewall rule change requests has many measurements associated with it. A few of these quantitative metrics and their purposes are outlined in Table 5-1.

Quantitative Metric	Purpose
Number of firewall rule change requests per month Number of firewall rule change requests per month by business unit	Obtain visibility into the pace of business-driven technology changes
Percentage of firewall rule change requests that do not comply with information security policy and standards or are associated with information security policy exceptions Percentage of firewall rule change requests that do not comply with information security policy and standards by business unit	Understand risk associated with firewall rule changes Can be used to manage risk and drive down the number of noncomplying requests
Average time to implement firewall rule change requests	Understand speed and performance Can be used to manage performance and improve the response time

Table 5-1   Quantitative Metrics Associated with Firewall Rule Change Requests

Quantitative Metric	Purpose
Percentage of CIS recommended secure configurations included in company host-hardening standard	Understand risk associated with internal information security policies and standards
	Can be used to manage risk and increase the percentage over time

Table 5-2   Quantitative Metric Associated with Host-Hardening Standards Review

Table 5-2 shows one metric for the example of reviewing host-hardening standards.

Later in the chapter, the section "Leveraging the Outsourcing and Offshoring Models" discusses the incorporation of these types of metrics into RFPs and contracts.

> **LINGO**
> **RFP** stands for Request for Proposal, a document that an organization uses to solicit proposals for a project that has specific requirements. The organization can then use the responses to the RFP evaluate and compare the proposals of multiple vendors.

Establish

This type of work occurs in areas of the information security program that are somewhat mature but lack an informal process and are performed ad hoc or as a best effort. The goal is to establish processes and documentation that make the work formal and repeatable.

Example

Patch and vulnerability management is an example of work that, in some companies and organizations, is done only partially or as needed. In such cases, the information security team may be interested in ensuring that the work is performed as a more mature, documented process.

Resourcing

If the information security management targets this type of function as a priority or as an area for improvement, then it may be best to bring in subject matter experts (SMEs) to assist with the effort to define the process steps and roles and responsibilities associated with this type of work. This is frequently contracted out as a consulting engagement, as the deliverables are clear and the project will have a clear start and end status.

Additional benefits of bringing in outside consultants to perform this work include specific subject matter expertise and an objective perspective. Resourcing the lead for this type of a project with in-house resources, especially resources who are actively engaged in part of the existing ad hoc process, may result in a final process definition that reflects the biases of the in-house resources. An outside consultant can objectively interview the resources and teams who are involved (or who should be involved) in the project, work with a big-picture view, and take prioritization and focus cues from information security management.

IMHO

In the example for this section, patch and vulnerability management, an outside firm may be able to provide consultants who have previously worked on this type of project at a variety of companies and organizations, each in a unique state of maturity and facing different issues and challenges. Such consultants bring a rich skill set to the table. In-house resources may not have the same breadth of experience, as they may be familiar only with their own organization and the way things work there.

The consultants may conduct interviews with the various stakeholders who will eventually play a consistent role in the finalized process. Through these consultations, the consultants may discover, for example, that the information security policy team wants two sets of requirements for patching, depending on whether the patching is performed under normal circumstances or under emergency circumstances. From the information security technical team, the consultants may obtain information about the types of technologies that are involved and the ease of use and practical use of those technologies. The consultants may also provide technical security consulting to the system administrators who will actually deploy (or roll back) the patches.

An outcome of the consulting engagement may be a process flow diagram that explicitly defines each of the steps required in patch and vulnerability management and the roles and responsibilities of each team.

Refer to the center of Figure 5-2 for where establishing work fits into an overall metrics and resourcing program.

Metrics

Initially, metrics in this area may be undefined. The definition of metrics should accompany the definition of the process, perhaps as a deliverable resulting from an SME consulting engagement. Because the performance and risk management being measured often involve the work of in-house resources, bringing in an outside consultant to help define these metrics can provide an objective perspective for the best outcome. And because these metrics are associated with a process that is still maturing, both quantitative and qualitative metrics will be useful.

One issue to address when talking about qualitative metrics is bias. In the security profession, we report both good and bad things, but because qualitative metrics often involve individual judgment calls regarding what should and should not be reported, a security professional might decide, based on personal bias, that certain results should not be reported. Bias is ultimately based in motive and incentive, and if one party is incentivized to fail to report certain data, then another party must be incentivized to report all the data. Quantitatively, this is much easier to handle because it can be done through logging and monitoring. Qualitatively, it must be done via review by other parties, such as auditors.

Tip

All data has bias. The question is whether or not you can correct for it.

Table 5-3 displays a few of these metrics and their purpose.

IMHO

One important thing to consider when reporting metrics is the meaningfulness of the metrics report to the audience. In my experience, I have seen many fancy and complicated-looking reports that, upon a closer look, don't seem to make any sense. Sometimes these useless but complicated-looking reports come from a vendor trying to sell a particular solution; other times they are the result of an information security team reporting the raw output from a vendor technology or are simply the result of a well-intentioned security professional who unfortunately has not taken the time to consider the meaning of the data that he or she is reporting.

One example of this type of report is patching reports that show on average how long it takes to patch systems. At first glance, this might sound like a meaningful report. But what can you do about the results of this report? How easy is it to determine what's desirable or undesirable, and how easily can you clearly direct a change for the better?

In my opinion, a report detailing how long it takes to patch systems is not particularly useful, given that the length of time to deploy different patches will vary depending on a variety of parameters, including criticality of the patch. Since patches have varying levels of severity and urgency, it is important to use patch-related security metrics accordingly. Commonly, an information security team will define SLAs for different types of patches. For example, it may be acceptable to deploy normal patches within 90 days, but for emergency patches, the time requirement may be as short as a week or 48 hours.

Quantitative Metric	Purpose
Percentage of patches deployed within the timeframe specified in the information security group's service level agreement	Compliance with information security standards and understanding of risk posture Can be used to manage risk and increase the percentage
Average time to deploy a normal patch	Understand risk posture, speed, and performance Can be used to manage performance and decrease the average time
Average time to deploy an emergency patch	Understand risk posture, speed, and performance Can be used to manage performance and decrease the average time
Comparison of protected areas versus honeypot areas	To show results of vulnerability scans, monitoring, and logging Can be used to help measure the benefit of the security program
Qualitative Metric	**Purpose**
Which business units receive network vulnerability scan reports from the information security team?	Visibility for process improvement Can be used to manage risk and improve performance
Which business units remediate their vulnerabilities based on the scan reports?	Visibility for process improvement Can be used to manage risk and improve performance
Which business units deploy patches within the timeframe specified in the information security group's service level agreement?	Visibility for process improvement Can be used to manage risk and improve performance
Which business units have high-criticality vulnerabilities that have not been remediated within 90 days?	Visibility for process improvement Can be used to manage risk and improve performance

Table 5-3   Quantitative and Qualitative Metrics for Patch and Vulnerability Management

Later in the chapter, the section "Leveraging the Outsourcing and Offshoring Models" discusses the incorporation of these types of metrics into RFPs and contracts.

Build

As described in Chapter 2, information security work is constantly changing due to the evolving nature of the attacks that hackers, fraudsters, and state-level opponents are devising. There are always new threat areas to explore, and new detection and prevention technologies and methodologies to counteract those threats. One type of work that information security practitioners will always be involved in is cutting-edge, innovative work that is intended to build completely new features. This strategic, forward-looking type of work is at the earliest stage of maturity because it is just being defined and is not ready for implementation.

Example

Two broad examples of cutting-edge build work at the time of writing are securing social media and securing cloud computing. However, this type of work may also be very specific to a company's or organization's particular business strategy and new areas of business.

A second type of build work involves high-level risk management and oversight functions. Making decisions or providing recommendations to executives about risk tolerance and mitigation, or creating and managing policy governance councils, should be in-house work.

Note

Because the build type of work is also usually the most creative and engaging, it should be "saved" for in-house resources, not only to exploit their talent, but also to keep the core team occupied working on the most enjoyable projects.

Resourcing: In-house and Outsourced

Build work can be handled in-house or can be outsourced. Outsourcing can provide the specialized expertise and intelligence of a team who is extremely focused (and resourced, globally and regionally as needed) on a particularly specialized area. An in-house model can provide the best insight into the organization's or company's business needs and the changes happening within that specific industry.

Refer to the center and right-hand side of Figure 5-2 for where building work fits into an overall metrics and resourcing program.

Metrics

Defining and using metrics for visibility and improvement of cutting-edge, innovative work may be difficult because the features are just being designed and created and typically are not implemented yet (at the next stage of maturity, it becomes the type of work described in the section "Establish"). Rather, the type of metrics defined here tend to measure broad success criteria that can be used to determine if the new development being done in this area is sufficient to meet the demands of the new problem that is being solved. These metrics will most likely be of the qualitative type, to fit the strategic nature of the work. Table 5-4 is an example of a few metrics that might be used to determine success criteria of security strategies in the area of cloud computing.

Qualitative Metric	Purpose
Can the confidentiality of information assets be protected under the cloud computing model? This query applies similarly to the following two metrics.	Broad strategic success criteria for evaluation of new security solutions
Does the cloud computing model allow for protection of the integrity of the information assets?	Broad strategic success criteria for evaluation of new security solutions
Does the cloud computing model allow for protection of the availability of the information assets?	Broad strategic success criteria for evaluation of new security solutions

Table 5-4   Qualitative Cloud Computing Metrics

Leveraging the Outsourcing and Offshoring Models

Addressing the volume and complexity of today's information security issues requires diversity of thought and collaboration. Often, in-house resources cannot meet the challenge alone and must rely on outsourcing and offshoring. This section reviews the benefits and concerns of outsourcing and offshoring and discusses ways to manage the risks involved.

LINGO
Outsourcing refers to contracting work to a third-party vendor, whereas **offshoring** refers to work done by resources in a different country (either third party or in-house).

Benefits

There are some huge benefits to creating and leveraging a multifaceted workforce. Today, global teams are widely used for many business functions, including information technology, development, and accounting. Why not information security?

The primary benefit and a common driver for using an offshoring resource model, of course, is cost savings. Resources in the United States (particularly in locations with high costs of living such as New York City, Los Angeles, and the San Francisco Bay Area) are some of the most expensive in the world. Although using local teams of experts is the most convenient model (because no language or cultural barriers exist, and because it is easier to walk down a hallway to speak to a coworker in person or have a conference call with someone in a nearby time zone), as businesses become more global in nature and pursue more effective cost models, leveraging team members who are located outside of the United States makes increasingly more sense from a cost perspective.

Budget Note

The same level of technical talent found in the United States is now increasingly available in Asia (particularly China and India) for 20 to 30 percent of the U.S. salary cost. EMEA (Europe, the Middle East, and Africa) resources with the same skill sets and expertise can also present cost savings (outside of large cities such as London). The salary cost of resources in Ireland and Israel is currently about two-thirds that of U.S. salary cost. For information security teams that are under-resourced, leveraging global resources can result in a significant, cost-effective increase in the number of full-time workers.

The second large benefit to leveraging a global team is the ability to serve increasingly global companies with global customers. Companies and organizations running a 24×7 operation can benefit from a "follow the sun" resourcing model, where working shifts are passed around the globe (rather than hiring U.S. local staff to work evening and early morning shifts, typically for a higher wage).

Note

In the area of information security, global resources may be most appreciated during a large incident (or an incident that occurs in or affects a region in another part of the world) that requires 24×7 attention, because they enable resources in the United States to go to sleep at night while resources in China or elsewhere take over.

Concerns

Many organizations and companies have serious concerns about offshoring or outsourcing information security work. Some common examples of their concerns follow:

- How can a team in India be managed by someone in the United States when the difference in time zones is nine or more hours?
- How will team members in China and the United States effectively communicate with each other despite different native languages?
- How can sufficient quality of talent and performance from global resources be assured?
- How will proper information protection be ensured as very sensitive and confidential data regarding security vulnerabilities and incidents is being passed to teams all around the world?

In Actual Practice

Some national governments are very concerned about cybercrime and thus have established a variety of committees and initiatives to combat it. For obvious defense-related reasons, these governments typically don't engage technical talent from outside their country for these programs. As with every business and security decision, the costs and the benefits must be weighed. For the most part, the recommendations given in this section regarding leveraging resources outside the country of origin for information security work apply primarily to industry rather than the public sector.

How to Manage the Risk

The use of RFPs and contracts can help to manage the risk involved in offshoring or outsourcing work. Both are described in this section.

IMHO

Security is one of those areas where a lot of money is spent on consultants and on technologies to put security capabilities in place, and security technology and professional services vendors take huge advantage of this (it's why they exist). Often security professionals receive cold calls or e-mails from vendors hoping to sell their services. From my experience, the ones I choose to seek out myself tend to end up being the most capable for performing what I need, since I looked for them once I identified I had a problem to solve and not because someone came knocking on my door trying to convince me that I have a problem that they can solve for me.

Request for Proposals

One way to ensure quality and performance from international (as well as local) outsourced or offshore resources is to conduct a formal Request for Proposal for a particular type of work, and competitively bid it out. This process ensures that all program or project requirements are met and that the best vendor for the engagement is selected. I recommend clearly defining the project deliverables and required timelines prior to sending the RFP so that responding vendor partners have something concrete to work with when formulating their responses. Refer to Chapter 4 for guidelines on how to specify project requirements. Clear engagement requirements will ensure the best evaluation by both the prospective vendor partners and your team when choosing the best resources to perform the work.

Budget Note

Security budgets can get quite complicated, with various types of consulting fees, capital expenditures, maintenance and license fees, and so forth. One easy way to simplify costs is to conduct an RFP to find the best fit for your requirements, at the best price. The primary advantage of using an RFP is to easily compare capabilities and the pricing of several different vendors at once—if you can find many different vendors who are capable of performing the work you need to be done, you can choose the lowest price and save money in your budget for use elsewhere.

RFPs can also be used over longer periods of time (one or more years) to identify key partners and establish set consulting rates for various levels of consultants. If there are specific types of work (such as task-oriented, routine work) that can be defined up front, one RFP form to identify the right security consultant can save time and money in the long run. This can also proactively establish good relationships with your company's or organization's procurement and legal teams, ensuring that going through the financial process to get the necessary work done runs smoothly each time.

Contracts

Meet with your organization's or company's legal team before you decide to outsource or offshore information security work. Contractual agreements and legal terms typically are an information security team's best defenses and risk mitigation tools when outsourcing or offshoring work. Contracts can be used to specify SLAs for performance and required security controls. Do not hesitate to specify everything that you expect from the vendor, from access control to physical security to encryption of sensitive or confidential data. Be sure to include the right to audit, as well as financial penalties for noncompliance. In some cases, you can require that the vendor provide (and pay for) third-party audits of their office locations and the environments in which your data is managed and stored.

Tip

The real issue is one of recourse. Make sure that if something goes wrong, you have specified terms for damages, reimbursement, an easy exit from contractual obligations, if needed, and so forth.

Your Plan

When putting together an RFP, ask the potential vendor partners to include information about the following:

Professional Services Capability

- Evidence of their expertise and applicable experience
- References regarding their past history and proven track record
- Which service level agreements and availability requirements they adhere to

Terms

- Whether they comply with your organization or company's RFP format
- Whether they accept your organization's legal terms and service level agreements

Strategic Value Add

- What industry knowledge and expertise they bring to the table
- Evidence of relationships with emerging technology vendors and other thought leaders

For business contexts in which outsourcing or cloud-based work is being done, it is absolutely critical to include the metrics in the contract. Without this type of engagement up front, establishing a metrics program in these areas is much more difficult to do after the fact.

Additional Recommendations

Even when the risk is mitigated up front by using RFPs and contracts, outsourcing and (especially) offshoring present unique challenges, whether the work is information security related or not. Outsourcing or offshoring may require the incorporation of a few completely new information security processes and will certainly take some focused attention and extra time from the information security team, especially at the start.

If your team expects to bring consultants onboard, even local consultants, you will need to introduce each of these new (though temporary) team members to your office logistics. Putting together an "on-boarding" packet for new hires and consultants that contains maps of the offices, badging procedures, instructions on how to obtain a company desktop/laptop, phone, or cube, and other administrative details may be very helpful to hiring managers and others who will help facilitate the process.

Hiring offshore team members, especially for long-term engagements or as permanent employees, presents special cultural and team-building challenges. In an environment where a team meeting may include folks not only from San Jose and Seattle but also from China and Israel, it is harder to build a sense of teamwork and team cohesion.

Into Action

Here are a few key recommendations to follow when assembling and managing international teams:

- Budget permitting, schedule some in-person time up front and periodically throughout the project so that the international team members can meet and develop personal relationships with the core local team. Sharing a meal or a few drinks can go a long way toward establishing a connection that goes beyond just the professional world. Hearing someone's personal stories and finding common ground with them (whether it be family life, extracurricular activities, or other interests) can help both international and local team members communicate better with each other via e-mail and the telephone.

- If the budget does not allow for in-person team-building activities, use video-conferencing to help build similar personal connections. Videoconferencing can also be used in addition to in-person time to enhance communication—it is easier to understand what someone is saying when you can see their lips move and watch their facial expressions. This is particularly useful for teams that do not share a native language.

- Use instant-messaging tools to augment conference calls if someone who does not speak the language of the organization or company natively has trouble understanding a team member who mumbles or uses local references when speaking. Having another team member available on Skype or another chat technology to answer the offshore team's questions in real time can help resolve this type of issue.

- Hold team meetings in which team members are encouraged to share and discuss not only professional activities but also personal activities. Having international and local team members put together and present slides of their personal hobbies, for example, gives each team member a sense of the culture that their international team members are coming from and gives international team members a chance to practice their verbal presentation skills in a team setting.

(continued)

- Assign a local "buddy" to each international team member. This should be someone who is not their manager, but whom they can feel comfortable reaching out to if they need assistance understanding something or obtaining access to information they need. Encourage frequent two-way communication through regular conference calls and chat tools such as Skype.

- Ensure that offshore resources receive appropriate training in their skill areas, specific job duties, and cultural/language areas.

We've Covered

Identifying information security core competencies

- Most information security teams have some of the core competencies described in this chapter. Use the worksheet provided in Figure 5-1 to determine which security-related core competencies your team handles, which of them are handled by other teams in your organization, and which of them your organization does not have in place yet.

Analyzing core competencies for metrics

- Analyzing core competencies is a good place to start when developing a security metrics program. You can measure the maturity of each core competency area and define goals for a desired future state.

Determining what should be measured and for what purpose

- Filling out the core competencies worksheet should give you some insight into what areas might have gaps or be broken. These are potential targets for a metrics project.

Resourcing information security work

- This chapter provided practical advice for the best way to resource different types of information security work appropriately.

Outsourcing and offshoring

- Leveraging outsourcing and offshoring as resourcing options can help you make the most of your limited information security budget by taking advantage of specialized expertise outside of your direct team and lower costs in other areas of the world.

CHAPTER 6

Identify Targets

We'll Cover

- Identifying targets for measurement, analysis, and reporting
- Identifying targets based on what's important
- Identifying targets based on areas for improvement
- Identifying targets based on what's basic
- Identifying targets based on what needs to be discussed
- Identifying targets based on what's new

As discussed in Chapter 5, identifying the core competencies of your information security program and figuring out how to resource each is one way to start an information security metrics program. This chapter provides further guidance on this topic and offers specific questions that you can evaluate to identify additional targets for measurement, analysis, and reporting.

The first step to beginning any security metrics program is to identify targets for measurement, analysis, and reporting. This chapter discusses a few different approaches that will guide you in identifying the appropriate targets for your information security metrics program. The chapter starts by revisiting from Chapter 1 the three objectives of having an information security metrics program. Throughout the chapter, I will point out which objectives are met by pursuing each recommended approach for identifying targets.

This chapter does not contain a specific list of recommended metrics, nor does it present in any particular order the metrics that are discussed. Metrics will differ significantly in the context of different business models and strategies and will vary greatly from one organization to another. For example, the metrics for a security program focused on policy and architecture will be dissimilar from the metrics for a security program focused on operations. Because no specific set of metrics fits all situations, I will instead walk you through general categories of questions that you can use to determine targets.

Revisiting Objectives of an Information Security Metrics Program

Before you attempt to identify which targets should be the focus of your information security metrics program, it is helpful to review the objectives of having an information security metrics program. You should keep in mind as you read this chapter that at least one of the following objectives should be fulfilled as a result of measuring, analyzing, and reporting each of the targets that you identify. If one of these objectives will not be fulfilled by focusing on a particular target, then there likely isn't a good reason for measuring it.

- **Visibility**   Information security metrics provide visibility into the current status or state of an existing area or process.

- **Education and a common language**   Information security metrics provide a lexicon for the information security team to communicate with and educate stakeholders and sponsors.

- **Improvement**   Information security metrics improve an information security program by enabling better management, promoting informed decision-making, and driving change throughout the organization.

Identifying What's Important

The first recommended approach to identifying targets for your metrics projects is to ask the question, "What's important?" If a particular area of the information security program has a particularly high priority and has a large impact on the overall organization, you will certainly want to obtain all the benefits of metrics (visibility, education, and improvement) for that area.

Here, I will discuss three common ways to evaluate what's important in your information security program. Another way to think about this is, how does my information security program add value to the business? Compliance is a very important factor to consider for public companies, companies that manage customer and employee information, and customers that manage credit card transactions. Risk management is another important factor. Security activities and projects can also manage and drive down risk for an organization. Finally ask yourself, how does my security program enable business? Each of these topics is discussed in the next few sections.

Compliance

In many organizations, complying with regulatory requirements is supremely important because of the potential impacts to the business if regulators deem it to be not in compliance. Regulations may apply to various corporate areas of responsibility, including HR, finance, and information security. Many regulations delineate a standard or a set of controls that certain types of organizations must adhere to. (In the absence of, in addition to, or as defined by such regulations, an organization may define controls internally.) These controls typically are tested on a regular basis by both internal and external auditors. Potential financial penalties and business strategy penalties are often a topic for discussion at meetings of high-ranking executives and boards of directors. These penalties can range from hefty fines to reputational damage to an inability to conduct business (for example, if a company fails to comply with the PCI Data Security Standard [PCI DSS], it may not be able to accept credit card payments).

It's very important for a company or organization to understand the status of its compliance to ensure that it is meeting regulatory requirements. Information security metrics provide visibility into compliance status as well as an opportunity for improvement if a company or organization is not meeting regulatory requirements. If compliance has not been achieved, defining and reporting these metrics can be used to drive the change required to meet compliance standards.

> **LINGO**
> **Compliance** means adherence to a set of policies or standards. Two broad categories of compliance are compliance with internal policies (specific to a particular organization) and compliance with external policies, standards, or frameworks.

Your Plan

One obvious question that may lead to a qualitative metric initiative is, "Will the organization pass or fail the next audit?" An information security team that manages multiple business units may want to evaluate this question for the individual business units. The team's findings can then be presented to the information security management team or external sponsors (such as executives or the board of directors) using a color-coded status system such as the following:

- **Red** The particular organization or business unit will likely fail the audit.

- **Yellow** The organization or business unit is in danger of failing the audit, but if certain issues are remediated in time, the organization or business unit will likely pass the audit.

- **Green** The organization or business unit is most likely going to pass the audit.

The specific metrics that are used to evaluate the controls and assign a color to each should be determined by the information security compliance team and can be collected and reported at an operational level.

Many audits are controls based, which means that when the internal or external auditor performs its examination, it will look at specifically prescribed process and technology controls. Organizations test these controls on an ongoing basis to ensure that when it comes time for the official audit, they are aware of their current status and have fixed any issues prior to the audit. Going one level more granular and tactical than "Are we going to pass or fail?" may include additional, quantitative metrics questions such as "What percentage of the controls have been tested?" and "What percentage of the controls that have been tested successfully passed?" The answers to these questions help to establish whether the organization is close to the edge of compliance and, if so, whether it needs to take additional action prior to the audit.

> **LINGO**
> An **audit** is a formal check to determine policy compliance. This may be done by internal auditors at an organization, or by an independent, third-party auditing firm.

The questions that may lead to defining information security metrics targets in the area of compliance are summarized in Table 6-1.

Highest Risk

Another way to answer the question "What's important?" is to identify the areas that present the greatest information security risk. A primary function of an information security program is risk management. Security metrics can fulfill all three objectives of visibility, education, and improvement in the sphere of risk management by assisting the overall organization in properly managing risk.

> **Note**
> Risk management is a complex topic. To learn more, go to Introduction to FAIR (Factor Analysis of Information Risk) at http://fairwiki.riskmanagementinsight.com/.

Qualitative Metric	Desired Outcome	Notes
Will the organization pass or fail the next audit?	Green	Red, yellow, or green status
Quantitative Metric		**Notes**
Percentage of controls that have been tested	100%	May be done on a quarterly basis
Percentage of controls tested that passed	100%	May be done on a quarterly basis

Table 6-1   Compliance Metrics

Your Plan

I recommend conducting a risk assessment to determine which areas present the highest risk, and then identifying those areas as targets for your information security metrics program. Many information security programs conduct annual risk assessments, either by using a consulting service or by performing one internally and leveraging a standard framework such as ISO or COBIT. The results of these risk assessments will provide insight into "the probable frequency and probable magnitude of future loss." A different but related way to think about metrics questions is to consider the maturity of an information security program. In this case, the question to ask in order to identify targets for your information security metrics program is, "Which areas of the organization currently are at the highest risk of their information being compromised?" The answer to the follow-up question— "How important is this area to the information security program and to the overall business strategy?"—will tell you if this is a good target for a metrics initiative.

Some organizations manage risk at the enterprise level. A Chief Financial Officer or a Chief Risk Officer may host enterprise risk committee meetings to review, discuss, and make decisions regarding all company risks, including technology-, financial-, and security-related risks. This group may have input and ideas regarding which specific areas, businesses, and processes should be considered high risk from an information security perspective. You should take cues from this group when you're starting to think about identifying targets for your information security metrics program. The question to ask is, "Which information security–related areas of risk are high profile for my organization right now?"

Another way to look at risk is to identify your most valuable assets. This is different from a risk assessment in that it has nothing to do with the functions of an information security program; rather, it has everything to do with understanding an organization's purpose and business model. Individual organizations value information differently, so each organization should have specific information classification standards that instruct employees how to treat various types of data.

> **LINGO**
> **Information classification standards** specify treatment of data (requirements for storage, transfer, access, encryption, and so forth) according to the data's classification (public, private, confidential, sensitive, and so forth).

Into Action

Start by identifying the organization's most critical information assets. This may require interviewing business stakeholders outside of the information security team to understand the processes of gathering, storing, transferring, and managing different information types.

Once you have identified critical assets to the business, you can begin to evaluate the controls protecting those assets. Areas where controls are weak or ineffective are great targets for a security metrics project.

Which information assets are important varies from organization to organization. One company may need to protect customer Social Security numbers, whereas another may need to protect employee credit card numbers, the source code of its website, or its intellectual property and confidential information about upcoming mergers and acquisitions. The questions to ask are

- Which information assets are important to my company?
- Who is responsible for managing those assets?
- What is the lifecycle of those information assets?

Tip

These questions are part of planning for failure and using metrics as tripwires that warn of potential failure.

Into Action

Your job is to identify which information assets are most important to your organization, find out how those assets are handled while under your organization's management, determine where they are located, and decide how to protect them. This involves researching business plans and strategies and interviewing business stakeholders to best understand what is valuable in your specific environment. The next step is to identify and interview application and infrastructure owners to understand the flow of information. The final step is to determine the best strategy for protecting those assets.

Qualitative Metric	Notes
Which areas of the organization have the greatest risk of information compromise?	This may be determined by performing an information security risk assessment.
Which information security–related areas of risk are high profile for my organization right now?	This may be discussed and determined by an enterprise risk group.
Which information assets are important to my company?	Interview business stakeholders.
Who is responsible for managing those assets?	Identify technical owners.
What is the lifecycle of those information assets?	Discuss with both business stakeholders and technical owners.

Table 6-2 High-Risk Metrics Questions

Table 6-2 summarizes the qualitative metrics questions related to identifying which information assets pose the highest risk within an organization.

Business-Enabling Security Practices

When attempting to identify targets for a metrics program by evaluating what's important to an organization, an increasingly significant question is, "Which information security practices enable the business to operate, and how can these be measured?" Typically, the primary objective of having an information security program is to protect and support the business, its product, its employees, and its customers.

An example of a metric in this category is the level of satisfaction of customers served by the security organization. Specific examples of this type of metric include measuring the turnaround time to requests from business units and measuring the turnaround time for vendor assessments.

Identifying What's Broken

Another approach to identifying a target for an information security metrics program is to ask the question, "What's broken?" This identifies a target for improvement, one of the objectives of an information security metrics program. Developing metrics for such targets not only guides improvement but also provides visibility into the progress of that improvement as a baseline is captured and tracked against.

Evaluating what's important is only one way to choose a target for a metrics project. A second way is to identify areas for improvement. This can be done based on process improvement, technology improvement, and audit findings. Metrics projects in target areas for improvement can be used to engage stakeholders to drive change in an organization.

Process Improvement

Processes performed as part of an information security program may be at various levels of maturity. Some processes may be informal and lack consistency, whereas others may be well defined, documented, and audited. Improving processes typically requires the cooperation of multiple individuals or teams. These stakeholders may or may not have the same understanding of how the processes should be run. Certain steps of processes may have SLA requirements associated with them that are met to varying degrees.

The following are several examples of information security processes that may be good targets for a metric:

- Vendor security assessments
- Business continuity assessments
- Patch and vulnerability management
- Policy development
- Policy exceptions management
- Incident response
- Security architecture assessments
- Security technology or product evaluation
- Secure development lifecycle
- Secure builds, configuration, and host hardening

There are numerous potentially applicable qualitative and quantitative metrics to consider in the sphere of process improvement. Table 6-3 lists only a few recommendations. Note that the metrics included here are very general. More specific questions should be asked depending on which process is being observed, measured, and potentially improved.

If your company or organization has more than one broken or issue-ridden process, there may be several target areas in Table 6-3 (and others not in the table) that are good candidates for developing metrics. Choosing to identify metrics for process visibility or improvement should be based on the answer to the question "What's important?"—areas of highest importance and/or highest risk.

Tip
Trend analysis is especially important to process improvement.

Qualitative Metric	Desired Outcome	Notes
Is this process defined and documented?	Yes	
Does each step in the process have clearly defined roles and responsibilities?	Yes	
Which steps or roles are unclear to or not agreed upon by the relevant stakeholders or process participants?	None	
Quantitative Metric		**Notes**
Number or percentage of steps in the process that all stakeholders agree upon	100%	This may be a count or a percentage.
Percentage of attempts to perform the process that are performed consistently	100%	Percentage—certain step-by-step measurement criteria may need to be specified for further definition of "performed consistently"; for example, "How often is the data capture involved in this process performed consistently?"
Percentage of SLA requirements defined for the process that are adhered to	100%	This may be measured as a percentage. A single process may have multiple SLA requirements defined, and this metric may be applied multiple times to a single process.

Table 6-3   Process Improvement Metrics

Another approach to improving processes through security metrics is to combine metrics to see what correlations may exist. For example, metrics for incidents and vulnerabilities may be combined with metrics for patches. If analysis of this combination shows that patching leads to incidents, it may indicate that the security team ought to investigate different protection strategies.

Technology Improvement

Another potential target for improvement is existing technology. (New technology deployments are addressed later in this chapter, in the section "Identifying What's New.") Your answers to the question "What's broken?" may be related to technology deployed specifically for security purposes (for example, a product to monitor and prevent data leakage) or to other company-wide technology deployments (e-mail systems, human resources on-boarding and termination systems, identity management systems, and so forth). Gathering metrics in this arena will also provide analysis and reporting to support visibility and decision-making.

Into Action

In most cases, best practices exist in each area identified for improvement. One method for generating metrics questions for specific process improvements is to compare a targeted process practice and components of the recommended best practice. To take it a step further, you can ask yourself questions such as, "What is the purpose of each of these best practice recommendations?"; "How can I further improve this process to optimize resources, time, and budget spend?"; and "In what ways can I further minimize the risk without obstructing business strategy and timelines?"

Discovering the answers to these questions may require some creativity and outside-the-box thinking. Do not worry about getting the questions exactly right the first time, but instead brainstorm, iterate on paper, and review your ideas with stakeholders before proceeding with any measurements and pursuing process changes. Stakeholders will provide you with a fuller perspective, but be aware that some stakeholders—particularly those who are outside the information security program or lack education in the field of information security—may be resistant to change, especially if it requires additional work on their part.

Budget Note

Not every information security process is intended to be at its maximum maturity level. Processes will always exist along a spectrum of maturity, and this is not necessarily a bad thing. Remember that you are not operating in a vacuum here; you want to use metrics to support planning and better management in the real world. The best use of resources and budget does not necessarily equate to equal distribution. Nor does it make sense to invest the entire security budget in one process simply because it's currently being reviewed. Rather, resources should be allocated as appropriate to ensure adequate distribution according to business and security priorities. Security metrics can be a useful tool for decision support.

Security Technology

What are some of the possible issues and challenges related to security technology? To answer this question, a good place to start is to apply some quantitative metrics to existing technology (for example, measuring the number or percentage of false positives generated by a vulnerability scanning and detection system). This should inspire qualitative questions about the scope of the technology and its accuracy and effectiveness. Table 6-4

Qualitative Metric Questions	Notes
What is the scope of coverage for this security technology? What are the advantages and disadvantages to increasing or decreasing the amount of coverage?	Does the scope of coverage include only headquarters, or all remote offices? Does it apply only to the development network, or to the production network? Does it apply only to corporate, or to production?
What are the functions of this security technology? What gaps in capability exist? Which functions are being performed by multiple different security technologies (overlap)? How effective is the technology?	In answering these questions, you may discover that you are paying for and resourcing technologies whose functions overlap. To find out which technology you can eliminate, proceed with an assessment and comparison of the two (or more) products. Alternatively, you may discover that a particular technology no longer works well.
Are the ownership, roles, and responsibilities associated with both the deployment and the ongoing maintenance of this technology clearly security related? If not, is this technology and what it delivers a priority for the team?	If the answer to the second question is yes, then resources need to be allocated to the technology. If the answer is no, then the technology should be decommissioned.
What are the intended functions of this security technology? How well does the security technology execute those functions? (That is, is it doing what it's supposed to do?)	To begin answering these questions, refer to the original project deployment plan for the technology or the RFP materials used to evaluate the technology initially. The answer to the second question may be as general as High, Medium, or Low Effectiveness.
What additional functionality is this technology capable of delivering? Does that functionality align with the priorities of the information security program? What is preventing this functionality from being deployed?	Many security products have capabilities beyond what an initial project to deploy the technology may require. Sometimes a security technology is deployed for a particular purpose, but it may be able to do much more. In terms of maximizing dollars and an investment in technology, look at the capabilities of existing technology before going out and buying and installing new technology to do what existing technology can already do.

Table 6-4   Security Technology Improvement Metrics Questions

Qualitative Metric Questions	Notes
Do the benefits of this technology deployment outweigh its ongoing maintenance cost, in terms of both annual licensing and team resources spent on maintaining the system? Are you spending in accordance with your priorities?	The first question is considered to be qualitative rather than quantitative because, depending on the situation, there may or may not be hard quantitative data with which to perform this analysis. Answering this question can at least start the thought process moving in the right direction. For example, do you have too many logs to actually review them? Is the resource burden too heavy to carry on? This speaks to the question of cost of ongoing maintenance. Oftentimes when a technology is deployed, folks may fail to think about how much it actually takes to keep it up and running. I have seen organizations buy and then not effectively use technology because proper maintenance costs (resources to support the processes required) were not taken into consideration.

Table 6-4   Security Technology Improvement Metrics Questions (*Continued*)

provides some recommended questions to identify targets for metrics work in the domain of security technology.

Non-Security Technology

Technology deployed outside of the information security program and with primary functions having little or nothing to do with security may still be a good target for an information security metrics project, if that technology deployment represents a significant amount of risk for your company or organization. Questions to ask here are similar to the questions proposed in the earlier "Identifying What's Important" section. You might also consider asking questions from the "Identifying What's Broken" section with security and risk management in mind. An identity management system may not be deployed or configured optimally. A database containing confidential customer information may not be properly configured with appropriate security controls or architected in a way that ensures secure flow and storage of data. Table 6-5 proposes a set of high-level questions that may be useful for identifying technology targets for your next information security metrics project that are not directly related to security.

Qualitative Metrics Questions	Notes
Have there been security incidents related to this particular technology? If so, how many? How often? Why? (Side question: Are you sure you would know whether or not security incidents related to this technology have occurred?)	Repeated incidents involving a particular technology may be a good indicator that it is a worthy security metrics project target.
Does this technology manage personal information or transactional data? Is the data that is stored, transferred, or processed by this technology system appropriately protected for its level of classification in the organization? How effective are the security controls currently in place? To what extent are security controls prescribed by the information security team adhered to by the teams who use and manage the systems?	The second question assumes an information classification standard is in place. If not, developing one may be a good place to start.
Who has access to the system? Are appropriate access controls in place considering the classification and uses of the data contained in this system?	The second question assumes an information classification standard is in place. If not, developing one may be a good place to start.
Does this technology have authentication and authorization controls? If so, how do they function? Alternatively, how does this technology manage passwords?	Depending on the sensitivity of information stored in this technology, you may want to take a look at the authentication and authorization controls. An example metrics project may be to identify and strengthen authorization and authorization controls for the most sensitive data types throughout your organization.
Who are the end users of this technology? Are the users of this technology customer service representatives or system administrators? Employees or just executives?	Different end users require different levels of controls for protecting information stored in and managed by a technology.
Does this technology integrate with third-party partners or providers?	If so, you may need to conduct a vendor assessment (if one has not already been completed) to review the security of this technology fully.
Does this technology accurately reflect the company's or organization's data retention (or anti-retention) policy?	You can assess the compliance of this technology with data retention standards. A gap may indicate an opportunity for a metrics project.

Table 6-5 Non-Security Technology Improvement Metrics Questions

Audit Findings

To find out what's broken in an organization, the audit findings produced by either external or internal auditors are a good place to look. Whether the auditors are internal or external, they have valid reasons for focusing on the areas that they audit. External auditors may focus on frameworks, best practices, compliance, and comparison of your organization to other clients. Internal auditors may have indicators from various sources (such as latest news or current events in an area, trends in high-risk areas to focus on, and company political influences) that affect which targets they choose for assessment. In all of these cases, the information security program has an interest in the auditors' findings because they answer the question, "What's broken?" When the focus is on a process or technology for which your team is responsible for managing the risk, consulting the auditors' findings is a good place to start so that you're prepared with metrics that can show progress and success.

PCI DSS is one example of an audit that is very pervasive and from which example metrics can be derived.

Identifying What's Basic

Another question to ask when identifying targets for your information security metrics program is, "What's basic?" Many security organizations would benefit from visibility, education, or improvement in an area that is considered "Security 101." Depending on organizational maturity, processes that are fundamental to the information security program may not exist (and thus need to be defined) or may exist at a lower level of effectiveness and maturity than is appropriate for a particular business or organizational strategy. In some cases, the best practices contained in controls frameworks may have been overlooked due to acute emergencies or a natural human tendency to focus on higher-profile issues.

Note

Processes that are fundamental to the information security program may not exist or may be at a lower level of maturity than is appropriate. This is especially true for data handling. In your organization, do you know how data is categorized and whether it is being handled accordingly?

In many cases, the maturity level of the information security program will be higher in some business units than in others. For example, a company may have in place strong information security practices for the corporate IT network but weak information security practices for the product division IT network.

Table 6-6 provides a few example metrics questions intended to identify "what's basic?"

In Actual Practice

I recommend considering basic information security program functions as initial targets for metrics, to ensure that you have the fundamentals in place. Then, if something bad happens, you can state matter-of-factly that your team has performed the basics, making it much less likely that the incident will be attributed to a lack of due diligence on your part.

IMHO

Another appropriate name for this section might be "Identifying What's Expected." Few executives or teams outside the direct information security organization are experts in the field of information security; however, most individuals who read the daily news are aware of some of the current threats and risks that the information security team must deal with. With that in mind, consider what your management might expect from the information security program (beyond ensuring that it's in place). Anticipating which metrics will interest management and having them available can help bolster conversations and enhance the credibility and reputation of the information security program with key stakeholders and sponsors.

Qualitative Metrics Questions	Notes
Which basic components of an information security program do not exist in the organization or are at a level of maturity lower than best practices dictate?	This question is about identifying gaps in the security program.
What units (product, corporate IT, customer service, etc.) of the organization lack one or more basic information security functions? Which functions?	This first question is similar to the first question but applies to more specific targets.
Based on recent news articles and mainstream trends in information security, which information security functions might management expect to have fully implemented? Are those functions currently at the expected level of maturity?	This first question is about identifying topics that may be on the mind of non-security professionals.

Table 6-6 Security 101 Metrics Questions

Budget Note

If your information security team already does a great job with security basics, consider the option of outsourcing or offshoring those functions to save costs. If your team chooses this option, you will want to develop metrics for the purposes of choosing the right vendor partner to perform the work and measuring that vendor's performance periodically. Be sure to include this information in the RFP used during vendor and product evaluation as well as in the contract offered to the selected vendor. Metrics can also be used to prepare a template for weekly reports that will save you time in the long run if the templates are defined up front in such a way that they are useful and meaningful.

Refer to Chapter 5 for examples of metrics that you can use in formulating a strategy for outsourcing or offshoring.

Identifying What Needs to Be Discussed

As described in Chapter 1 and reiterated at the beginning of this chapter, one of the benefits of an information security metrics program is that it provides a common language to communicate with and educate stakeholders and sponsors of the information security program. Therefore, a good method for choosing targets for an information security metrics project is to identify areas and issues the information security team will need to discuss with people outside of the team: with sponsors of the program, to justify budget and resource requests; with other risk managers in the organization, to raise issues regarding areas of high risk and provide visibility into the high-risk areas; with stakeholders, to discuss information security processes or controls their teams may be involved in performing; with the board of directors, to highlight and address any concerns they may have due to recent news of malware incidents at competitive organizations; and so forth.

This is also related to the "What's expected?" question in that metrics can be used not only to begin and maintain a conversation about what the information security program does to add value to the overall company or organization, but also to provide a common language for talking about it. Chapter 9 reviews in detail a number of specific stakeholders with whom the information security team might be interested in talking, as well as specific examples and recommendations for what to discuss.

Tip

Consider integration information from security-related news feeds into your reporting.

Identifying What's New

Another method for determining targets for your information security metrics projects is to look at what's new in your program. What areas are you just beginning to develop or thinking about developing? As discussed in Chapter 4, defining success criteria and metrics during the planning phase of a project can be useful in justifying the budget and the resources required for the project as well as showing continuous progress and success during the pilot and actual implementation. Success criteria and metrics can be useful even if they don't paint a happy picture—they can be used as feedback into your process early on to make educated decisions about how and what to change in order to achieve the original project objective. In this case, metrics based on targets identified by asking the question "What's new?" will provide visibility, an opportunity for improvement, and a common language for communicating with stakeholders. For new areas, the latter benefit may prove to be the most important as information security is constantly changing and stakeholders and sponsors constantly need to be updated and provided with information about what's new.

Another way to think about "What's new?" is to look at what's going on in the security metrics industry. Industry statistics integrated with internal numbers can paint a richer picture for the intended security metrics audience. Especially when you are working on developing new areas in your program, having supporting measurements to compare with your own data can help you verify your results. Consultants who provide anonymizing services for information sharing may be particularly useful in this regard. In addition to providing an external baseline, engaging industry stakeholders can also broaden your own ideas for which metrics to use. Organizations such as ISSA, ISC2, CIS, and so forth are great starting points. Social networking sites such as Facebook and LinkedIn can be great places for industry professionals to share information on security metrics.

Tip

Be sure to check out www.securitymetrics.org for information, resources, and events intended for information security professionals interested in and working on metrics initiatives.

Technology Evaluations

When you are looking to choose a new technology product to deploy in your environment, metrics used to assess and compare one vendor partner against another will be critical to making the right decision for your company or organization. Table 6-7 provides a few questions that might be incorporated into an assessment of a new technology.

Qualitative Metrics Questions	Notes
How much does this technology cost, both up front and ongoing? What resources will this technology require for the build phase and for maintenance?	Cost will always be a factor. Managing how the information security budget is invested must be done carefully in order to properly fund the program priorities.
What are the functional requirements for this technology? What is it expected to perform and deliver?	Answering these questions will help ensure that you specifically evaluate the new technology to ensure it meets all of your requirements.
What are the service levels provided by the vendor? Do these meet your needs?	Answering these questions will help ensure you're getting the level of service you need from the vendor once the technology has been deployed.
Is the vendor financially viable? Will the vendor be able to sustain your needs in the short and long term?	Answering these questions helps you determine if the vendor will be around long enough for you to use their technology when you need it.
Does this vendor adhere to the legal requirements that you set forth?	Your legal team may require an answer to this question. This is a good question to ask up front.

Table 6-7   Technology Evaluation Questions

Cloud Provider Metrics and Evaluations

The questions that you should ask become more complex when outsourcing security-specific functions or choosing a vendor to provide infrastructure-, platform-, or application-hosting services. When utilizing a business model that relies on cloud providers, metrics play the important role of assisting with assessment and comparison. See Chapter 17 for more on security metrics for cloud computing.

We've Covered

Identifying targets for measurement, analysis, and reporting

- This chapter discusses different methods for identifying targets for metrics projects.

Identifying targets based on what's important

- Compliance, risk management, and business enablement are all good factors to consider when determining what areas of your program are most important.

Identifying targets based on areas for improvement

- Another way to identify a target for a metrics project can be to identify areas for improvement. This can be done based on process improvement, technology improvement, and audit findings.

Identifying targets based on what's basic

- You can choose a target for a metrics project by identifying basic components which are missing or weak in an information security program.

Identifying targets based on what needs to be discussed

- You can choose a target for a metrics project based on what messages you want to convey.

Identifying targets based on what's new

- You can choose a target for a metrics project based on new initiatives.

Endnote

1. Jack A. Jones, Introduction to FAIR, http://fairwiki.riskmanagementinsight.com/ ?page_id=6.

PART IV

Get Started

CHAPTER 7

Define Project Objectives

We'll Cover

● Defining what it means to have an objective tied to a metrics project

● Reviewing the benefits of a security metrics program

● Defining clear project objectives

● Practical tips for succeeding in a metrics project once an objective has been defined and the project has begun

hapter 6 discussed various approaches you can take to identify appropriate targets for your particular information security metrics program. These approaches include determining what's important, what can be improved, what's basic, what needs to be discussed, and what's new. Part of that identification process involves ensuring that at least one of the benefits of a security metrics program is fulfilled by measuring, analyzing, and reporting a particular target. After you have identified the appropriate targets for your program, the next step is to determine specifically what you want to accomplish through projects aimed at those targets, which is the focus of this chapter. I'll begin with the simple analogy that deciding what you want to accomplish in a security metrics project is like deciding that you want to run a marathon: you need to determine the final goal so that you can prepare properly to reach that goal.

Training for a Marathon

A few years ago, I decided to train to run a marathon. Prior to that decision, I had never run more than 7 miles continuously in my life. I decided that I wanted to condition my body to the point that it could cover 26.2 miles in one run. I perceived several benefits to accomplishing this specific objective: creating an athletic discipline in my life that did not exist previously, improving my health, making new friends, developing more confidence in my physical self, and achieving one of the loftiest ambitions of a runner.

I signed up in February for a race in June, so I had a total of four months to train. I joined a program called Team in Training and worked with coaches who put me through a specific workout regimen during which we ran one "long run" every two weeks. Each long run was a few miles longer than the previous one, and the long runs were scheduled such that by June 1, I would be able to complete 26.2 miles. Participants in the program checked in weekly with the team and coaches to benchmark against each other and track our progress. In the end, I did complete the marathon, accomplishing my objective of running 26.2 miles.

Whether it's in the realm of physical fitness or an information security program, to achieve measured improvement in an area (or to gain better visibility or provide a common language for educating stakeholders), you must define thresholds and bounds and devise a reasonable plan for accomplishing the stated objective. The first step to doing this is to define an objective—in this case, I wanted to be able to run 26.2 miles after four months of training. I talked to my coaches and doctors (my physical health stakeholders) about the feasibility of pursuing this goal, and after evaluation and assessment, they determined that this would be a reasonable undertaking.

How does this relate to an information security metrics program? Any metrics program, whether in the information security industry, the traffic security industry, or in the area of personal health, can benefit from the shared characteristics of a clearly defined goal or objective. Here are a few of those specific parameters from my marathon-training experience:

- I wanted to increase the distance that I could run by a specific length, in a specific amount of time.

- I measured a baseline of being able to run seven miles at the start of my training.

- Throughout my training, my coaches and I measured consistently the distance that I ran.

- I checked with subject matter experts (my doctors and coaches) regarding what was reasonable in terms of achievement based on benchmarking and assessing my physical health condition.

- As a primary stakeholder, I was well aware of the training schedule and milestones required to accomplish my goal.

- I planned periodic check-ins with my coaches to ensure that I was on track, and made adjustments as needed throughout the training schedule.

In this chapter, I will take you through the steps to define the objectives for a security metrics project.

IMHO

What might have been the result if my training program to achieve better physical fitness was haphazard? Suppose each week I had done a few dozen sit-ups, run a few miles, and taken a yoga class or two. Although I might have seen short-term, minor improvements to my physical health over the four months, I likely would not have been able to achieve a long-term, sustainable change in my lifestyle.

Similarly, I advise against starting an information security metrics program haphazardly by randomly gathering data. With so many different security technologies deployed, intelligence reports from various sources, and data feeds to manage, it can be tempting to simply make a list of all the different types of data that you could potentially collect and then start collecting it. This is a bit like training for a marathon by walking out of your house one day and running down the road as far as you can until you're out of breath and collapse. These approaches end similarly too—consuming and exhausting resources, burning out, and ultimately not making any real progress.

This is why it is so important to start with an objective when beginning any metrics project. It may sound simple (this is, after all, a beginner's guide), but to get anywhere, you have to start by figuring out where you want to go. To figure out where you want to go, you should figure out what benefits you will achieve by getting there.

Mapping a Target to a Benefit

Chapter 6 discussed various techniques for identifying a target for a security metrics project. As shown in Figure 7-1, the next step is to map that target to a benefit that can be achieved by making the target the focus of a security metrics project. As the figure

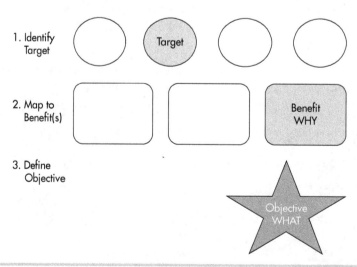

Figure 7-1   Metrics target, benefit, and goal

suggests, by mapping the target to a benefit, you establish a reason for why the project should be initiated. With that reason for the project established, you can turn your attention to defining the goal or objective of the metrics project—what you want to accomplish, as discussed in the next section.

Tip

When identifying the benefit of a security metrics project, consider whether the "end justifies the means." In other words, you should determine whether the benefit of executing the project justifies the amount of work and resources that will be required for the project.

To justify a project, you should be able to map it to at least one of the following benefits of an information security metrics program:

- **Visibility**   Information security metrics provide visibility into the current status or state of an existing area or process.
- **Education and a common language**   Information security metrics provide a lexicon for the information security team to communicate with and educate stakeholders and sponsors.
- **Improvement**   Information security metrics improve an information security program by enabling better management, promoting informed decision-making, and driving change throughout the organization.

Defining the Objective of a Security Metrics Project

In this section, I will discuss how to define the objective for the security metrics project. You'll define an objective desired direction, a metrics project distance, and a metrics project timeline. *Objective desired direction* is the direction in which you want to change the target you're measuring. *Metrics project distance* is how far you want to change the target. *Metrics project timeline* is the duration of time you want to spend to get the target to achieve the metrics project distance.

Objective Desired Direction

To grasp the concept of objective desired direction, think of a traveler who is looking at a map, with a destination in mind and a compass in hand. Once the traveler has identified where she needs to go (her objective), she needs to determine in which direction she needs to go to get there (her desired direction).

There are different ways to portray objective desired direction. Here I present two common methods: Up or Down and Red, Yellow, or Green.

Up or Down?

In some cases where you're measuring a target quantitatively, you'll have a good intuitive sense of whether you want the number to go up or down.

LINGO
The **objective desired direction** of a metrics project refers to the direction in which you want the measurement to go to achieve the benefits of an information security metrics program, especially the benefit of improvement.

For example, if you're measuring the number of vulnerabilities on a site or network or the number of laptops stolen from your company, the direction in which you desire the measurement to go is straightforward: down.

In other cases, the desired direction is not quite as straightforward, even if the measurement is quantitative. Measuring the number of security incidents and anomalies is an area in which it may be difficult to determine whether an increase or a decrease is desirable. An increase in the number of incidents and anomalies detected may indicate that detection capabilities are improving. However, a decrease in the number of incidents and anomalies detected may indicate the effectiveness of preventive controls that have been implemented.

Ultimately, when defining the goal of a project, you can determine whether the objective desired direction is up or down by considering the benefit that the project is meant to achieve. For example, if you want to improve detection capabilities, you need to keep preventive controls static and experiment with new detection processes and technologies. If you want to improve preventive measures, keep your detection controls static and experiment with new preventive controls. Measurement will be most effective if your project concentrates on one particular facet of a problem. Figure 7-2 provides a visual depiction of this concept.

In Actual Practice

Keeping one set of controls stable while measuring another set for the purposes of "clean" measurement may not always be a straightforward choice. You may find yourself in a situation where it would be advantageous to increase detection capabilities and improve preventative security controls simultaneously. In such cases, you must determine which will be most beneficial to your overall information security program: keeping one set of controls static for the purpose of focusing on improvement of the other, or deploying both with a limited ability to measure, report, and communicate the effectiveness of the work you're performing.

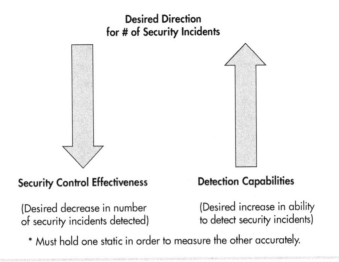

Figure 7-2   Desired direction for security controls vs. detection capabilities

Red, Yellow, or Green?

When measuring the health of an information security project or compliance with a specific standard or framework, red, yellow, and green colors are typically used for status reporting (see Figure 7-3, which includes labels to identify the colors for purposes of this grayscale book). In this case, identifying which color is the objective desired status (or direction) is very straightforward: green universally means good, whereas red universally means bad. Yellow is typically used to depict a status at risk of becoming red.

Red, yellow, and green can also be used to represent quantitative measurements more clearly, with defined start and end points corresponding to each color. For example, if you're measuring something on a scale of 1 through 10, where higher numbers are desirable, you could define green to represent anything with a status of 7, 8, 9, or 10, yellow to represent anything with a status of 4, 5, or 6, and red to represent anything with a status of 1, 2, or 3.

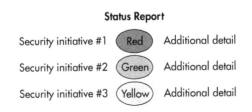

Figure 7-3   Green is the objective desired direction when measuring health or compliance.

Metrics Project Distance

When defining the objective of a security metrics project, the metrics project distance represents how much improvement you want to accomplish by the end of the project. For example, for a project targeting the number of open vulnerabilities on a particular platform, the metric project distance might be a specific percentage decrease in vulnerabilities from the start of the project to the end, such as a 20 percent decrease in the number of web application vulnerabilities on a customer-facing website. In the marathon example from earlier in the chapter, the project distance would be defined as the difference between the 26.2 miles I wanted to achieve and the 7 miles that I was already able to accomplish (or 19.2 miles).

> **LINGO**
> **Metrics project distance** refers to the amount of change you want to achieve in your target measurement by the end of the metrics project.

Metrics Project Timeline

The distance and time components of your metrics goal must be defined together. In the marathon example, I had a project timeline of four months to improve my endurance by the 19.2 mile project distance.

Project timelines are just estimates. It's impossible to say exactly how many hours or how many days will be required to complete any project. A few factors to take into consideration include:

- **Historical data**   How long have similar projects taken to complete in the past?

- **Vendor/partner team expertise**   Ask the team responsible for doing the work how long they think it will take. They may be able to give you better estimates than you could come up with yourself.

- **Resource and budget availability**   Consider vacation schedules and time to obtain budget approvals as needed.

- **Issues and risks**   Make a list of the items that might cause a delay and build those delays into your estimates.

At this point in the chapter, we've identified three components to include when defining a metrics project objective: desired direction, project distance, and project timeline. To give you a general

> **LINGO**
> **Metrics project timeline** refers to how long you want to spend to achieve the metrics project distance.

Target	Desired Direction	Distance	Timeline	Notes
Number of web application vulnerabilities	Down	20% reduction	1 year	This number will need to be normalized to take into account the changing number of code lines
Percentage of security incidents with formal postmortems	Up	Increase from 25% to 100%	6 months	Criteria for determining what is a security incident should be defined up front.
PCI compliance	Green	Improve status of compliance, from red and yellow to green	9 months	The timeline may depend on the date of the next audit.
Number of compromised user accounts	Down	10% reduction	3 months	This assumes that detection methods stay the same. This is a relatively short timeline because detection methods are likely to change frequently.
Percentage of patches deployed within the timeframe specified in the information security team's SLA	Up	Increase from 10% to 25%	3 months	The short timeframe may be driven by an internal audit finding.

Table 7-1   Examples of Metrics Objectives, with Defined Target, Direction, Distance, and Timeframe

overview of how your definition should be developing, Table 7-1 provides a few examples that define these components for particular targets. You can use a table similar to this when you are defining objectives for your own security metrics projects.

The remainder of this chapter is spent discussing practical advice based on the lessons I've learned implementing metrics objectives.

Lessons Learned

In this section, I will present some lessons learned from my experience in running metrics projects. I'll discuss metrics lifetimes, setting a baseline for a metrics project, and stakeholders. Metrics lifetimes is a topic about which security professionals have a variety of opinions. I'll present my thoughts. I'll also discuss the advantages of setting a baseline at the beginning of a metrics project and engaging stakeholders early. Some folks in the security community demand that once a security metric is defined, it be executed and measured in the exact same way forever. I strongly recommend against this static approach. Today, the speed of the attacker in terms of developing and deploying new exploits is accelerating. To keep up with the attackers, information security professionals must begin to think of metrics in terms of each having a specific lifetime, ranging anywhere from a few weeks to a few months to a few years. The static way of tracking metrics might even be detrimental to an information security program because it may inhibit further changes toward improvement if those changes deviate from the original metrics approach. Because new hacking and fraud techniques are being devised faster and faster and the number of attackers is ever increasing, we need to move faster to catch up, keep pace, and eventually get ahead.

Simply defining a metric at the beginning of a metrics project and sticking with it is no longer sufficient. We need to think one step further and contemplate exactly how long that metric will need to be in effect. Ultimately, the length of time for "keeping" a security metric will depend on the benefit you're trying to achieve and the business model and strategic environment that you're working in. It makes sense to define a specific timeline to match a specific distance for a single phase of a metrics project. At the completion of that metrics project, you can always decide to adjust any of the parameters as needed for the future phases.

For example, consider the previously introduced example of a metrics project that is intended to drive down the number of web application vulnerabilities on a customer-facing website. Suppose your initial objective is to decrease the number of vulnerabilities by 20 percent in the first year, but you find at the end of that year that the bug-fixing team was able to reduce the number of vulnerabilities by 50 percent. If you choose to pursue a similar project in the next year, you may want to increase the distance or decrease the timeline for this same metric.

IMHO

I am a strong proponent of retiring metrics appropriately when they are no longer useful or relevant. However, you should not change metrics too often. You should measure a target for a sufficient length of time to achieve an objective (whether it be visibility, improvement, or change) and establish that the target of the metric is stable.

Setting Baselines

Once you've defined the target, objective desired direction, metrics project distance, and metrics project timeline for your metrics project, the next step is to measure and report a baseline. A baseline is a current measurement of the target on the start date of the project. This will be the starting point for your metrics project distance.

You'll need to measure consistently throughout the lifetime of the project in order to preserve the integrity of the metrics. To achieve consistent measurement, when you are

In Actual Practice

Tracking security metrics trends in particular can be very useful in achieving all three benefits (especially visibility and education) for various areas of the information security program. Education in this area must be continuous; having complete data to show trends is more convincing than with an incomplete dataset. The most important thing to ensure when collecting and reporting trend information is that the data is collected and reported in a consistent manner. This will support not only the integrity of the trends you're reporting but also any conclusions you may draw from the trend lines. Data quality and presentation is discussed further in Chapter 15.

setting the baseline, make sure to document the sources of data and standard procedures for collecting, analyzing, and reporting the data. This will set up your metrics project to ensure that the steps are repeated in the same manner no matter who is responsible for performing the metrics work. You can also use this documentation to discuss the metrics project with key stakeholders and sponsors, educate them about the metrics project, promote the metrics project, and ensure that you obtain necessary buy-in.

Ensuring that everyone involved in the metrics project understands how the baseline data (and future data) is collected, analyzed, and reported will also set your team up to produce and report on trends in the data as you measure at various intervals in the future. In other words, the team responsible for gathering, analyzing, and reporting data associated with the metrics project will need to gather data regularly and consistently to accurately show the trend of the data being measured; for example, is the measurement trending up or down as time passes?

Initial Buy-in from Stakeholders

As discussed in previous chapters, every information security metrics project will have a set of key stakeholders and sponsors. It's very important to engage the key stakeholders and sponsors early in the process, during the initial phase when you define objectives and goals (and each of the related parameters: direction, distance, and time).

The teams who are involved in managing the information or performing the processes that you are targeting for your metrics project will be able to tell you most precisely whether your goals are reasonably achievable. Discussing the parameters of distance and time up front with these stakeholders may make the difference between a successful metrics project and a failed project. Ideally, you want your metrics goals to be aggressive but also attainable. Obtaining the stakeholders' perspective and understanding their day-to-day work, issues, and concerns will also enable you to communicate more effectively when discussing the different components of your metrics project.

Achieving improvement through a metrics project requires that something change from the way it's been done in the past. In many cases, the information security team will not be the only people involved in making that change happen; rather, success will largely depend on other teams changing their historical and current behavior. Engaging stakeholders and sponsors during the objectives definition phase sets up a follow-on conversation about how the necessary changes will be achieved.

Recurring Checkpoints with Stakeholders

In addition to meeting with stakeholders as you are initially defining the objectives for your metrics project, you'll also want to meet with them periodically throughout the duration of the project. This will give you an opportunity to present progress reports along the way and will facilitate ongoing discussions of issues, risks, and concerns. You

Your Plan

The following are some sample questions that you can ask when meeting with stakeholders to gather their input and incorporate it into your metrics project objectives. These questions are open-ended by design because they are intended to be starting points for a deeper, two-way conversation.

- What is your role relative to the target identified for this metrics project?

- What do you see as potential risks, issues, and dependencies that may impede visibility, improvement, and education in this area?

- From your history related to the target identified for this metrics project, what can you tell me about what has worked and what hasn't worked in the past?

- What are historical distance and time parameters in terms of changes for this particular metric? What is a reasonable objective based on what's been accomplished in the past?

- What do you believe would be a reasonable goal in terms of distance and time for what we need now?

- What changes will need to be made in order to achieve these objectives?

can discuss whether the changes initially recommended to achieve the objectives of your metrics project appear to be working. These meetings will allow for course corrections that may be needed during the project. There's nothing wrong with changing one of the goal or objective parameters (direction, distance, or time) as long as all the stakeholders and sponsors understand why the change is being made and agree that it should be made.

We've Covered

Defining what it means to have an objective tied to a metrics project

- I advise against starting an information security metrics program haphazardly by randomly gathering data.
- Starting with an objective in mind before starting a metrics project sets you up for success.

Reviewing the benefits of a security metrics program

- **Visibility**   Information security metrics provide visibility into the current status or state of an existing area or process.
- **Education and a common language**   Information security metrics provide a lexicon for the information security team to communicate with and educate stakeholders and sponsors.
- **Improvement**   Information security metrics improve an information security program by enabling better management, promoting informed decision-making, and driving change throughout the organization.

Defining clear project objectives

- Defining objectives and goals at the beginning of any metrics project is essential to achieving success.
- Clearly defined objectives have direction, distance, and a timeline.

Practical tips for succeeding in a metrics project once an objective has been defined and the project has begun

- It is important to measure consistently and set baselines for trending.
- Engage stakeholders and sponsors up front, during the objectives definition phase.

CHAPTER 8

Define Your Priorities

We'll Cover

- Importance of prioritizing security metrics projects

- Factors to consider when prioritizing security metrics projects

- Techniques for prioritizing security metrics projects

- The benefits of prioritizing security metrics projects

Chapter 7 discussed how to define clear objectives for your information security metrics projects. This is critical to setting up an information security metrics program for success right from the beginning. This chapter describes how to prioritize projects within a security metrics program, to ensure that you're focusing on the most important targets.

One of my major intentions in writing this book is to provide information security practitioners with good, practical guidance in the area of security metrics. As you probably know all too well, in the area of information security, we always have more problems than we have the budget and resources needed to manage those problems. Fooling ourselves into thinking we can change this fact is pointless. Therefore, the best course of action is to acknowledge the reality of a limited budget and limited resources and to focus on clear and consistent prioritization when allocating that budget and those resources. Security projects typically don't generate revenue, so developing an ROI for security projects is impossible. Rather, management decides on a budget for security, and it is up to the security team to use that budget effectively.

In this chapter, I'll discuss the importance of prioritizing projects within an information security program, define factors to consider when prioritizing projects, show you techniques for prioritizing projects, and review the benefits of project prioritization. First, though, I'll give you an example of a prioritization process from my own experience.

A Real-World Prioritization Example

When contemplating how I would write about the topic of prioritization, one particular prioritization exercise that I participated in stood out in my mind. At one point in time, when I was on the security management team of another company, we were taking a look at what little existed in the area of information security (basic audit and compliance, with many key functions missing) with the goal in mind of developing a full-fledged information security program from the ground up. As a brainstorming exercise, we posed some questions for consideration:

- What current security projects are in progress?
- What are the security risks to the organization?
- What are known gaps in the security program or in the security posture of the organization?
- Which of these areas do we want to fix sooner rather than later?
- Do we have the resources required to tackle these issues?

We began to build a spreadsheet filled with the initiatives, projects, and tasks that each of the managers was currently working on, planned to work on, or thought was a good idea. This initial list did not have a threshold for size—we included everything from small tasks to large, strategic programs. We also included new ideas and functions that didn't currently exist. As we put items on the list, more new ideas came up and the list grew and grew. By the end of the first working session, we had a list of 200 items.

We decided to use a scale from 1 to 10 to guide our prioritization. Assigning a 10 meant that the project, initiative, or task was an "absolutely must do" and a very high priority, whereas assigning a 1 meant that it was a "nice to have" and a low priority. We went through the 200 items on the list, one at a time, and discussed each item and assigned a priority to it. By the end of a few working sessions, we ended up with about 100 "absolutely must do" items with a priority of 10 assigned to them and about 100 items with a priority of 1 to 9.

This was not an ideal outcome. Determining that half of the 200 items were things we "must do" was unrealistic when considered in the context of budget and resources constraints. Therefore, we decided to do another sweep through the items rated 10 to determine which items within those 100 were the highest priority, medium priority, and lowest priority relative to each other.

The approach that we took in this particular session was fairly one-dimensional and instinct-based, with a lot of emphasis and weight placed on the fact that the management team, as clear subject matter experts and with years of experience, would have a sense of what was important and what was not. We discussed and documented many factors (the details of which aren't relevant at this point in the chapter), including resource allocations and how much time each of the items would require not only from our functional teams but also from partner and vendor teams both within and outside of the organization.

An important point to note here and keep in mind throughout the chapter is that the process of discussing prioritization is useful in and of itself. Laying out all the work for the management team to analyze and discuss laid the framework for many good discussions about what we were working on, why we were working on it, and what each item required in terms of resources, dollars, support, and so forth. It brought us closer as a team in terms of our understanding of the overall program and provided each manager with a big-picture look at the program. This is decidedly different from each manager simply managing their own work in a silo and not having discussions with the rest of the team.

The primary objective of starting with this example is to show you that usually there are a lot of different items to prioritize, and that prioritization is not easy. (In this case, we ended the first round with 50 percent of the items listed as the highest priority, which required us to get more granular in order to manage the program properly.)

Why Is It Important to Prioritize?

Prioritization is absolutely essential in the area of information security. As technology changes and hackers and cybercriminals continuously develop new attacks, the problems to solve and the protections to put in place become unlimited. Information security professionals not only must protect against and neutralize the latest emerging threats, but must also cover all the bases in terms of basic and existing threats. Attaining perfect information security is impossible, so as real-world security practitioners, we must strive to do the best we can with the limited resources, headcount, and budget that we have. Ultimately, prioritization is an exercise in determining relative importance of tasks, projects, and initiatives. This requires us to recognize that classifying everything as important and setting out with the goal of accomplishing everything would only result in failure.

IMHO

Looking at your security environment realistically, not everything that you want to get done will get done. Therefore, your security team should openly and honestly discuss what they can and cannot accomplish. Identifying what cannot be accomplished enables the team to dedicate the time and resources to what can be accomplished, and is just as important as defining what is the highest priority.

The prioritization process also is important because it involves all key stakeholders. It requires defining a clear list of all the possible tasks, projects, and initiatives and then submitting it for open and transparent discussion by the information security management team. Key participants in this type of activity may also include stakeholders outside the direct information security team, such as Legal, HR, IT, Risk, Operations, Business Development, and so forth. I will go through more specific recommended steps for this process a bit later in the chapter. This type of exercise allows the information security team and stakeholders to manage proactively rather than reactively.

In Actual Practice

The approach, requirements, and process for prioritization optimally will be unique to each organization depending on that organization's business model, future business strategy, and attack surface. It is important to take each of these factors into account to get the most highly optimized roadmap for your specific team and organization.

Key stakeholders for the prioritization discussion will also differ from company to company. For example, a highly regulated bank may prioritize compliance with required standards, with the internal auditing team playing a key role, whereas an online retailer may prioritize web application security, in which case the leaders of the development teams may play a key role.

There is something to be said about benchmarking, and many organizations participate in annual surveys to identify the top priorities for the current year. I find these surveys to be somewhat useful, as participating in the surveys and reading the reports allows information security management to review items that they might have otherwise overlooked or failed to review and evaluate. However, I do not believe that one organization should take its annual roadmap from another or from a group. That would be like choosing clothes from a clothing store based on the average size, color, and style of everyone who shops there. This might keep you roughly up to date with fashion trends, but the direct value to you as an individual would not be as great as if you had gone in for a personal fitting specific to your body and style preferences.

Advantages of Effective Prioritization

As mentioned in the preceding section, prioritization allows a management team to manage proactively rather than reactively. Clear and transparent prioritization helps to establish a schedule, a roadmap, and resource allocations. It avoids allowing the projects to run the team in such a way that, instead of completing the high-priority items on time, they partially complete everything.

Another huge advantage to prioritization is that, with the information security management team and key stakeholders engaged up front to help define specifically what should be done (and what should not be done), team members can be held accountable for their high-priority projects. This also means that project leads will not inadvertently focus on low-priority work while allowing higher priorities to slip (an unfortunate but not uncommon result come performance review time). Documenting the results of the prioritization exercise and ensuring that the document is both properly distributed and regularly updated keeps everyone in the organization aligned on priorities. It also gives everyone involved the opportunity to raise concerns about what is being prioritized and clearly discuss any changes to prioritization as the work begins, which is likely to happen.

Factors to Consider

This section offers several factors that you may want to consider in your prioritization discussions. This list is by no means comprehensive, but rather is intended to guide the beginner-level security metrics professional.

Compliance

Compliance is a very common factor to consider during a prioritization exercise, for obvious reasons. If an organization fails to comply with a regulatory requirement, the result may be significant negative impacts to the business, including high fines and penalties as extreme as no longer being allowed to do business in a certain way or with a certain asset (for example, a potential penalty for failing to comply with Payment Card Industry Data Security Standard [PCI DSS] is to be barred from handling credit cards transactions on the Internet). Failures in the compliance area also tend to affect public relations negatively, which can impact the reputation and credibility of executive management and the company.

Into Action

Here are some questions I recommend asking when considering compliance as a factor in a prioritization exercise:

- Is this project, task, or initiative directly tied to a regulatory compliance requirement that must be adhered to?

- If so, how important to compliance is this item?

- What negative impact on the organization's compliance status could result from not performing this project, task, or initiative?

- What are the negative consequences if the organization fails to comply in this area?

As I've discussed in earlier chapters, I believe that compliance is sufficiently important that regulatory requirements ought to be used as a starting point in designing an information security program and, where appropriate, a foundation upon which the rest of the information security program is built. Compliance typically relates directly to a type of business or a manner of performing business and therefore inherently has some reasonable alignment with business strategy.

IMHO

Not all compliance-related projects, tasks, and initiatives are created equal. Some may have a very large impact on an organization's compliance posture, whereas others might be only indirectly related. When using compliance as a prioritization factor, make sure to give it an appropriate level of importance in the context of your specific business strategy and organizational needs, such that anything and everything related to compliance does not get a "free pass" simply because it may be vaguely related to compliance efforts. A subject matter expert familiar with the particular compliance regulation in question should make decisions on what projects are in scope and which are out of scope. If something is labeled "compliance" but is only vaguely related to compliance, make sure that it is appropriately prioritized, even if that means assigning it a low priority.

Risk Reduction

As information security professionals, we are in the business of managing risk; specifically, if necessary, we must reduce the current level of risk in the information security area to align with the level of risk the company is willing to tolerate. How this alignment should be achieved is not always easy to identify quantitatively, but even very qualitative judgments with respect to risk reduction are useful during prioritization exercises. A well-rounded management team that is staffed appropriately for a given business or organization usually has a good sixth sense of what will reduce risk and what will not. This may sound unusual in the context of a book about information security metrics, but not everything has to be about the numbers.

Note

Security professionals often are forced to make qualitative judgments. In such cases, it is important that we document the decision-making process so that, in the future, we can recall the factors that led to the decision and perhaps find metrics related to those decision factors and move to a more quantitative risk management approach.

Into Action

Assigning a priority level to a project from a risk-reduction perspective may be as simple (though not as easy) as asking the following questions:

- What type of attack or negative impact will this project, initiative, or task eliminate?
- What is the probability of this attack occurring if this project, initiative, or task is not deployed?
- Is that probability increasing or decreasing?
- What is the potential severity of this attack (estimated in dollars, if possible)?
- Is the potential severity increasing or decreasing?
- What is the risk reduction associated with deploying this project, initiative, or task? (Should be calculated by Probability × Severity if the attack or negative impact can be completely eliminated, or as a percentage if it only partially reduces the impact.)

Threat Analysis

Threat analysis is a topic worthy of its own book, so I will not delve deeply into it here, but for the prioritization discussion, it is certainly worth mentioning as a valuable tool. The same questioning and analysis used in threat analysis can be used in prioritizing security metrics projects.

LINGO
Threat analysis is one component of risk management. This approach involves identifying and analyzing potential attacks, threats, and risks and preparing countermeasures accordingly.

In Actual Practice

Both the security risk management models and the threat analysis models have one common challenge: the security experts developing these models only know what they know, and there is no way for any single person or group of people to exhaustively know everything. It's important to admit and acknowledge what one does not know.

Tip

There will always be events that are highly improbable and, therefore, likely to end up at the bottom of the list of priorities. These are sometimes called "black swan" events. I recommend Nassim Taleb's book, *The Black Swan: The Impact of the Highly Improbable, Second Edition* (Random House, 2010), for further reading on this topic.

Alignment with Top Business Objectives

An information security program is not an end in and of itself, but rather a means to protect the business. The information security program can best protect the business by addressing the top strategic initiatives of the business, including the support structures, infrastructure, information flow, and technology needed to make those initiatives happen.

Many organizations define and distribute strategic roadmaps for the next three years, one year, or quarter. It's important for the information security program to be informed of what's happening companywide and what's being done to drive the business. This can be used as direct criteria for prioritizing information security tasks, projects, and initiatives. Items that relate to or support top company initiatives ought to be prioritized above others.

Specific Prioritization Factors for Security Metrics Projects

Prioritizing metrics-related projects within an information security program can prove to be a unique challenge, as most of the time you don't know what results you will achieve before you begin to work on the project. You don't know what your measurements look like before you begin measuring, you don't know how clean your data is before you begin analyzing it, and you don't know how effective you will be in effecting change and informing management decisions before you have the project results and begin working with the stakeholder teams to make change happen.

Into Action

You can ask the following questions to identify top business objectives during your prioritization exercise:

- What matters to the top executives at your company?

- Is the task, initiative, or project being prioritized directly or indirectly associated with or supporting a top company priority, goal, or objective? To what extent?

- Will the company goal be negatively impacted if this item is not completed?

Of course, sometimes you may be prioritizing in-progress security metrics projects against new projects. In that case, the following questions may be useful.

What's the Point?

This question can be applied to both existing and new information security metrics projects. It helps to eliminate and deprioritize projects, initiatives, and tasks that do not have clearly defined goals, objectives, and benefits. Sometimes information security professionals, with the best of intentions, pursue projects that turn out to be pointless or a waste of time (when compared with the positive results that might have been achieved by reallocating the budget, headcount, and resources dedicated to the original project).

Will We Potentially Do Anything Differently Once We Have This Data?

This is one of my favorite prioritization questions to ask when it comes to information security metrics. It is related to using metrics to effect change and especially to inform management decisions.

Start by considering what the data might tell you once your data gathering and analysis is complete. Enumerate the various possibilities. If you discover that there is only one possibility, then you can stop doing the project because you will not do anything differently once you receive the project results. You will proceed along the exact same path if there is only one possible outcome of the project and you already know what it is. This project should be eliminated or deprioritized. However, if there are several possibilities to what might be done as a result of different metrics project outcomes and you are deploying the metrics project with the specific intent to determine what course of

Budget Note

One of the key points of this chapter is to recognize that each project that the team undertakes not only has value in terms of what positive outcomes and results occur at project completion, but also has relative value to what might have been accomplished if the resources used for that project had been otherwise allocated. The cost of anything is the foregone alternative. This is similar to a financial investment concept that considers money sitting in a savings account as "wasteful"—even though no dollars are being lost while the money is in the savings account, no dollars are being earned because they are not being invested.

action to take, then the project is as valuable as the decision that will be made based on the data once the project is complete.

Please note that I am not advising against determining "how bad" a particular function or area is with the intent of improving it from that point on. In this case, the project goal or objective may be to measure a baseline that can then be used as a starting point for improvement.

The following are a few examples to demonstrate how the question "will we potentially do anything differently once we have this data?" can be used in a prioritization exercise.

Example: One Possible Known Outcome   If an organization knows that it is failing a regulatory compliance standard, then what good is performing an exercise to test further for compliance status? That type of a project is useless at this point, as it only confirms what the team already knows to be true. If the only outcome is one that is already known, then the resources and time that would be spent in a redundant manner are better spent on a separate project (in this case, perhaps a remediation project to achieve compliance).

Similarly, if a security organization has identified through a risk management or threat analysis exercise a large attack, threat, or risk that currently is not being appropriately mitigated in the environment, spending valuable resources on a project to try to show that it's a big threat is just wasteful. Those resources might be better spent trying to solve the problem rather than trying to show that what is already a known problem is a problem.

Example: Many Possible Known Outcomes   A situation in which there are many possible outcomes and the team does not know which will be the final result may be as straightforward as testing for compliance against a particular standard (regulatory or not) to measure compliance status. Unlike the previous example, with one possible known outcome, in this case the team does not already know for sure if the result will be compliance or noncompliance. Because there are multiple potential outcomes, once the outcome is determined, that information will be used to inform important decisions. These decisions will be different based on which outcome turns out to be true. If the program is found to be compliant, then the decision and plan of action may be not to take any action at all, or it may be to document the findings and put together an annual or quarterly testing schedule. If, however, the program is found to be noncompliant, the decision and plan of action will most likely involve building and driving a remediation program, or a heightened focus on remediation if a program already exists.

The initial project used to determine compliance or noncompliance in this case is very valuable as it informs further important program prioritization and roadmap decisions.

Example: One Possible Known Outcome Requiring Baseline There is a third type of situation, in which the single outcome is already known, but there is additional value in performing the project anyway. The key to adding value if an outcome is singular and known is to have defined, specific objectives related to the project. For example, in the case where noncompliance is already known and there is no chance of compliance, the team may need to document the status of noncompliance in a specific manner in order to file a required report. In this case, the value of the project is not the outcome of the testing (which will show noncompliance, as known) but rather the documentation itself. Another potential value might come from defining a baseline from which to improve upon, as a starting point for a remediation program. Then, once the remediation program is underway, it will be easy to look at the initial findings and report on progress made since that time.

Does Anyone Look at This?

Especially for metrics projects involving reporting, the straightforward question "does anyone even look at this?" is very important for prioritization. If relevant teams, stakeholders, and sponsors are reading and using the information generated by the project to make better decisions and to do their work optimally, then the project priority should be high. If no one even bothers to read the e-mail that contains this report, but instead automatically redirects it to a junk mail folder, then it may be time to stop doing the project or reprioritize that work and ask yourself a few more questions.

Into Action

If no one is looking at the reports generated from a security metrics project, the following are a few potential follow-up questions your team may want to consider:

- Who is the intended audience for this metrics project reporting?
- Why don't they look at the reports?
- Do they understand the data?
- Do they care about the data?
- Do they understand what the data means for their team and for the overall organization?

How to Prioritize

In this section, I will walk you through a specific exercise used to prioritize information security efforts. Ultimately, an information security management team will most likely balance a project portfolio of a combination of both reactive and proactive efforts in order to effectively manage the program.

Prioritization Representations

There are many different ways to prioritize. A few common approaches include:

- Use a number system of 1 through 10 to represent least important (1) through most important (10). You can also use decimals in this system if you choose to.
- Use the representations High, Medium, and Low (meaning high priority item, medium priority item, and low priority item).
- Use the representations Must, Should, and Nice (meaning must do, should do, and nice to do).

The type of representation you choose should not affect the outcome of your prioritization exercise. Prioritization is much more art than science, and all of these representations are simply tools for guiding the prioritization exercise. I recommend that you choose one that "feels right" and makes sense for you and your team. For folks who think in a big picture, conceptual kind of way, either the second or third set may work best. You can also choose to define "in-between" prioritizations, such as High– ("high minus") or Medium+. There are no rules here and no reason to stick to a strict way of doing this; it is only a way to get the team started thinking about relative importance of items.

Phase 1: Brainstorming and List Generation

The first thing to do in one of these prioritization exercises is to generate a list of all the potential issues, items, projects, initiatives, and tasks that are on the table for discussion and make that list available to the entire information security management team for review. This process can be done offline, where each member of the team sends in their suggestions individually. However, I personally recommend an in-person or conference-call live discussion, which helps to generate new ideas through team brainstorming. The interaction between team members during the simple exercise of generating the list is itself valuable, adds value to the prioritization exercise as a whole, and helps to ensure sign-off from key stakeholders.

IMHO

Generating this list can be frustrating and overwhelming. With a huge list of things to do, sometimes the mountain of work can seem impossible to climb. Stay patient and stick with it—the list itself is likely to be too much to accomplish, but remember that the point of this exercise is to narrow it down to what can be accomplished with the means available to the team.

Phase 2: Top-Down Prioritization

The next step is to ask each of the members of the information security program's management team to list their top three, five, or ten priorities.

Tip

Do this independently with each member (meaning secret-ballot style). This will prevent them from influencing each other's priority lists.

How many priorities you should ask them to specify depends on how many items you have overall to prioritize, how many resources you have to dedicate to working on those priorities, and the size of the management team. The number of top priorities each lists should be small enough that not every single project has the possibility of being one of the top priorities—this eliminates the purpose of the prioritization exercise in the first place. On the other hand, the number should be large enough that the members of the management team can sufficiently cover what they believe to be the top priorities for their area or from their perspective.

Once these are specified, you can have meeting where you go around the table (or send individual e-mail requests to the team) in order to ask each person to state their top priorities. Write these priorities on a whiteboard, and place a check mark next to a priority each time it is repeated. At the end of this exercise, which projects are the top priorities for the team will be clear.

Here are a few other suggestions for how to conduct the prioritization exercise:

- Ask the members of the management team to write down their top three (or five, or ten) priorities on sticky notes and take turns putting them up on the board. If a member of the team sees that someone has already posted one of their priority projects, they simply put their sticky note on top of or below the first iteration of the project. The items with the most sticky notes are the top priorities.

In Actual Practice

A security program in a company with many different lines of business may find itself trying to prioritize different security activities according to different business units. As a sanity check to make sure there is business alignment in this type of situation, I recommend that you map your prioritization list to the revenue for each of the different lines of business. That way, you can avoid the embarrassing problem of finding that 80 percent of your team's priorities apply to only 20 percent of the business revenue. Another key to this point is good communications; if your security program is prioritizing a low-revenue area, make sure that you explain why and stay in sync with the priorities of the business.

- One variation on this phase is to list all the different projects for consideration on a whiteboard or a poster, and then to distribute three, five, or ten stickers to the team. Ask each team member to go to the board and put stickers by each of their most important projects. This is another way to enable easy counting of the top priorities.

- If you want to avoid the potential territory grab or politics that can sometimes arise when team members are asked to prioritize projects in their area of ownership versus areas they do not own, then enforce a sticky-note voting rule where each team member is only allowed to vote on issues not in their direct area of responsibility. This can be done independently or in conjunction with a simpler voting method to show where bias may exist for political reasons.

Phase 3: Comprehensive Review

In some cases, phase 1 and phase 2 may be sufficient to identify the top priorities of the team. However, in many cases, these phases do not account for "run the business" or "keep the lights on" type of work, and this may need to be addressed separately. Some teams choose to set aside a percentage of their time, budget, and headcount specifically for this type of day-to-day work, whereas other teams choose to prioritize it against other projects that are more of the "build" or "strategic" nature.

In phase 3, the team goes through the entire list of priorities, one by one, and assigns a value to each item (1–10, High/Medium/Low, or Must/Should/Nice). Although this process can take quite a bit of time, depending on how long the list is, it is usually worth the effort in order to get everyone's input and gain a totally comprehensive understanding of each person's argument for prioritizing a particular item as high or low.

This phase also offers the benefit of developing an understanding of the priority of items relative to one another. This relative understanding makes it easier during the final phase to identify which items should be deprioritized. As previously mentioned, determining which projects should not be done is just as important as determining which projects should be done, in order to make the most of limited time and resources.

Phase 4: Draw the Line

At this point you should have a list of prioritized projects, determined both from input by top management and by your comprehensive review. Now you need to draw a line in the list, meaning that every item above the line will be funded and resourced, and those below the line will not. During a prioritization exercise, it is just as important to identify what projects will *not* be done as it is to identify which projects will be done. Being very explicit about the work that will not be performed ensures that the limited resources and budget will be focused on the highest priority projects in order to set them up for success.

This can be a complex task to carry out, as each project will probably require different resources from different teams, and different sources of money (capital, consulting, or maintenance) at different times. You can go as deep into the specific resource, skills, and budget allocation as is practical. There are many different factors to consider, including time, resources, cost, and executive support.

IMHO

Remember that not everything that needs to be done needs to be done right away. If something can be put off for a while, perhaps more dollars and resources can be dedicated toward it in the future. If you're planning for a year of security projects, not every high-priority project must be done in the first quarter. The security budget may be distributed over a year, so you may be able to fund only a few high-priority projects in the first quarter. Other projects will need to be implemented in the second quarter and later in the year.

What you will end up with is a prioritized list that everyone can agree upon and everyone has participated in to create. If the information security program budget is cut, you can move the line up the list accordingly. Similarly, if more funds become available in the budget, you can move the line down the list accordingly.

Publication and Recurring Reviews

The list of priorities should be made available not only to the information security management team, but to the entire information security team and any stakeholders and sponsors of the program. The more that stakeholders and sponsors know about information security priorities, the more support that can be garnered from the teams required to make them happen.

The information security management team should review this list periodically, as it will undoubtedly change as company priorities and the threat environment changes. Tracking the number and frequency of priority changes over time is a metric unto itself! Changing the list and moving things around isn't a problem—what's important to remember is to include all the right team members so that changes to the prioritization list are transparent. Transparency in making changes to the prioritization list is key for deployment of the projects. You may choose to make the recurring review process as formal or as informal as works for your team culture. Some teams may work well with a formal document that needs to be filled out in order to justify a change, whereas others may simply need to reach a verbal consensus in a staff meeting.

We've Covered

Importance of prioritizing security metrics projects

- Prioritization is necessary to focus limited resources on the most critical activities that will produce the most value.

Factors to consider when prioritizing security metrics projects

- Key factors to consider in prioritization include compliance, risk reduction, and alignment with business objectives.

Techniques for prioritizing security metrics projects

- Some techniques you can use to help you conduct a prioritization exercise include brainstorming and list generation, top-down prioritization, comprehensive review, drawing the line, and recurring review.

The benefits of prioritizing security metrics projects

- Clear and formal prioritization enables transparency and keeps stakeholders all on the same page.

CHAPTER 9

Identify Key Messages and Key Audiences

We'll Cover

- The concept and importance of stakeholder engagement

- Useful questions for identifying key messages and audiences

- Examples providing key questions for key audiences

In a security metrics program, reporting often supports a key message that is intended for key stakeholders of the information security program. This chapter discusses how to identify key messages for key audiences. This includes advice for determining what you will say, who you will say it to, what security metrics you will present, and what issues you'll discuss. Multiple scenarios of this type are provided as examples. Easy-to-use worksheets are also provided in the Appendix to guide your brainstorming process. You will define your key audiences and the key messages you want to communicate to those audiences to build the foundation of your security metrics program.

Why Stakeholder Engagement Is Important

Some security metrics will be used exclusively by the information security team. However, securing a company's information assets frequently requires participation, buy-in, and work effort from more than just the information security team. Therefore, many security metrics are published to people outside the immediate team, particularly key stakeholders of the information security program.

After you have defined the targets, objectives, and priorities for the security metrics program, you must identify key stakeholders throughout the organization. By effectively engaging key stakeholders and getting their commitment early in the process, changes driven by the information security organization are more likely to be effective and sustainable.

Stakeholder engagement also decreases risks and costs associated with security initiatives by presenting the right

> **LINGO**
> **Stakeholders** of an information security program are the leaders who are responsible for critical decision making and the key supporters who will drive change throughout the organization.

information and security metrics to stakeholders up front and opening the communication channel to ensure both sides understand each other—stakeholders understand the security team, and the security team understands the stakeholders.

Stakeholder Engagement

Chapter 1 discussed the two primary benefits of a security metrics program: to inform decision making and to drive change. These help you to identify the key audiences to whom you should be promoting security in an organization: the decision makers who need to be informed and the people who are responsible for making changes. In addition to the people who drive these objectives, a key audience may also be someone you need data from.

Information security does not happen in a vacuum, and every company or organization has key people and teams whose support is required to run an effective information security program. These key people and teams are the stakeholders in the security metrics program and typically include roles such as CEO, CFO, CRO, CTO, BU leader, CIO, Director of Physical Security, and Director of HR. Security metrics require support from stakeholders to be successful, just like any other component of an information security program.

This section presents a series of questions to kick-start your brainstorming process and help you to formulate the key messages that you'll want to convey to key stakeholders.

What's This Person's Area of Responsibility? Why Is This Person Important to Information Security?

This person should add value to promoting security in your organization. They should be able to help you drive change and make decisions. For example, the team they manage may perform important security work to drive improvement of your security posture. Alternatively, a person may be a key stakeholder if the team they manage will make decisions and behave differently based on information you provide to them.

This chapter provides brief descriptions of typical job titles and roles of key stakeholders for an information security program. However, job descriptions vary greatly from organization to organization. For example, the responsibilities of a Chief Technology Officer (CTO) at a small technology start-up in Silicon Valley may be very different from the responsibilities of a CTO at a large, established manufacturing company in the Midwest.

Into Action

The following are some recommended techniques for gaining a richer understanding of how to best communicate with the key stakeholders in your organization:

- Look up the key stakeholder in your corporate directory. Their specific job title may provide insight into what they do.

- Look up the job title of the manager of the key stakeholder in your corporate directory. This will help you to understand the broader context of the key stakeholder.

- Related to the job title and role of the stakeholder, find out what their budget responsibilities and contributions to revenue are, how long they've been with the company, and any cultural issues you may need to understand before presenting to the team or individual stakeholders. Understanding this will help you know how to best communicate with them and to understanding their history and biases, which can influence the scope of their responsibility.

- Visit a library, bookstore, or check out online resources to take a look at professional development books and magazines written for this particular role. These resources may give you insight into some of the typical personality characteristics that you will want to be aware of before meeting with the stakeholder.

- Look up the job titles of the person's peers (other people who report directly to the manager of the key stakeholder). This will shed light on related topics that the key stakeholder is likely to be familiar with.

- Look up the job titles of the direct reports of the key stakeholder in your corporate directory. This provides additional detail on the stakeholder's areas of expertise.

IMHO

Doing research on a stakeholder is almost like conducting an informal background check on them. I like to joke that the best way to prepare for a meeting is to "stalk" the person you're presenting to by finding them on LinkedIn, Facebook, and other, similar websites. The more you know about the person, the better you will be able to tailor your message specifically for them.

What's Valuable to This Key Stakeholder?

Information security comes down to protecting assets. A key stakeholder of the information security program will be responsible for and care a lot about assets that are important to the company. Understanding which assets are relevant to this person will help you to tailor your key message to their interests so that it is relevant and effective.

IMHO

An important but subtle point is what information *not* to share with a key stakeholder. Telling that person about something they don't care about or do not understand will not promote or benefit security in the organization. In fact, it may hurt the organization if the person is confused or if your key message is diluted by information that is irrelevant to that person.

You may have only limited visibility and opportunity to make an impact. Before your meeting, find out what is most important to the key stakeholder so that you can deliver your message in terms that will catch their attention immediately, thereby maximizing the brief time that you have to meet with and influence that person.

What Are Their Security Needs?

Just as various business lines in the organization have differing security needs, so too do the key stakeholders. Individual roles in the organization have varying levels of responsibility and expertise that affect their security needs. Some will be focused on protecting financial information, while others will be focused on protecting code. What the CFO needs from a security program is distinct from what the Director of Physical Security needs.

For What Purpose Do You Need Their Buy-In? What Do You Need Them to Approve?

Information security teams frequently need the support of stakeholders who are outside the immediate control of the team. The ability to promote security in the organization through enhanced controls depends on using processes that require buy-in from the management of the teams doing the work.

Note

The most effective security must be pervasive throughout an organization. To make this happen, every employee must understand the expectations for their own behavior and play a role in securing the company's assets.

Influencing the organization requires buy-in and approval from stakeholders on security projects, initiatives, and behaviors.

What Information Do You Need from This Person?

The information security team does not have access to all the company systems and information. Therefore, gathering security metrics often requires obtaining information from people and systems, which requires having access to both. For example, patching data must be obtained by system administrators or through a product deployed for this purpose. Similarly, testing controls in a network requires access to that network or access to the people who manage the network.

Examples

This section provides real-life examples of how to formulate key messages for key audiences, using the questions from the previous section to guide the process. Each example identifies the key audience and provides guidance on how you can define key messages and supporting metrics for that audience.

Note

Please keep in mind that these examples are not applicable to every situation. Every organization has a unique structure and unique security needs. These examples are meant to give you a few potential paths for defining key messages for your own key audiences. The Appendix includes checklists and a summary for easy reference and a template to perform your own analysis.

Key Audience: Chief Executive Officer

Here are some thoughts you'll want to consider as you tailor your security presentation for meeting with the Chief Executive Officer (CEO).

What is this person's area of responsibility? Why is this person important to information security?   In this example, the CISO is meeting with the CEO of the company. The CEO is responsible for total management of the company, including the generation of both product and capital value.

Note

Generally you should assume that the CISO or someone assisting the CISO is the one having these conversations.

A security metrics conversation with a CEO managing one organization will be similar to a security metrics conversation with the leader of an individual business unit. In this example, the CEO manages multiple lines of business and oversees the individual BU leaders.

What's valuable to this key stakeholder?   CEOs are interested in appropriately managing risk throughout all the business units. The CEO knows how much revenue is generated by each business unit, and has a keen understanding of the value of assets in each business unit.

The CEO is also interested in understanding generally how the work that the information security team performs affects overall company performance and specifically how the program impacts overall company metrics. In meeting with the CEO, the key message that an information security professional delivers might be one that shows how security metrics tie to and influence company metrics in a positive manner.

IMHO

Generally speaking, CEOs are risk takers. They tend to like extreme sports such as auto racing and endurance events such as triathlons. We as security professionals have to understand that they will still like some intuitive decision making, along with metrics reporting data. One approach is to use analogies. One common analogy you may have heard regarding the value of an information security program to a company or organization is "brakes are there to make the car go faster," which may be more akin to the terms they're used to thinking in.

What are their security needs?   What a CEO may not be aware of is how the individual business units relate to and affect each other at a technology level, and what security risks exist for each. Factors such as a recent merger or acquisition, rapid company growth, or a change of business model all play a role in the different level of risk each business unit faces.

You may want to present metrics about the sophistication of emerging threats. A key message here may be that the sophistication of the threat is rapidly increasing, an appropriate introduction to which might be to provide the CEO with industry-level metrics on the number of new malware programs detected per day.

For what purpose do you need their buy-in? What do you need them to approve?   You may want to improve a company's security posture by driving process and technology changes in each business line. The CEO's approval and guidance will be important in (1) driving prioritization of security projects and (2) setting the culture and

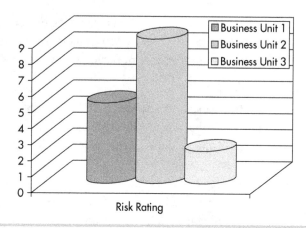

Figure 9-1 items legend:
- Business Unit 1
- Business Unit 2
- Business Unit 3

Risk Rating

Figure 9-1 Comparison of risk scores of business units

tone for the leaders of each business unit. One metric for discussion may be a comparison of the risk scores of the different business units. These BU-level risk scores are composed of risk scores for different areas of security per business line. Figure 9-1 shows an example of what this might look like.

At a quick glance, the CEO will be able to see which business units are secure, and which aren't. The CISO then has data as a starting point to begin explaining the security situation of each BU and highlighting to the CEO what he or she may need to be aware of.

What information do you need from this person?   CISOs may also approach CEOs with the objective of obtaining an understanding of the strategic direction in which the business is going, to forecast where security will be needed in the future.

Key Audience: Chief Financial Officer

Here are some thoughts you'll want to consider as you tailor your security presentation for meeting with the Chief Financial Officer (CFO).

What is this person's area of responsibility? Why is this person important to information security?   If you're a security professional and you're meeting with the CFO of your company, you're likely going to be discussing how much your team spends on security and how much it will need to spend in the future.

What's valuable to this key stakeholder?   Most CFOs are not interested in spending more on security than peers or competitors spend, since security does not add value to the bottom line as clearly as sales and other areas of the company do. However, most CFOs also do not want to spend much less than peers or competitors spend, because they want to ensure that their company's defenses are at least as strong as peers or competitors, to protect against fraudsters who are looking for an easy target.

The CFO is often one of the most important stakeholders for any security program. The CFO is the one who determines how much investment to make in security and doles out the headcount and budget. CFOs measure and quantify everything. To cut costs, CFOs may use methods that are not popular with employees, such as outsourcing. They respond best to hard numbers and data.

What are their security needs?   CFOs want to understand how much they should be spending on security. The CFO may be interested in benchmarking data against other like organizations to see how much they are spending on security and maturity data for your organization. The CFO is also going to be interested in understanding what their investment in security "buys" them. They will want to know what peers and competitors are doing about security, including what types of actions they are taking and which programs they are running. A CISO can provide this information to the CFO.

For what purpose do you need their buy-in? What do you need them to approve?   CFOs do not have the data discussed in the preceding paragraph on hand, since it is not their area of expertise. It is the responsibility of the CISO to obtain and present this data to justify annual security budgets. An example of metrics that a CISO can present to a CFO are maturity assessments of the organization over time, to show that the state of security is improving (or not, depending on the situation).

What information do you need from this person?   CISOs may need to work with CFOs to understand revenue generation for different business units in order to understand which assets in the company are most valuable. They may also obtain their annual budget from the CFO.

Key Audience: Chief Risk Officer

Here are some thoughts you'll want to consider as you tailor your security presentation for meeting with the Chief Risk Officer (CRO).

What is this person's area of responsibility? Why is this person important to information security?   The CRO is responsible for governance of significant strategic, reputational, operational, financial, and compliance-related risks for a business.

As the manager of both risks and opportunities in the organization, the CRO can be an important advocate of the information security program and the funding it requires.

What's valuable to this key stakeholder? The CRO may be interested in a discussion of regulatory compliance requirements related to information security. Today's busy regulatory compliance environment includes the Health Insurance Portability and Accountability Act (HIPAA), Family Educational Rights and Privacy Act (FERPA), Gramm-Leach-Bliley Act (GLBA), Payment Card Industry Data Security Standard (PCI DSS), Safe Harbor, and the EU privacy regulations, to name just a few.

You may provide the CRO with information on the status of compliance with any of these regulatory requirements. Metrics to support your meeting may include, for example, the percentage of controls tested and the percentage of controls failed. If your company has multiple business units, then you might want to display a simple red, yellow, or green status for each business unit and its level of compliance.

Additionally, the CRO may be interested in your perspective of the top ten information security risks. This can be displayed graphically for easy consumption, and typically involves points on a chart showing probability of occurrence and size of impact. Figure 9-2 shows an example of what this might look like.

What are their security needs? You may be the expert in the organization who is responsible for providing the CRO with information on new and recently released regulations and alert them to the level of preparedness for your organization. Even if the CRO is already aware of the regulatory compliance requirements for your company, you can demonstrate the level and current status of compliance related to information security requirements. This information allows the CRO to make and influence financial and prioritization decisions to support information security initiatives as he or she sees fit for

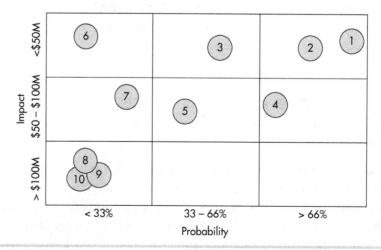

Figure 9-2 Top ten risks

managing overall company risk. Additionally, in the case of risks that exist due to a gap in the information security program, the CRO must be aware of, sign off on, and approve plans to mitigate or accept the risk. Notifying the CRO of risks arising from a failure to comply is an important message for the information security team to deliver.

For what purpose do you need their buy-in? What do you need them to approve?   The buy-in of the CRO can provide support, funding, and proper prioritization of the information security program in relation to other company objectives.

What information do you need from this person?   The CRO may define the risk tolerance for the company or, in the case of a company with many business lines, assign appropriate risk tolerances to distinct business units. A start-up company that collects no personal or financial information from its customers will likely be more risk tolerant than an online e-commerce site that facilitates transactions between total strangers. This information is important to the information security team in understanding how to best design and enforce security controls in alignment with overall company objectives.

Key Audience: Chief Technology Officer

Here are some thoughts you'll want to consider as you tailor your security presentation for meeting with the Chief Technology Officer (CTO).

What is this person's area of responsibility? Why is this person important to information security?   The CTO manages technical and security aspects of an organization. The CTO is typically responsible for overseeing the technical staff of a company and the development of new technologies.

What's valuable to this key stakeholder?   A CTO who is responsible for software development may be concerned about the quality of their code. In this case, you may want to discuss topics such as secure coding practices and training for developers, and present trend information about the number of security vulnerabilities that exist in code. One metric for this audience may be a graph showing the trend of the number of security vulnerabilities per million lines of code. Another metric may be a chart showing coverage of vulnerability scanning.

What are their security needs?   CTOs differ greatly from company to company in their areas of focus and responsibility. For example, one CTO may be focused on technology research. This CTO may work with external organizations (such as vendors, research organizations, and industry partners) to purchase or develop new technologies. The CTO may want to know about the type of information involved in these new developments (Is personal or financial information being transferred to an external organization?) You may want to come to the meeting prepared to discuss information about security assessments of research partners and vendors. Relevant metrics may include the percentage of security assessments that are high risk, or the percentage of high-risk security assessments for which found vulnerabilities are remediated within an SLA defined by the information security team.

For what purpose do you need their buy-in? What do you need them to approve?   Both examples in this section (security vulnerabilities in code and security assessments) are related to driving change in the organization. Securing an organization may involve decreasing the number of security vulnerabilities in code and limiting the number of high-risk partners the organization is doing business with. You may need the CTO's research organization to run new vendor partners by your team so that you can perform security assessments on their products and networks prior to doing business with them and sharing confidential employee or customer data.

Reducing vulnerabilities in code will require approval of the CTO for training in secure coding practices and developer time set aside to fix known vulnerabilities.

What information do you need from this person?   Security leaders responsible for ensuring the security of a company's technical assets should meet regularly with the CTO both to understand their technology roadmaps and to provide them with information about relevant security topics in their area.

Key Audience: Business Unit Leader

Here are some thoughts you'll want to consider as you tailor your security presentation for meeting with the leader of a business unit (BU).

What's this person's area of responsibility? Why is this person important to information security?   A BU leader is responsible for managing a line of business within a company or a particular region that the company does business in. It will be important to go into the meeting with a solid understanding of that particular business unit.

What's valuable to this key stakeholder?   What is valuable to BU leaders will vary greatly. To understand what's valuable to the leader of a particular BU, ascertain the answers to the following questions before you meet with them:

- What does the business unit do?
- Who are its customers?
- How does the business unit generate revenue?
- What assets are valuable to the business unit?

- What are the key processes that support revenue generation for the business unit?
- What are the outsourcing and offshoring strategies of the business unit?
- How does the business unit relate to other business units? What are their interconnections and dependencies?
- What is the language of the business unit?

What are their security needs?   A recently acquired start-up will function very differently from an older, more established business. Security requirements and policies will also be different. The security standard for a recently acquired business unit will likely be lower than the standard for a business unit that has been part of the company for a longer period of time.

A conversation with the leader of a recently acquired business unit may involve a review of the security evaluation performed during acquisition activities and prioritization of projects required to bring the new business unit up to meet the security standard.

For what purpose do you need their buy-in? What do you need them to approve?   Security professionals may request business unit leaders for their help in distributing policy and auditing against a security policy.

What information do you need from this person?   A CISO may need to request access to distribute security policy to that business unit.

Key Audience: Chief Information Officer

Here are some thoughts you'll want to consider as you tailor your security presentation for meeting with the Chief Information Officer (CIO).

What is this person's area of responsibility? Why is this person important to information security?   One group typically managed by a CIO is system administrators. System administrators are responsible for the maintenance and operation of computers or networks.

What's valuable to this key stakeholder?   CIOs are often concerned about availability and resiliency of their systems. They want their systems to be available continuously to support business projects and technology, and they want their systems to be robust so that there are fewer problems to fix or broken systems to replace.

What are their security needs?   Security conversations with this particular audience may focus on vulnerability management, configuration management, standard builds, antivirus protection, business continuity, and disaster recovery. Providing relevant metrics can bolster conversations with system administrators to ensure that they understand why security-related work is related to availability. System administrators who are aware of the importance of security can prioritize security-related work and projects appropriately within their operational duties.

For what purpose do you need their buy-in? What do you need them to approve?   Most likely, a meeting with this audience will relate to driving change and improving existing security processes (or putting them in place if they do not already exist). A CISO may meet with a CIO to request resources to work on key information security projects related to the technical infrastructure. Metrics to support this discussion may include the number of patches deployed within the requirements of the SLA, the percentage of new systems deployed according to a standard secure build, the percentage of systems in compliance with secure configuration standards, the percentage of systems with up-to-date antivirus protection, and the percentage of unmanaged systems. Trend lines over time will be useful to determine if security status is improving or getting worse.

What information do you need from this person?   If the security team does not already have the access required to obtain the metrics it needs, part of your key message to the CIO would be that you need access to deploy a product to gather the data or need the CIO to provide the data directly.

Key Audience: Director of Physical Security

Here are some thoughts you'll want to consider as you tailor your security presentation for meeting with the Director of Physical Security.

What is this person's area of responsibility? Why is this person important to information security?   The Director of Physical Security is responsible for preventing and deterring attackers from accessing company facilities, resources, and information stored on physical media. This leader of the physical security team will be very familiar with fundamental security practices and likely will have greater security expertise than many of the other key audiences in the previous examples.

What's valuable to this key stakeholder?   The director of the physical security team will be interested in designing structures and processes to thwart attacks on the company's physical facility and assets. One example may be the protection of easily stolen devices, such as laptops. The physical security director will want to know that a device has been stolen from the premises. The information security leader will want to know that a device, possibly containing personal or confidential information, belonging to a company employee or customer is now in the hands of a potentially malicious individual. The physical security and information security teams may meet to discuss this issue and share metrics data such as trend lines showing the number of stolen laptops at various corporate campuses.

Another metric that may be of interest to both information security and physical security teams is the trend of tailgaters at various corporate campuses. Physical security will be concerned that an outsider is trespassing and that the safety and well-being of company employees and their belongings may be at risk. The information security team will be concerned that someone who has followed a legitimate employee through a door requiring a badge or ID may be able to access corporate systems and steal company information.

What are their security needs?   Laptop security can be a shared responsibility between the physical security director and the CISO. The CISO may be responsible for notification of customers in the event of a security breach and may inform the physical security director of these requirements. As of July 27, 2009, 45 states, the District of Columbia, Puerto Rico, and the Virgin Islands have enacted legislation that requires companies to notify customers of security breaches that involve personal information.

For what purpose do you need their buy-in? What do you need them to approve?   Penetration tests and audits of different company offices may require notification of and approval from the physical security team, especially if the information security team is sending in an investigator or auditor who may be exhibiting behavior that appears to be malicious in order to test physical security controls.

What information do you need from this person?   For the example metrics previously provided in this section (number of stolen laptops and tailgaters), the information security and physical security teams may need to coordinate with each other to determine which of the two groups will be collecting, trending, and reporting this data for sharing between the two teams. In some cases, the physical security team may be the

In Actual Practice

There is a growing convergence between traditional security and IT security. Sometimes this relationship is competitive, as each of the leaders of these organizations carves out their specific areas of responsibility and draws the lines between the two. This is something to be aware of when approaching the folks in charge of physical security. It may be advantageous to team up with them and present whatever you're interested in communicating as both a shared task and a shared reward.

organization who has deployed and is monitoring the technology or the people in place to detect these incidents, and the information security team may need to request that this information be shared.

Key Audience: Director of Human Resources

Here are some thoughts you'll want to consider as you tailor your security presentation for meeting with the director of the human resources (HR) department.

What is this person's area of responsibility? Why is this person important to information security?   The HR Director is responsible for the processes involved in managing people in the organization. This includes processes related to employment, development, utilization, compensation, and policy.

What's valuable to this key stakeholder?   The HR Director may be responsible for managing corporate behavior of employees in order to promote a particular company culture. This may include deployment of training to company employees in various areas (ethics, sexual harassment, and so forth). One of these areas should be information security training, particularly education about social engineering and the classification and protection of information.

The HR Director is also likely to be responsible for the confidentiality of employees' personal data.

What are their security needs?   Broad security training intended for new hires and all employees will most likely include a discussion of social engineering and information classification and protection of information. Training implemented by the security team to educate personnel on these subjects should be accompanied by a method of measuring the effectiveness and impact of the training.

Metrics in this area may include the results of a survey given to employees after information security training is complete to test their retained knowledge, and trend charts showing the number of security incidents resulting from social engineering tactics over time. Providing these metrics to the HR Director when you meet establishes a starting point for a discussion on the importance and effectiveness of training.

For what purpose do you need their buy-in? What do you need them to approve?   The information security team may be responsible for communicating the importance of creating a culture of security to the HR team. This often involves working closely with the HR team to design training that will be aligned with overall company culture. The HR Director may need to approve information security policy before it is given to and signed by all company employees.

What information do you need from this person?   You may need help from the HR Director to obtain distribution lists for implementing training and communicating policy requirements and guidelines.

Note

In general, when trying to influence a key stakeholder, keep in mind that they can influence their C-suite peers by sharing the data that you provide. In other words, the person you are trying to influence is also a key influencer. If you can't meet with the key stakeholder who has decision-making authority for what you want to get approved, then consider meeting with a key influencer, in an attempt to deliver your key message indirectly.

Chapter Summary

Table 9-1 summarizes all the examples from this chapter. These examples do not represent a comprehensive list of all possible audiences, messages, and metrics that an information security professional may identify. They simply illustrate how you may begin thinking about stakeholder engagement as a context for designing and building security metrics. Additional key audiences may include management from the customer service department, privacy department, legal department, or other departments.

Key Audience	Key Message	Security Metric(s)
Chief Executive Officer (CEO)	Present information on security posture of multiple business lines	Comparative security score reporting
Chief Financial Officer (CFO)	Justify funding for the information security program	Benchmark data of peer companies
Chief Risk Officer (CRO)	Present an update on the status of regulatory compliance	Percentage of controls tested Percentage of controls failed
Chief Technology Officer (CTO)	Educate on risks of outsourcing and obtain buy-in for vendor security assessments Request remediation processes to manage vulnerabilities	Percentage of vendor security assessments resulting in a status of high risk Percentage of high-risk security assessments for which found vulnerabilities are remediated within an SLA defined by the information security team Percentage of security vulnerabilities per million lines of code

Table 9-1   Summary of Key Audiences, Messages, and Metrics

Key Audience	Key Message	Security Metric(s)
Business unit (BU) leader	Drive further compliance with information security policy	Trend of audit results over time
Chief Information Officer (CIO)	Improve patching, secure build, and antivirus procedures	Percentage of patches deployed within SLA
		Percentage of new systems deployed according to standard secure build
		Percentage of systems in compliance with secure configuration standards
		Percentage of systems with up-to-date antivirus
		Percentage of unmanaged systems (and trends for each)
Director of Physical Security	Define a joint process for managing physical device and information loss related to laptop theft	Trend in number of laptops stolen by office location
		Trend in number of tailgaters by office location
Director of Human Resources (HR)	Promote a culture of security for company employees	Trend in number of social engineering–related security incidents
		Trend of percentage of employees completing information security training

Table 9-1   Summary of Key Audiences, Messages, and Metrics (*Continued*)

We've Covered

The concept and importance of stakeholder engagement

- Stakeholders are leaders responsible for critical decision making and key supporters who will drive change throughout the organization.

- Once key stakeholders are effectively engaged and committed, changes driven by the information security organization are more likely to be effective and sustainable.

Useful questions for identifying key messages and audiences

- To identify your key audiences and the key messages that you'll want to convey, consider the following questions:

    - What is this person's area of responsibility? Why is this person important to information security?

- What's valuable to this key stakeholder?

- What are their security needs?

- For what purpose do you need their buy-in? What do you need them to approve?

- What information do you need from this person?

Examples providing key questions for key audiences

- Include metrics and thoughts for each of the roles: CEO, CFO, CRO, CTO, BU leader, CIO, Director of Physical Security, Director of Human Resources.

CHAPTER 10

Obtain Buy-In from Stakeholders

We'll Cover

● The concept of buy-in and why it's needed for the success of a security metrics project

● How to prepare for a buy-in meeting with stakeholders

● A step-by-step process for obtaining buy-in for a security metrics project

A big mistake that some security professionals make is not engaging stakeholders early enough and, therefore, failing to obtain stakeholder buy-in for security metrics projects. This applies in general to many security projects, but because this book is about security metrics specifically, here I will discuss the importance of obtaining stakeholder buy-in and their commitment to timelines for security metrics projects.

What Is Buy-In and Why Do You Need It?

Most security metrics projects cannot be done in a vacuum using only resources, budget, and time from the security team. Due to the comprehensive nature of information security and the capability of today's technology to store, transfer, and retrieve information in so many different formats and in so many different places, we as information security professionals are often faced with situations in which we need support from other teams to achieve our objectives. Obtaining buy-in involves first identifying all of the different stakeholders whose support is required for a security metrics project to be successful and then ensuring that they understand the goals of the project and are committed to achieving them. A security metrics project may have only one stakeholder but typically has several. When identifying stakeholders, it is important to note their roles and responsibilities, such as owners and end users of systems or facilities involved in the security metrics project, audit team members, and so forth.

The information security team's job is to protect the information assets of the organization or company. An information security program is most effective if it aligns with business strategy by ensuring that the security metrics projects are adding value and that the value is clear to stakeholders and sponsors.

IMHO

Sales and communications are not necessarily the first skills that come to mind when thinking about the traits required for an effective information security team; however, both of these skills will play a role in any job you take as an information security professional. Information security is an area where expertise can be very specialized, and conveying the value and the "why" of security metrics projects to sponsors and stakeholders is not always straightforward or easy to do.

What happens if you don't have buy-in from your stakeholders? Too often, security metrics projects are set up for failure because buy-in is not obtained before it's needed. By the time stakeholders are properly identified and looped in, they don't have time to participate in the project or don't consider it a priority.

If stakeholders don't understand the "why" behind security metrics projects and aren't committed to achieving the same goals as the security team, then security metrics projects that need help from IT, operations, or any other supporting team may continue to be deprioritized (and won't get done) quarter after quarter.

Tip

Security will not be embraced by all, so buy-in is most necessary at the highest levels of stakeholders and not always necessary with the end-user community. Focusing on the highest-level stakeholders and obtaining their buy-in can give you leverage over lower-level stakeholders who might not be as willing to embrace the project.

Preparing for a Buy-In Discussion with Stakeholders

In this section, I describe "the homework" you'll need to do as you prepare for a meeting with stakeholders. You may get only one or a few chances to sell your security metrics project. The best way to approach this conversation is to have a comprehensive understanding of both what you're trying to communicate and what will work best for your particular audience.

Understanding Your Part

The first thing to do before approaching stakeholders is to understand what you are doing and what you will need.

What Are You Doing?

To obtain stakeholder buy-in and get your stakeholders to commit to timelines, you must be clear and convincing when you make your presentation. This requires that you have a solid understanding of what you're trying to achieve through your security metrics project. If you've read the previous chapters in this book, you should be well prepared. In Chapter 7 you learned how to define your goals and objectives, which should help you to explain to stakeholders the "why" behind your security initiative. Chapter 8 explained how to prioritize your security initiative within the context of both information security and overall company priorities, providing you with solid arguments for why this project is important to the company and why now is the right time to do it. Chapter 4 provided you with the necessary business justification and project proposal framework to answer most of the questions that you may encounter as you begin your selling journey. All of this upfront work will come in very handy when you're selling the project to your stakeholders.

To help you organize your presentation of what you're trying to achieve through your security metrics project, here's a summary of the things you've developed in previous chapters that you'll want to have available for review as you're preparing to obtain stakeholder buy-in:

Chapter 4	Brief Objective Statement Type of Change Proposed Start and End Date Roles and Responsibilities Project Name Problem Statement Solution Statement Priority/Principle Supported Scope Project Description Change Details and Impacts Risks of Not Implementing This Project Dependencies Metrics/Success Measures Major Deliverables and Deadlines Required Budget Resources Required
Chapter 6	Target
Chapter 7	Objectives/Goals
Chapter 8	Priorities
Chapter 9	Key Messages

With your homework done, you're ready to provide a clear agenda for the discussion with your stakeholders. During the actual meeting, I recommend presenting the information in the following order:

1. Key Messages

2. Problem Statement and Solution Statement

3. Target

4. Objectives/Goals

You can then follow this discussion with a more detailed presentation of the project plan components from Chapter 4.

Into Action

You also have requirements for the project, and depending on the role that the stakeholder team plays, they may have requirements too. You'll need to discuss both.

First you'll need to lay your requirements out on the table with regard to resources, budgets, and timelines. If you're pursuing a project with stringent deadlines and deliverables, such as a compliance remediation that is needed to pass regulatory requirements, then you will need to take a hard approach where you state what absolutely must be done and what you need to accomplish it. Because the project is mandatory, you should not meet stakeholder resistance to your requests. Your task, then, will be to work with the stakeholder teams to figure out the best way to meet those requirements. On the other hand, if you're proposing a project that is not mandatory, you'll have to take a more delicate approach when you lay out your requests, and then work within the means of your stakeholder to get what you need. Without the compliance requirements of the first example, you'll need to convince your stakeholder that your project is enough of a priority to dedicate the required resources and budget.

If the stakeholder team that you're meeting with is a customer of the security team, you'll need to obtain their requirements to ensure that your team delivers what they need according to their specifications. This meeting is the perfect place to do so, and you can use the project proposal/business justification form in Table 4-1 of Chapter 4 as a guiding document to facilitate the discussion.

What Do You Need?

The second step in preparing your presentation to obtain stakeholder buy-in is to identify your potential stakeholders and sponsors.

Access   Sometimes, to accomplish your objective, the only thing you need from a particular stakeholder team is access to their systems. Your information security team may have the bandwidth and the expertise to do the work that needs to be done, but you may need to request and gain access to certain systems or applications to get the job done. Your work may change or impact the systems and applications that you're accessing, in which case you'll need to request from the stakeholder team the access and permissions to make the changes.

Resourcing and Budget   The two biggest things that you will likely be requesting from your stakeholders to accomplish your objectives are their resources (specialized expertise and work from their team members) and their budget for hardware, software, consulting, or maintenance costs to support your project objectives.

Outline your requirements first and then ask the stakeholder team to define the specific resourcing required. You are the security expert and they are the expert in their field, so when it comes to allocating their resources and how much time it takes for things to get done, they know best. Similarly, if you're putting forth security requirements for a big technology purchase that will be chosen and deployed by the stakeholder team, it's best to center the discussion on security requirements rather than prescribing pieces of the project, which is their area of expertise.

IMHO

It's important when talking about resourcing and budget to communicate your requirements to the stakeholder team and then ask them for the resource and budget estimates. It is critical to ask how much it will take rather than specifying it yourself—with this approach you're more likely to get something closer to what it will actually take as they know the historical data best. Additionally, you're protected against blame for scope issues down the road.

Timelines   One of the critical things for which you need stakeholder buy-in is the timeline for your project, particularly regarding the phases during which the stakeholder teams will need to perform work, grant access, or have their systems affected by other work involved in the project. Timing is one of those project management components that may or may not be flexible, depending on the project needs and situation. For example, an audit project that has a tight deadline will have very strict timeline requirements, and to meet those requirements, other project parameters such as budget and resources must adapt to the timeline. On the other hand, another project may exist that has limited budget and resources but is more flexible in terms of the timeline. In that case, the project may ration its budget and resources over time to deliver the project successfully.

Tip

If you have a rigid timeline, communicate that fact to the stakeholder team and explain why time is of the essence. If you have a flexible timeline, begin by outlining your requirements and then ask the stakeholder team what they estimate for resourcing needs.

Understanding Your Stakeholders

As discussed in Chapter 9, you need to understand your stakeholders prior to meeting with them. Make sure you have as much information as you can gather beforehand regarding what they're responsible for, what they care about, what they're working on, and the history between your team and theirs.

Why is it important to understand the history between the teams? Understanding past relationships and events that have occurred can give you insight into both what's worked and what hasn't worked

> **LINGO**
> A **pain point** is exactly what it *sounds* like—a problem that has been particularly difficult to solve.

and help you to shape your presentation accordingly. Success stories can provide a context to which you can refer as you present your current case for a new security metrics project, and pain points and conflicts from the past can guide you in formulating a new approach.

As an example of why it's important to understand the history between the teams, suppose your team previously initiated a secure coding training project for developers that resulted in fewer application vulnerabilities on the corporate website and, consequently, more time for the developers to work on other issues (instead of fixing vulnerabilities and taking the heat for any that might have been exploited). The next time you approach the development team with a security idea or a new project, they're likely going to listen to you as a trusted authority. If, however, your team previously deployed onto the corporate network a monitoring tool that ended up breaking business-dependent systems and

Into Action

In addition to the resources listed in the table in "What Are You Doing?" here are some guiding questions that you can use to identify which teams you'll need buy-in from:

- Which teams will need to provide support?
- From which teams will you need resources and time to make your project happen?
- Which teams will be affected during the implementation and rollout of your project?
- Which teams will need to be informed about the project deployment and results?
- Which teams are the customers to whom you will be providing services?

Into Action

Discuss success stories in a quantitative manner by including details about the number of hours, dollars, and headcount involved in the past projects. Also, recruit an advocate within the group of stakeholders prior to the meeting, to help keep the meeting on track and continuously refer to past successes. Finally, address past negativity up front. Let your stakeholders know that you understand their pain points and that your team will avoid past mistakes or obstacles to ensure the success of the project.

causing downtime, then the next time you approach the IT team with a request to evaluate or implement more security tools on the network, you're going to have a tougher time convincing them. You will need to research the new tool and present information to the IT team that convinces them the new tool is not going to interfere with their systems and customer needs.

Finally, when deciding whom to include in your meeting with a stakeholder team, there are two different roles to consider: the decision-maker and the worker.

Including the decision-maker ensures that the person who is responsible for allocating resources and making approval decisions is present. Getting that person to understand why your project is valuable and is a priority is often very important to obtaining buy-in. The downside is that, depending on the level of the decision-maker, that person may lack the specialized expertise to know exactly how long something will take or to give you insight into additional specifics, risks, and issues related to the "how."

The advantage of including the worker who will be performing the actual tasks is that they will know all about the "how," including technical intricacies, specific historical information about what has worked and what hasn't in the past, and the different players who will need to be involved to get the job done. It will be important for you to specify your requirements to the team members in this role so that they know what to do. They will most likely be able to provide more accurate input than the decision-maker in terms of scope and what additional resources outside of their team may be required. The disadvantage is that they may not hold the decision-making power required to utilize their time (even if they think that your project is a great idea, their boss may have them working on something deemed to be a higher priority).

My recommendation is to include both of these types of stakeholders in your meeting, if possible. If not, start with the folks in the worker role to get an accurate scoping, and

In Actual Practice

How do you learn about the history between the teams? If you have a senior security team member who has been around for a long time, you might be able to simply ask them, either during a casual conversation or a quick meeting that you set up specifically for that purpose. If you know someone within the stakeholder team that you are trying to engage who might be able to provide insight into what's happened in the past and how the relationship between the two teams works, then you might want to consider reaching out to them as well prior to kicking off your stakeholder buy-in meeting.

If no one on the security team has been around long enough and you don't have contacts on the stakeholder team, consider reaching out to vendor contacts who have been doing business with your company for some time. Often, security vendor partners or resellers also have relationships with IT and network operations teams, and if the vendor is well established and has been doing business with different groups in your company for some time, then they may be able to provide you with some information.

then follow up with the folks in the decision-making role in order to get final buy-in and management approval. Getting stakeholder buy-in from only one or the other may lead to unnecessary friction and project hold-ups down the line.

Tip

None of this "soft research" is intended to dictate your specific actions or approach; rather, it's just good information to have when going in to ask for stakeholder help on a project.

The Steering Committee

If multiple stakeholders are involved in a single project, program, or initiative, a steering committee type of format may be best. A steering committee typically consists of decision-makers from various teams (although other formats include workers, or perhaps two separate but related committees of decision-makers and workers). This type of group may meet on a monthly or quarterly basis to guide and direct major company initiatives, ensure that initiatives are aligned with organizational growth and drive competitiveness, ensure alignment with industry best practices and standards, and provide a forum for reviewing, discussing, and approval project requirements, scope, priorities, and resource allocations. A steering committee may be focused on a particular aspect of the company or organization, such as risk management or technology.

If a steering committee whose charter is relevant to your security metrics project exists, you may want to present your project proposal to that committee for their discussion and approval. If one does not exist, you may want to consider creating one for the purposes of meeting the objectives previously described. This type of committee can evaluate and prioritize project proposals, determine prioritization, scope, and resource allocations, and follow up on ongoing projects to check their progress and calibrate prioritization against other existing and new projects.

Meeting, Explaining, Asking, Documenting

After you have prepared to meet with stakeholders by identifying what you're trying to achieve through your security metrics project, identifying what you need to request from stakeholders, and gathering as much information as you can about your stakeholder group, it's time to meet with them. This section addresses what you'll need to discuss with your stakeholders and get their input on.

As discussed, the first thing to present to your stakeholders is a description of what you're trying to achieve through your security metrics project. The second part of the presentation is an explanation of what you need. It's important to note that the second stage should be a two-way conversation: while you're specifying what you need, you must also find out what the stakeholders can provide, to ensure that the teams are aligned.

Documentation and Commitment

After you've outlined your project proposal and requirements and your stakeholder has filled in the gaps, make sure that you ask specifically for the stakeholder team's commitment to what's been estimated in terms of resources and timelines. Ensure that this buy-in is also documented in meeting minutes. You can then easily distribute the minutes via e-mail to make the information available to anyone who was not present in the meeting. More importantly, you can refer to this documentation as the project progresses in order to ensure that the stakeholder teams follow through with their commitment as things change and priorities shift. When the project is underway and questions arise, you'll already have the answers, and these will be transparent and already agreed to. Think of it as a security contract, and use it as such.

Note

After you've obtained and documented stakeholder buy-in and launched your project, don't forget to follow up with your stakeholders on a regular basis, communicating the project status and ensuring that commitments are being followed. You can also communicate project accomplishments, risks, and issues on a weekly, biweekly, or monthly basis. This topic will be discussed further in Chapter 13.

We've Covered

The concept of buy-in and why it's needed for the success of a security metrics project

- Most security metrics projects cannot be done in a vacuum using only resources, budget, and time from the security team.

- Obtaining buy-in involves first identifying all of the different stakeholders whose support is required for a security metrics project to be successful and then ensuring that they understand the goals of the project and are committed to achieving them

How to prepare for a buy-in meeting with stakeholders

- Organize your presentation.

- Make sure your description of what you're trying to accomplish and what you need from stakeholders is very clear.

- Make sure you've done your homework on your stakeholders—who they are and what they need.

A step-by-step process for obtaining buy-in for a security metrics project

- The key steps to obtaining buy-in are understand what you are doing, understand what you need, and understand your audience.

PART V

Toolkit

CHAPTER 11

Automation

We'll Cover

- The benefits of automating a metrics program, security or otherwise

- A general workflow for metrics automation

- Functions that typically comprise a metrics automation workflow

This chapter is about automating the collection, computation, and communication of metrics, whether or not they are specifically targeted at security. The first section provides a general discussion of the benefits of automation. The following section will cover specific technologies and tools within the context of common metrics program requirements.

Automation: Benefits

Almost any metrics program, even the smallest and least ambitious, will be required to process significant amounts of data. While in some cases it might be feasible to use manual means, automation will almost always be preferable due to the many benefits it can deliver. This section will identify and discuss several of those benefits.

But first it is important to realize that automation, by definition, is work that is performed by computers. If you don't know what you need, the computer can't help you. So, your first responsibility is to create the overall plan for the program and clearly define the role that automation will fulfill. Earlier chapters in this book address how to do this—how to establish the essential components, define objectives, and set priorities, roles, and responsibilities. These need to be firmly in place before comprehensive automation is possible.

An effective strategy is to introduce automation incrementally as the program gains clarity. Ad hoc tools such as Excel can be useful for prototyping or limited-scale automation while project staff members are learning the best ways to collect, cleanse, transform, and integrate data from multiple heterogeneous sources. After staff members understand these processes better, they can be introduced to additional tools such as databases, computational engines, and reporting packages. Each new technology should be added only if its benefits are relevant to the goals of your metrics program.

This section provides a general discussion of the benefits of automation. The following section will cover specific technologies and tools within the context of common metrics program requirements.

The most important benefits of automation can be itemized as follows:

- **Accuracy**   Computers, once program steps are verified, can be counted on to process data correctly. This is critical for establishing trust in metric results.

- **Transparency**   At the very least, the instructions for all automated tasks must be spelled out in detail for a computer to execute them. It is possible to ensure that at least one accurate source exists that describes exactly what processing was performed.

- **Scale and scope**   With automation, you can process more data, more calculations, more metrics, and more complex reporting in terms of quantities, execution frequencies, and breadth of function.

- **Repeatability**   Computers can be counted on to repeat a process exactly, so results can be reproduced.

- **Reliability**   Operations performed by computers are much less error-prone than when performed by humans.

- **Auditability**   Automation can incorporate logging features that document every step taken and every encountered error or exception.

The preceding benefits of automation serve to instill trust in the metrics that they deliver. They also make it possible to address quantitative analysis tasks of large enough scope and scale to be meaningful. It is hard to imagine a successful metrics program without automation.

IMHO

Automation is not equivalent to spreadsheets. It is much more. Spreadsheets, as wonderful as they are, do not support collaboration in which multiple users can contribute to metrics content. Chapter 12 provides an example of one company's evolution from spreadsheets to a truly automated metrics program. The company started with spreadsheets and quickly learned that, while convenient, familiar, and apparently low cost, they really handle only one function well: calculation. Calculation is important but it is only a small, perhaps the smallest, function needed to implement a sustainable and credible metrics program.

Automation: Workflow

Given that automation is an indispensible component of a metrics program, what types of functions should candidate automation tools support and how should those functions work together?

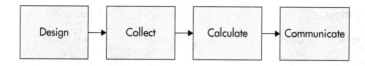

Figure 11-1 Automation workflow

The first observation we can make is that the vast majority of metrics automation processes will implement the simple workflow depicted in Figure 11-1.

The *design* step identifies and defines the questions that you want metrics to help you answer. The *collection* step involves acquiring and preparing data for metric calculation. The *calculate* step performs the computational logic to generate results. The *communicate* step tackles all the issues associated with presenting the data to authorized audiences of end users.

A capability not shown in Figure 11-1 is overall *orchestration*. Orchestration comprises functions such as scheduling and coordinating the workflow—making sure that the preceding steps are completely specified, that they occur in the correct order, and that errors are caught and reported.

The terms workflow and orchestration became common in the 1990s to describe processes composed of multiple distinct steps. The steps in such processes may be a combination of both automated (computer based) and manual (person based) units of work. Relationships between steps are modeled to capture common requirements such as sequential execution (step 1 must be completed before step 2), parallel execution (steps 6–10 can be performed simultaneously), and conditional execution (do not perform step 9 if step 8 did not complete successfully). The term *workflow* typically refers to the final model for a process, while orchestration refers to the administrative oversight that ensures the workflow is executed as specified.

The following sections discuss general requirements of a metrics automation tool, organized into the preceding workflow steps.

LINGO

Workflow is a collection of rules that govern the relationship of steps required to complete a process. Relationships might include sequence order, branching conditions, looping, and number of repetitions.

Orchestration is the administrative oversight that ensures a workflow is properly executed. Oversight might include ensuring that all criteria are satisfied for proceeding from one step to the next, error detection, error reporting, and even recovery from discovered errors.

Design: Hypothesize and Strategize

This is the most creative step of the workflow and usually the least automated. In this step, you first decide which questions are important (hypothesize) and then decide which quantitative analysis and metrics would be helpful in either answering those questions or at least providing insight (strategize). Automation can help in three key areas:

- Metrics catalog
- Content management
- Social networking

Let's look at each of these in more detail.

Metrics Catalog

A *metrics catalog* is simply an online, searchable repository that holds definitions and, optionally, implementations of metrics. It is designed to provide complete and unambiguous definitions of a set of metrics—metrics that you have implemented, may implement, or just think are interesting. There is no industry standard for what constitutes a metric definition, but there is an emerging consensus that is supported by several organizations. This consensus metric definition is called the MetricML Framework.[1] MetricML includes specifications that cover attributes for defining a metric and an XML schema for sharing metric definitions. Several organizations, such as the Center for Internet Security (www.cisecurity.org), the Cloud Security Alliance (www.cloudsecurityalliance.org), the Unified Compliance Framework (www.unifiedcompliance.com), and securitymetrics.org, have adopted MetricML for their own use. Attributes of a metric definition include a name, author, description, audience, frequency of measurement, units of measure, suggested target values, limitations, references, and more. Figure 11-2 provides a screenshot of the MetricsCenter Catalog. Note that the MetricsCenter Catalog is one implementation of a metrics catalog that was implemented at PlexLogic. Each metric is defined using the MetricML schema, which lends uniformity and completeness to the definitions of all the metrics contained in the catalog.

The left panel provides a hierarchical list of business contexts to which the metrics can be linked via a Web 2.0–like tagging scheme. The right panel holds the definition of the metric. Additional panels can be displayed to perform searches, make comments, and define new entries in the catalog.

The following are a set of frequently asked questions (FAQs) about metrics catalogs:

What information does a metrics catalog contain? Catalog entries can describe contexts, metrics, datasets, surveys (for obtaining metric values manually), comments, and

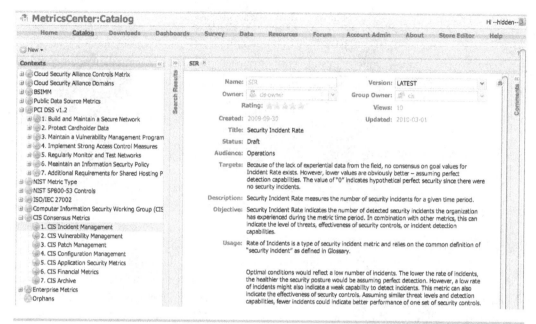

Figure 11-2 MetricsCenter Catalog

dimensions (attributes that are used for aggregation as well as linking together multiple datasets). All of these catalog entries can be associated with each other. For example, metrics are associated with the datasets that they use in their computation. Comments can be associated with any object, a dataset, a metric, a dimension, a survey, or a context. Metrics are associated with the business contexts to which they are relevant. The diagram in Figure 11-3 shows the associations that are implemented in the MetricsCenter Catalog The black lines with arrowheads reflect many-to-many relationships while the gray lines indicate one-to-many relationships. For example, the relationship between datasets and metrics is many-to-many because one dataset can be used by many different metrics and one metric may require many datasets to compute it. Similarly the relationships between context and metric, metric and survey, dataset and dimension, and survey and dimension are all many-to-many. The relationship between contexts and comments is an example of a one-to-many: one context may have many comments posted about it but each comment can be associated with exactly one context. Similarly the relationships between comment and metric, comment and dataset, comment and dimension, and comment and survey are all one-to-many.

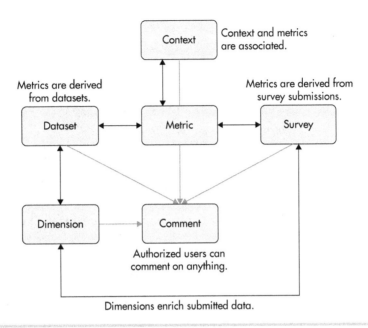

Figure 11-3   MetricsCenter Catalog data model

What features can a metrics catalog support?   The MetricsCenter Catalog also implements various features normally associated with content management and social networking. Here are a few examples:

- Every object in the catalog has a URL, making it individually addressable as web content.
- Users can register for RSS feeds to be notified of changes to individual objects or groups of related objects.
- References to other web objects (internal or external to the catalog) can be embedded in a metric definition.
- Users can rate metrics and share comments.
- Workgroups can be set up to control access to metric definitions as they progress from early draft through review and final release.
- A versioning system tracks changes and the comments that triggered the changes.

Does a metrics catalog need to support all of the preceding content and features?   To be effective, a catalog does not need to support all the features in the preceding list. However, combined, they are quite helpful when groups of stakeholders want to collaborate and arrive at consensus definitions. What is most important is to formally record complete and unambiguous definitions of the metrics that you are using. The case study in Chapter 12 gives a concrete example of the loss of productivity and trust that can occur when such definitions are not readily available.

What are the three primary benefits of using a metrics catalog?   The primary benefits of using a metrics catalog are as follows:

- *It provides an online searchable resource for metrics.* A catalog with just the objects depicted in Figure 11-3 provides a simple and effective resource for finding suitable metrics for almost any purpose.

- *It provides means to map metrics to key business requirements.* A catalog with just the objects depicted in Figure 11-3 enables users to link metrics to almost any type of business requirement ranging from compliance with standards such as PCI or ISO to security management disciplines such as vulnerability management or access control.

- *It provides clean separation between metric specification and implementation.* A catalog with just the objects depicted in Figure 11-3 provides clean separation between a metric definition and its potential other incarnations, such as scripts or code to automate it and the results that are calculated when the code is executed. This is not to say that a catalog cannot or should not contain such objects. Rather, it need not contain them. And, if it does not, then the catalog has the potential to be entirely agnostic with respect to any implementation or operational considerations about the metric program. It is not inconceivable that you could select distinct automation tools for the catalog and the rest of the steps identified in Figure 11-1.

IMHO

The concept of a metrics catalog is new. Yet, for some reason, most quantitative analysis programs and tools fail to implement one. A pet peeve of mine is to see a graph with no clear units of measure. Related to that are graphs where a metric's name is provided but there is no clear and unambiguous definition of how it was derived. I suppose this is yet another form of lying with statistics, so eloquently identified by Mark Twain in his famous quote: "There are lies, damn lies, and statistics." Providing a complete definition of a metric often can take lots of space—more than just one or a few sentences. There should be a standard for defining metrics. This standard should identify everything from its name to a detailed description of the data required to compute it. PlexLogic has been working with several organizations to create and openly publish a standard XML schema for defining metrics. You can find out more about this at www.metricscenter.net. There you can see the MetricsCenter Catalog, which is the first and only implementation of a catalog that is uniquely tailored to the needs of a metrics program.

Content Management

A content management system is web-centric software that automates many of the mundane tasks associated with creating and updating a website. Most typically, metrics and analytics are published via the Web—perhaps internally only, but possibly, in the case of benchmarking, to users across administrative boundaries. In many cases, the content of a metrics website will be created by many sources, some of which are automated (such as those that crunch numbers and store results) and others of which are manual (such as written commentary, analysis, and annotations about the metrics).

A content management system facilitates important and common web tasks such as the following:

- Creating and updating web pages with static and dynamic content by a potentially large number of contributors

- Controlling access to both web content and functions for managing web content

- Implementing a flexible information architecture in which hierarchies of topics can be assigned to sections and subsections with intuitive navigation between areas

- Establishing a modular software infrastructure in which specialized functions (such as search, dashboards, and catalog management) can be plugged in

Using an off-the-shelf content management system provides the technical infrastructure that is needed to support a very collaborative metrics program, which leads us to the next topic: social networking.

Social Networking

Social networking in this context essentially means collaboration among the various groups that typically are involved in a metrics program. These groups include

- Metrics designers, who define metrics that will pass the "who cares?" test

- Quantitative analysts, who provide expertise on techniques from math and statistics

- Operational staff, whose actions are influenced by metric results

- Line managers, who use the metrics to evaluate the performance of the systems for which they are responsible, make changes, investigate the effects of those changes, and identify actions for correction and/or improvement

- Internal and external auditors, who are looking for hard evidence of compliance

- Executives, who usually may want to look only at summaries and narrative reports, but sometimes may want to drill down to higher levels of detail

These groups have differing information requirements. It is conceivable that each group would both consume and produce content about metrics. Some may have data to provide, some may have questions, and some may have answers. Capturing this content in a well-organized and centralized system is critical for capturing a record of why certain decisions were made and how they affected performance over time spans of months, quarters, and even years.

Whether a group of collaborating metricians is "social" or not, many of the features and functions of social networking are certainly applicable.

Collect: Extract, Cleanse, Transform, Merge, and Load Datasets

The capability to collect data is the most fundamental requirement of a security metrics automation tool. Getting accurate data is typically by far the most time-consuming task in metrics programs. Having powerful data management tools can yield huge benefits not only in the obvious value of delivering accurate metrics, but also in minimizing the time it takes to prepare the data to create the metrics. Data management is not the function on which you want to skimp.

Figure 11-4 shows a typical workflow for collection.

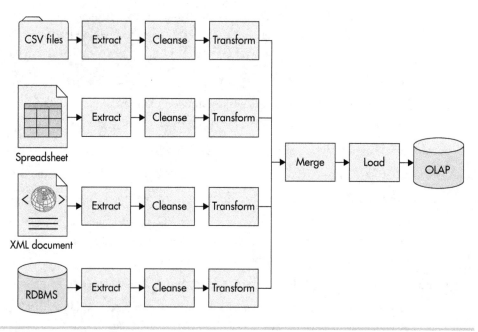

Figure 11-4 The collection workflow

An additional function that is important is *curating* data. Curating is an administrative function that is designed to accomplish several very important tasks:

- Cataloging datasets so that people know they exist and what data they contain. The Metrics Catalog can help with this via the Dataset object. The key is to establish a well-known authority on existing datasets so that reuse of clean, authoritative data is maximized and people who want metrics can easily find the data needed to compute them.

- Establishing standards for data content. For example, if metrics are to be aggregated along lines such as Business Unit or Product, a curator would establish the collection of names to be used so that different spellings or abbreviations don't interfere with proper aggregation. A more subtle function, but critical, is the establishment of rules on how to handle integration of historical data into current categorical structures that may have changed due to administrative reorganization or changes in data granularity. For example, it is common to want to introduce additional levels of granularity as the amount of data grows. Projects that can aggregate by a coarse-grained category, such as Commercial vs. Government vs. Nonprofit, in the beginning may evolve to more fine-grained categorization that divides Commercial into Finance/Manufacturing/etc., which could, in turn, evolve into looking at Banking vs. Insurance within the Finance category.

IMHO

Data is everything. Data collection is essential to a security metrics program. Eighty percent of the work in creating a metrics program involves data. You have to understand it, organize it, ingest it, update it, and improve it. The importance and effort associated with these tasks is almost always underestimated. Yet, doing these functions carefully and diligently will pay rewards that can potentially far exceed the cost. These rewards include being able to stand up to the highest and most intense scrutiny, with results that are accurate and insights that are based on verifiable, hard, ground truth. Take care of your data and it will take care of you.

Note the "merge" function depicted in Figure 11-4. This function specifically addresses the situation when a metric requires data from more than one source. Some of the most valuable metrics are created based upon data from more than one source. Let's look at some examples of such metrics and the types of questions for which they can provide insight.

Merging Data Sources: Why Do It?

- **Metrics that correlate two independent processes** What is the relationship between security awareness training and certain types of security incidents? What is the relationship between a business unit's use of a centralized internal audit service and the number of external audit findings? Is there a relationship between application language and discovered security flaws?

- **Metrics that measure "treatment effect"** What is the difference in security incident frequency before and after installation of a security information and event management (SIEM) solution? What is the difference between service desk workload and installation of a new identity and access management system? What is the difference in percentage of e-mail traffic that is spam before and after introduction of new antispam technology?

- **Metrics that identify key factors that influence the value of an outcome metric** Which factor is most influential in creating secure applications: language, software development life cycle (SDLC) structure, type of supplier, or other factors? Where is the point of diminishing returns in a multilayer protection (security-in-depth) strategy? How much better is three layers than four layers?

By their very nature, metrics derived from multiple data sources are complex. This section focuses on the data aspect. The metrics and analytics will be covered in subsequent sections.

Merging Data Sources: Physical Considerations

With respect to data, it quite commonly resides in separate and distinct "islands," or data storage formats, that were never intended to be integrated. At the lowest level of incompatibility is the physical or technical interface required to read the data. This interface varies depending on the data storage format, some of the most common of which follow:

- **Comma Separated Value (CSV) files** Text files that typically are organized into records and fields. One row in the file represents a single record, with multiple fields represented as ASCII text and separated by a special character such as a comma, colon, or pipe symbol (|).

- **Excel spreadsheets** Proprietary files that are created and managed via Microsoft Excel. A useful feature of Excel is the Export to CSV option that renders one spreadsheet as a CSV file.

- **Relational database management systems (RDBMSs)** Proprietary formatted disk files that present a standard Structured Query Language (SQL) interface that can be used by either humans or programs to access the data. The data is organized into tables that are linked to each other via common attributes called *keys*.

- **Extensible Markup Language (XML) documents**   Files that consist of ASCII characters that follow the XML standard for representing objects and their attributes. The data is organized as a hierarchy in which a parent object can have one or more children.

- **Web services and Representational State Transfer (REST) interfaces**   The physical attributes of data storage are hidden behind standard application programming interface (API) calls that are used to access it. The program that accesses the data can be located on a different server from where the data physically is stored. The data is described via a standard called Web Service Definition Language (WSDL), and the APIs and remote access protocols are defined via the Service Oriented Architecture Protocol (SOAP), which runs over HTTP or HTTPS.

- **Structured logs**   Files and data streams such as syslog on computers running the UNIX/Linux/MAC OS X operating system or Microsoft event log formats on computers running Microsoft operating systems.

- **Lightweight Directory Access Protocol (LDAP) repositories**   Structured data that typically describes users, their affiliations, applications, computers, and who can access what. LDAP is a standard API for accessing data in these repositories. Microsoft Directory is an LDAP repository.

- **Simple Network Management Protocol (SNMP) management information bases (MIBs)**   A hierarchical storage scheme commonly used by network devices and computer systems to hold data related to performance, faults, configuration, accounting, and security.

- **Really Simple Syndication (RSS) feeds**   A combination of structured and unstructured data that is typically delivered on demand as part of the dynamic content of a website.

- **Proprietary APIs**   Application programming interfaces that are created and supported by a single software vendor to provide access to data associated with its products.

Each of these data storage formats has an associated extraction technology that would be part of the implementation of the workflow diagrammed in Figure 11-4. Extraction technology is potentially a huge consumer of engineering resources—not because each individual data source is hard to integrate, but because there are so many of them. There are standards, some of which are mentioned previously, and they do lighten the resource drain.

For enterprises, the collection of systems that are potential data sources for metrics is finite and can probably be prioritized. If you are running an enterprise metrics initiative, a key task (part of curating) is to identify what sources exist and what data they can contribute. Once that is done, you can begin to look at ways to integrate the sources that

In Actual Practice

In practice, dealing with the multitude of technical interfaces is the easiest hurdle to overcome in data integration for metrics processing. *Physically* extracting the bits from wherever they live can typically be accomplished by a competent software developer in less than a day or two. The hard part is *logically* merging independent sources to create a picture that is greater than the sum of its parts.

you have. For example, do two sources, say for incident tracking and asset inventory, have a common identifier that can be used to merge these two data sources and perhaps calculate metrics about asset risk?

For commercial metrics tool developers, the list of possible data sources is finite but very, very long—so long as to be practically impossible to cover completely. Prioritization is typically assigned based on a combination of factors: market share and customer need.

In addition to the technical aspects of just physically extracting the bits from a data source, there is the additional issue of what the bits actually mean. This issue is typically referred to as *logical extraction* as opposed to *physical extraction.*

Merging Data Sources: Logical Considerations

This section describes the logical considerations required for merging disparate datasets by looking in detail at some examples. Two of these examples are projects that are funded by the U.S. Federal government as part of its overall cybersecurity program managed by the Department of Homeland Security (DHS). The last examples discuss specific aspects of the more general concept of an overall risk model.

With respect to the first two DHS projects, the National Institutes of Science and Technology (NIST) is responsible for defining and disseminating the resulting standards, whereas MITRE is the engineering organization that implements and operates the technologies (as well as provides important insights into their design). Both projects deal with naming. The first project names vulnerabilities and the second project names products in which the vulnerabilities have been discovered:

- **Common Vulnerabilities and Exposures (CVE)** CVE (http://cve.mitre.org) is a free and open dictionary of common names, called *CVE identifiers*, that uniquely and universally identify security vulnerabilities that have been discovered. CVE was launched in 1999 as a solution to the problem that information security tools built by different authors were using their own names for security vulnerabilities. As a result, there was no easy way to determine when two different products were referring to the same vulnerability. CVE currently is the industry standard for naming vulnerabilities and exposures. A typical CVE identifier takes the form CVE-*nnn*, where *nnn* is an integer that is sequentially assigned by the CVE Candidate Numbering Authority.

- **Common Platform Enumeration (CPE)**   CPE (http://cpe.mitre.org) is a free and open structured naming scheme for information technology systems, platforms, and packages. It is based on the generic syntax for Uniform Resource Identifiers (URIs) and a dictionary that is used to cross reference vulnerabilities (CVE identifiers) with software products (CPE identifiers). CPE currently is the industry standard for naming software products.

Thanks to the existence of CVE and CPE identifiers, products that identify IT assets and the software running on them have a common, nationally accepted way to identify both the software assets and any discovered vulnerabilities. This is a big improvement, but it represents only one solution to a much bigger problem. There are many other entities associated with measuring security and developing a complete model for managing risk that need a similar naming solution. Here are a few:

- **Threats**   There is no analog to CVE, in part because this is such a broad topic. There are many types of threats, ranging from spam, to botnets, to viruses, to disgruntled employees.

- **Countermeasures**   There are generic names for tools and techniques for preventing threats (such as firewalls, intrusion detection systems, patch management systems, and so forth), but no standards exist for naming them.

- **Regulations**   The specific compliance requirements mandated by these documents are difficult if not impossible to identify in a common manner. Work is being done in this area by several commercial product vendors, but no widely accepted standard exists.

- **User accounts**   The manner in which a user and his or her accounts are identified often varies depending on the operating system, identity management system, and application. A key feature of identity and access management tools is to rationalize these identifiers of not only the "actor" but also the target object and actions that can be performed.

In addition to the generic objects in the preceding list, there are also enterprise-specific entities such as the business unit hierarchy, locations and offices, product categories, and instances. All of these need a coherent naming strategy so that metrics can be mapped to the business that they are measuring.

This mapping of metrics to business context is enabled via a logical model in which entities and all of their attributes are identified. Associations between entities are identified and characterized as to whether they are one-to-one, many-to-one, or many-to-many.

Loading Datasets

Once a logical data model for the metrics is defined, it can be loaded as a collection of associated generic dataset definitions in a metrics catalog. This has the huge advantages of not only integrating an overall business context model with the definitions of the metrics that the data will drive, but also clearly identifying how associations are made between datasets—what attributes are used and how they are acquired from the raw data sources.

Figure 11-4 from earlier in the chapter shows a repository with OLAP as the last stage of the collection process. This is a typical final outcome of the collection process, but the process need not always operate as portrayed in Figure 11-4. Storage of temporary or intermediate results may occur throughout the collection process, as well as at the end. In some cases, the collection process does not store anything and just streams results directly to the calculation step. OLAP is shown as the final result of the collection process because it appropriately suggests the type of preparation, and therefore the proper final product of collection, that is needed for calculation, the next step in the workflow.

Calculate: Slice, Dice, and Model

This is the most mathematically intensive step, in terms of both analytical sophistication and compute power. OLAP products often are used at this stage because they specialize in "slicing and dicing" data along multiple dimensions.

For example, OLAP is commonly used to facilitate sales reports that are aggregated along dimensions such as time, location, organization, product, and salesperson. Note that some of these dimensions, such as time and location, are hierarchical. Time can be decomposed into a hierarchy consisting of years, quarters, months, and weeks. Location can be decomposed into a hierarchy based on country, region, state, and city.

> **LINGO**
> **OLAP**, which stands for online analytical processing, refers to a specific type of data storage and retrieval mechanism that is optimized for swift queries that involve summarization of data along multiple factors or dimensions.

If you think about it, metrics reporting can greatly benefit from the technical capabilities of OLAP. Metrics are often much more interesting when reported along hierarchical dimensions such as time, location, and business unit, to name a few. Additionally, OLAP

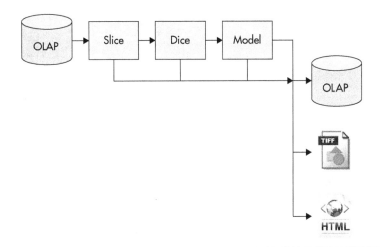

Figure 11-5 The calculation workflow

provides valuable security features, such as restricting visibility based on a user's position within a hierarchy. For example, a user in one business unit can be restricted to viewing metrics only for that business unit and (perhaps) the company as a whole and will not be able to see the metrics for a different business unit.

Figure 11-5 shows a typical workflow for calculation.

Using the optimized facilities of an OLAP (or RDBMS) repository, you can select the data to be used in a metric (slice) and then aggregate it (dice) by counting, summing, weighting, and performing other simple arithmetic operations. Adding models to the slicing and dicing calculations was covered in Chapter 3. Suffice it to say here that modeling is important if you want to add confidence levels to your statements, perform forecasting or cluster analysis, or identify trends and correlations.

As Figure 11-5 indicates, the results of the calculations can be re-stored in the repository (for reuse by other metrics) or be packaged as images (such as TIF format) or web page visualizations (HTML format) and other possible presentation options (not shown). This is not the only way calculations can be performed, but it is certainly one of the most common ways. The key result is material that is ready to be presented to end users.

Communicate: Visualize, Annotate, Publish

Communicating results is the most visually demanding requirement for metrics automation tools. The functions and features that are most useful fall under the generic categories of content management and, for workgroup collaboration, social networking.

Figure 11-6 shows a typical workflow for communication.

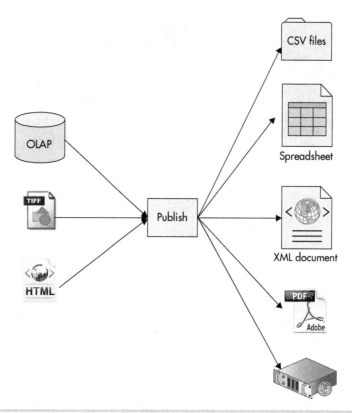

Figure 11-6 The communication workflow

The result of calculations is either more data or *widgets*, pieces of content that may or may not stand alone. In either case, these elements of content need to be organized, formatted, and presented to end users that are authorized to see them. A release cycle may follow. For example, if a collection of results is about the performance of a particular business unit, then the owner of that business unit should be able to review, comment, and/or correct those results prior to publication to a wider audience.

Another common publication workflow deals with annotation and interpretation. If the quantitative analysis is to be part of a large report, then both graphics and prose will need to be integrated, reviewed, revised, beautified, and published.

Orchestrate: Deploy, Schedule, Execute, and Coordinate

Unlike design, collect, calculate, and communicate, orchestrate is not really a workflow step. Rather, it is an overall management capability that synchronizes the flow of tasks from initial metric creation through ultimate delivery of results to authorized consumers.

In Actual Practice

A key decision about communication is how much interactivity end users should be allowed to have. At one extreme, you can just publish static reports—such as PDF documents or static web pages. The other extreme is to allow unfettered access to the metric results and the raw data that was used to compute them. In general, neither extreme is common practice. Here are two very common tensions that need to be resolved in order to deploy the right level of interactivity:

- **Anonymity vs. detail**   If there is information associated with individuals that needs to be protected, then the more level of detail that you release, the more difficult it is to protect or anonymize confidential facts about individuals. There is a famous case where Netflix released what it thought was an anonymized dataset of user movie preferences to researchers for analysis.[2] Despite the fact that the dataset was large (over 500,000 Netflix subscribers), it was demonstrated that identification of so-called anonymized records was easily possible by combining only a small amount of data from other sources. The moral to this story is that when you release enough detail, you are arming potential adversaries with access to external sources over which you have no control. By combining the data you released with these external sources, adversaries may have enough to cause serious harm. This very question of how much is too much is an active and difficult area of anonymization research. There is no simple answer.

- **Interactivity vs. focus**   Almost all analysis involves following many avenues of investigation with only a few discovered nuggets to show for all your work. The primary value added by metrics to raw data is precisely this analysis. One effective way to rescue your audience from traveling the same unproductive paths that you did is to not give them the opportunity. On the other hand, there is benefit to be gained by even limited interactive exploration. For example, providing options for viewing aggregation along, say, three or four dimensions is far more effective than generating tens or hundreds of static images.

Your Plan

Automate a metrics program by implementing software that performs one or more of the following tasks:

- Designs metrics that identifies hypotheses and strategies for gaining insight
- Collects raw data that extracts, cleanses, transforms, merges, and loads datasets that will drive metric calculation
- Calculates results by slicing, dicing, and applying models
- Communicates results by creating for a variety of audiences consumable reports that include both graphics and annotation
- Orchestrates a workflow that coordinates design, data collection, calculation, and communication of results

As such, orchestration includes functions such as signing off on a metric definition, deployment of its implementation, scheduling its calculation at regular intervals, and executing and delivering updates. If a system that was supposed to contribute raw data fails to do so, the orchestration function needs to capture this exception, stop downstream tasks, and report the error to a metric system administrator.

In the early stages of a metrics program, when the number of metrics is low, it is feasible to manually perform orchestration. As the numbers of data sources, the number of metrics, and communication complexity increase, the benefits of automating orchestration become greater.

We've Covered

The benefits of automating a metrics program, security or otherwise

- Accuracy, transparency, scale, and scope
- Repeatability, reliability, and auditability

A general workflow for metrics automation

- The workflow decomposes into four primary functional areas: design, collection, calculation, and communication.
- Orchestration is the glue that binds together the four functional areas.

Functions that typically comprise a metrics automation workflow

- Key design functions are a metrics catalog, content management, and social networking.
- Key data collection and calculation functions include interfaces to data sources, anonymization, and packages of math and statistical functions.
- Key communication functions include dynamic and static visualization, annotation, and publication.

Endnotes

1. MetricsCenter Catalog, www.metricscenter.net.

2. A. Narayanan and V. Shmatikov, "Robust De-anonymization of Large Sparse Datasets," *Proc. IEEE Symp. Security and Privacy, 2008*, pp. 111–125, May 2008, userweb.cs.utexas.edu/~shmat/shmat_oak08netflix.pdf.

CHAPTER 12

Analysis Technologies and a Case Study

We'll Cover

- Some representative automation technologies that are commonly used to implement the automation workflow of any metrics program, whether it is specifically targeted at security or not

- The strengths and weaknesses of common technologies in light of requirements

- A case study that illustrates a range of programs, automation efforts, and experiences associated with establishing a metrics program in a range of companies

This chapter discusses options for implementing automation of metrics collection, calculation, and communication to stakeholders. There is a range of possibilities, depending upon how much of the process you wish to automate and how much you want to develop in-house or purchase as a commercial-off-the-shelf product. Each option has advantages and disadvantages. In particular we look at the strengths and weaknesses of security metrics programs implemented with spreadsheets, homegrown systems, and a purpose-built commercially available metrics cloud service.

Automation: Technologies

This section describes the technologies that must be integrated to deliver a complete metrics automation solution, whether or not it is specifically targeted to implement security metrics. Figure 12-1 shows a high-level architecture diagram of the major components.

Starting at the bottom of the diagram, the three servers are generators of raw data that will be used to compute metrics. The bulleted list under the servers provides examples of security management systems that are likely data providers for metrics. These are all operational systems that typically live in a data center that may or may not be co-located with the server used to generate metrics. The raw data that the servers generate is collected via an Extract Transform and Load (ETL) function. Each ETL function has two interfaces: the raw data generator interface and the metrics system interface. The raw data generator interface is often implemented using an Application Programming Interface (API) provided by the vendor of the raw data generator. Similarly, the metrics system interface may be based upon proprietary technology of the metrics system's developer. Both interfaces may

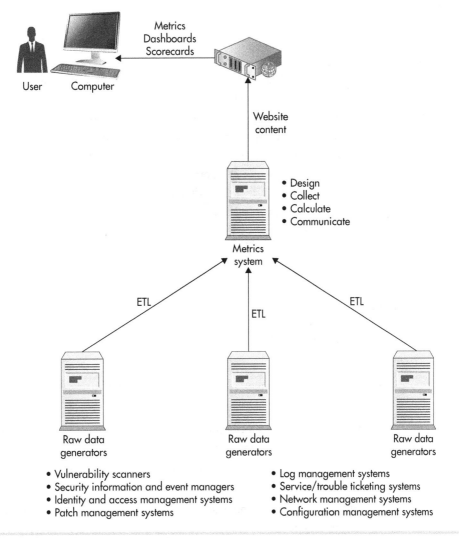

Figure 12-1   Metrics system architecture

also be based on standards such as XML/XML Schema, comma-separated value files, or others. Once the data has been ingested by the metrics server, it is further processed to ultimately deliver metrics content to end users. The diagram shows a web server as the component for delivering this content. Other delivery mechanisms include static documents, presentations, and spreadsheets such as MS Word files, PowerPoint slide decks, or Excel worksheets.

Budget Note

It is common for the data collection portion of a metrics project to dominate the budget in both cost and effort. In medical research, it is not unusual to see a budget that allocates as much as 80 percent of the cost to data collection, with the remaining 20 percent dedicated to design, calculation, and communication. From my experience, you should expect a similar 80-20 ratio for security metrics projects. As you develop your initial plans for a metrics program, spend significant time on understanding what data you have, what shape it is in, and what time and effort will be required to prepare it for analysis.

Your Plan

As discussed in Chapter 11, the five functional areas that you can automate in a metrics program are as follows:

- **Metrics design**   Implement a metrics catalog and collaborate with your peers to obtain a collection of metrics that will pass the "who cares?" test.

- **Data collection**   Identify the sources of data that you have to work with and learn everything you can about each source—how it is created, what it means, what is counted and what isn't, how it is updated, and how amenable it is to change or improvement.

- **Calculation of results**   Identify simple calculations as well as additional models to enrich your results, explore the data, and learn about relationships and what seems to be normal.

- **Communication of results**   Know your audience; be sure to include review cycles before wide publication of results (particularly controversial ones).

- **Orchestration of the preceding workflow**   Identify steps that do not require human intervention and automate them. Eliminate manual effort wherever possible.

Similar to the discussion of functions in Chapter 11, this section is organized around the four workflow steps: design, collect, calculate, and communicate. The technology for implementing a metrics program has been available for years. What is new and creative is how orchestration technology is used to integrate and repurpose these generic steps specifically for security metrics.

Note

Whenever a book cites specific manufacturers and products, there is always the danger of failing to mention excellent products, for any number of reasons. Omission of a product from this discussion should not be interpreted as anything other than lack of space.

Design

Metrics design is perhaps the least addressed of the four automation workflow steps. Table 12-1 identifies some functions, common technologies, and example products used to implement the automation of metrics design. The corresponding remarks provide additional information such as prevalence of use and strengths or weaknesses.

Function	Technology	Example Product	Remarks
Social networking	Social networking	CIS Consensus Security Metrics[1]	Developed using Basecamp (http://basecamphq.com), a popular collaboration technology. CIS used Basecamp to coordinate review and comment from over 50 experts. Prevalence of use: High. Basecamp is a widely used collaboration platform.
		CSA[2] Metrics	Developed using open source wiki software. CSA used this software to coordinate review and comment from over 50 experts. Prevalence of use: High. There are many open source wiki platforms.
Content management	Document publishing	CIS Consensus Security Metrics[1]	Final publication of this product can be downloaded free of charge as a PDF document. Prevalence of use: Growing since the release of the CIS metrics in early 2010.

Table 12-1   Metrics Design Technologies

Function	Technology	Example Product	Remarks
		NIST SP800-53 Controls[3]	Final publication of this product can be downloaded free of charge as a PDF document. Prevalence of use: Growing. Most widely adopted by government agencies.
		MetricsCenter Catalog[4]	A proprietary technology from PlexLogic LLC, offered in two formats: a free, read-only, online catalog of metrics such as those from CIS and NIST, and a commercial cloud service. The two implementations use open source content management software from Joomla (www.joomla.org) and Drupal (http://drupal.org), respectively. Both implementations allow collaboration on metric definitions and comments by authorized reviewers. Prevalence of use: Growing since introduction of the service in 2009.
Metrics catalog	RDBMS with Web 2.0 user interface	CIS Consensus Security Metrics[1]	CIS metrics were also published as MetricML XML documents and loaded into an online catalog. A MetricsCenter.net account is required to view the metric definitions. Prevalence of use: Growing since release in 2009.

Table 12-1 Metrics Design Technologies (*Continued*)

Without a purpose-built solution such as MetricsCenter, the work products of the design step are not integrated with the work products of the other steps. As a result, the risk is greater that the documentation and actual implementation of the metrics may drift apart. Like all documentation of IT systems, maintaining synchronization between documentation and implementation requires ongoing investment.

Tip

Technology candidates other than MetricsCenter Catalog for design collaboration include free cloud services such as Google Apps and open source wiki packages.

Collect

The collection step comprises three primary functions: acquiring raw data, transforming it, and mapping it into a model that provides a business context. As with the design step, integration across the collection functions is a key issue. If the data modeling function is not well integrated with the acquisition and transformation functions, then discrepancies can develop. Furthermore, if the modeling function is not integrated with the metrics catalog, then it may be difficult to identify exactly which datasets were used to compute the metrics and exactly which operations were performed on the raw data prior to metric calculation. Generic tools to perform these functions have been available for years from the database management technology space. Table 12-2 gives some examples.

Function	Technology	Example Company or Product	Remarks
Data acquisition	Extract, transform, load (ETL)	Pentaho, SAP BusinessObjects, and SAS	ETL technologies typically are delivered as part of a larger solution, such as an online analytical processing (OLAP) product (for example, Pentaho or SAP BusinessObjects) or statistical analysis packages (from companies such as SAS or IBM SPSS). ETL solutions typically include facilities for remote access.
Data transformation	ETL	Pentaho, SAP BusinessObjects, and SAS	ETL solutions typically include common data transformation operations such as folding to uppercase, string operations, and very simple mathematical functions.
Logical data modeling	Data modeling tools	Microsoft Visio and Altova XMLSpy	Many technologies are commercially available to support various techniques. Visio supports models such as Entity-Relationship (E-R) and the Unified Modeling Language (UML). Altova has tools such as XMLSpy to support XML-based web services modeling.
Data storage	Database management tools	MySQL, Microsoft SQL Server, and Oracle RDBMS	MySQL is an open source relational database management system (RDBMS). SQL Server and Oracle are commercial products.

Table 12-2 Metrics Data Collection Technologies

Pentaho and MySQL are open source solutions that you can use without incurring license fees. The other products are licensed from their respective manufacturers.

The underlying logical data model of the repositories for data storage is an important consideration when selecting a collection technology. The two most commercially significant models are described next.

Relational Model

The relational model was first introduced in the late 1960s by Dr. E.F. Codd, a mathematician who defined 12 precise rules for creating a "normalized" relational database. The relational model organizes data into tables with rows and columns. Tables are related to one another through the existence of common columns. For example, data about vulnerabilities found in an enterprise might be described using these two tables:

- **Vulnerability Types**   Includes one row for each CVE ID (CVE is described in Chapter 11). Columns of this table hold the CVE ID as a key, a weakness type name (such as cross-site scripting or buffer overflow), and identifiers for the vendor, product, and version of software that has this vulnerability.

- **Vulnerability Instances**   Includes one row for each discovered vulnerability on a specific host. Columns of this table hold a unique identifier of the host (such as its hostname), the CVE ID of the discovered vulnerability, and possibly the number of vulnerabilities discovered, owning business unit, and the criticality of the host.

Relational tables are easy to visualize, and they map quite naturally into spreadsheets. A relational database management system (RDBMS) is an automated data management system that implements the relational model.

OLAP Model

Similar to the relational model, the online analytical processing (OLAP) model defines a basic data structure for organizing data—namely a cube, which is also called a *hypercube* or *multidimensional cube*. Cubes, like RDBMS tables, are defined via a schema. Most often, cubes are defined as an extension of a relational schema called a star schema. A star schema separates numeric *facts* or *measures* from categorical *dimensions*. Dimensions allow you to very quickly slice and dice measures along one or more dimensions. (Does this sound perfect for metrics, or what?)

As an example, a simple two-dimensional hypercube model for the relational model for vulnerability names and instances (from the preceding section) would identify the following:

- One numeric fact: the number of discovered vulnerabilities

- Two categorical dimensions: weakness type and owning business unit

It is easy to visualize a two-dimensional cube that has one row for each type of weakness and one column for each business unit. The cells hold a value based on the measure, the number of discovered vulnerabilities. The cell values could be as simple as a sum or as complex as a difference between actual observed counts and a forecasted value. If you extend the model to include one more dimension, then you get a 3D cube. With more than three dimensions (called hypercubes), visualization gets less intuitive. Another key capability that is supported with hypercubes is hierarchical dimensions. So, for example, if it is useful to represent a business unit as an entire hierarchy of divisions, departments, and groups, this is inherently supported in the OLAP data model. For metrics, treating time as a hierarchical dimension is extremely useful because it enables you to very conveniently display metrics on yearly, quarterly, monthly, weekly, and daily time intervals.

Tip

The primary advantages of RDBMS over OLAP modeling are simplicity and the broad availability of knowledgeable technical staff. The primary advantages of OLAP over RDBMS are execution speed of slicing and dicing when using large datasets and flexibility (hierarchical categories being a prime example).

Calculate

Calculation technologies often include functions to address the collection step. For example, the SAP BusinessObjects, Pentaho, and SAS products all include data repositories that support query languages that perform slice and dice operations. The primary differences in these technologies are derived from their underlying data model (is it relational or is it cubes, for example). SAP BusinessObjects, Pentaho, and SAS support OLAP hypercubes. Pentaho provides OLAP functionality as a layer on top of a relational database, such as the open source RDBMS MySQL. This is the same approach as that taken by Microsoft with its OLAP data analytics support implemented as a layer on top of SQL Server.

The underlying data model has a strong influence on the types of slicing and dicing supported. While OLAP can easily offer hierarchical aggregation of measures using hierarchical dimensions, this capability is less convenient (but not impossible) for RDBMS-based systems.

The biggest influence over modeling support is probably best identified when looking at the primary target market for a product. Products with the most sophisticated modeling capabilities tend to target more academic- and research-oriented users, while products that offer less sophisticated modeling capabilities often target business users.

One interesting exception to this last statement is the Microsoft Excel spreadsheet application. Out of the box, it supports lots of basic math and statistics functions and, with plug-ins from third parties, can support quite sophisticated and specialized analytics.

Table 12-3 provides examples of technologies that can be used to implement, slice, dice, and model functions needed in calculating metrics.

Note

Pentaho, MySQL, and R are open source products. R is a very popular language for modeling that is derived from research at Bell Laboratories. Excel, SAP BusinessObjects, Oracle, SAS, and IBM SPSS are all commercially available software products that have been on the market for many years.

Function	Technology	Example Company or Product	Remarks
Slice	Spreadsheets	Microsoft Excel	Excel's capabilities for operating with multiple tables and row and column filtering are weak compared to those of RDBMS or OLAP repositories.
	Structured Query Language (SQL)	MySQL and Oracle	SQL is most widely adopted but is limited when compared with OLAP slicing functionality. Oracle offers an OLAP extension to its RDBMS repository.
	Multiple Dimension Expression Language (MDX)	Pentaho and SAP BusinessObjects	MDX is less widely known than SQL but is definitely worth the effort for the types of operations commonly required in metrics calculation.
Dice	Spreadsheets	Microsoft Excel	Excel is best for prototyping simple calculations that require little conditional logic. Since it is possible to publish a spreadsheet without formulas, the risk of loss is heightened but can be mitigated with special care.
	SQL	MySQL and Oracle	RDBMSs are not strong on mathematical calculations because their primary focus is on table and row operations as opposed to operations on individual cells.
	MDX	Pentaho and SAP BusinessObjects	With respect to mathematics and modeling, OLAP products have many of the same limitations as RDBMS products.
Model	Modeling software	R, Excel, SAS, and IBM SPSS Modeler	The best products for modeling have that as their focus. The manufacturers of the best modeling software promote development of specialized extensions by experts and provide frameworks so that third-party extensions can be easily installed and used.

Table 12-3 Metrics Calculation Technologies

Integration between modeling engines and software for collection and communication is typically available for the most common scenarios—RDBMSs for storage, and web pages for publishing results. With respect to integration between collection and calculation, the existence of built-in features for accessing data in modeling engines is sufficient for most metrics programs.

Integration between the calculation and communication steps typically takes significant effort. First, the individual metric results need to be packaged as "widgets" suitable for incorporation into an overall presentation framework, which requires that you make several decisions. Will they be tables or graphs in a web page? Will they be static or dynamic? Will they be organized into a dashboard that contains many other widgets? If they are dynamic, does a change in one widget have a ripple effect on other, related widgets? Are there specific navigational requirements within and between widgets? How will textual narrative be incorporated?

Just as glue is needed between raw data and data that is ready for metric calculation, glue is needed between raw metric results and widgets that are ready for the communication step. Design and implementation of the glue takes into account characteristics of both of the steps that the glue is integrating. The advantage of a purpose-built metrics platform is that this glue has been designed and built. This, of course, means that many decisions have been made regarding which types of widgets are supported and which options exist for assembling them.

IMHO

If you elect to perform your own integration with components such as relational or OLAP repositories and modeling engines such as SAS or R, then I need to warn you, it takes time, resources, skill, and buy-in from your company. Attempting to do it on a shoestring or as an extracurricular unofficial project rarely yields success. The good news is that when you build a homegrown custom metrics system you get exactly what you need. The bad news is that it can be very expensive.

Communicate

The last step is to communicate results to a potentially wide range of consumers: the operations team, which needs enough detail to troubleshoot an issue and deploy staff to resolve it; managers, who want enough information to make decisions and assign responsibility; and executives, who need high-level status information and recommendations. Table 12-4 provides some example companies and products that include technology that is useful for communicating metrics results.

Function	Technology	Example Company or Product	Remarks
Publish static reports	Image generators	R, Eclipse BIRT, Microsoft PowerPoint, and Adobe Photoshop	For metrics that are reported relatively infrequently, a website that is updated on a schedule that is synchronized with metric updates provides a very controlled mechanism for presenting "pre-cooked" analysis. Static graphics also afford the greatest protection of anonymity.
	Report generators	SAP Crystal Reports	It is important to provide capabilities for both hardcopy printed reports and dashboard displays with flexible navigation. As a result, report generators are often used in conjunction with web content frameworks or business collaboration platforms.
Publish interactive reports	Visualization products	TIBCO Spotfire, Wolfram Mathematica, and SAS	Interactive publishing products provide either a rich client or a web interface. In many cases they provide both. A key differentiator for these types of products is their support for modeling. Spotfire offers a commercial version of R called S+ as its support for modeling. SAS and Mathematica use their own proprietary modeling engines.
	Business collaboration platforms	Visual Mining and Microsoft SharePoint	Visual Mining offers limited capabilities but can leverage third-party modeling components. SharePoint relies on a faceless Excel server for modeling.
Publish unstructured annotation	Business collaboration platforms	Microsoft SharePoint	Integration of unstructured text along with quantitative metric results is absolutely crucial. The text needs to describe what the results show, any key assumptions, special circumstances, actions recommended or to be taken, and any other "color commentary" that is appropriate.
	Web content frameworks	Drupal and Django	There is almost always enough of the preceding type of information to exceed the limitations of common mechanisms such as tooltips and pop-up windows. Using a web content framework to provide full web pages with navigational links is most effective.

Table 12-4   Metrics Communication Technologies

Note

R, BIRT, Drupal, and Django are open source products. The rest are proprietary commercial products.

When you deploy automation for metrics, the most common ultimate deliverables are documents (such as PDF files), slide decks (such as PPT files), and websites. All of these have technical requirements for creation. Spotfire, for example, supports a feature to automatically generate a Microsoft PowerPoint file from a collection of graphs. You can create SharePoint web pages from all Microsoft Office products. This type of commercially supported integration can save lots of time. It is worth doing the research needed to determine if such features exist in the technologies that you select for automation of your metrics program.

Orchestrate

The most sophisticated metrics programs incorporate two key attributes that drive them to automating orchestration: lots of metrics and a commitment to generate results regularly and repeatedly at scheduled intervals. Some metrics might be scheduled for daily collection, some weekly, and some quarterly. As this number grows, manually implementing orchestration becomes less and less feasible.

Table 12-5 lists orchestration technologies at the simple end of the spectrum.

In Actual Practice

There is a large and vibrant community for defining standards for workflow management that is documented in many articles and whitepapers available on the Internet.[5] To leverage workflow products, you have to package each step to be performed in a manner that meets the integration requirements of the workflow engine that will be managing it. Some very simple engines require that each step be a runnable file, such as an executable shell script in the UNIX operating system. Other, more sophisticated workflow engines require a web services definition that includes detailed specifications of input and output parameters as well as protocols for remotely invoking actions.

Function	Technology	Example Products	Remarks
Deploy	Install packaging	WinZip	When a new metric is ready to be placed into production, a formal packaging mechanism, such as .zip format files, is desirable to ensure repeatable results.
Schedule+Execute	Schedulers	Unix Cron	A scheduler ensures that metric computations occur regularly and repeatedly.
Coordinate	Workflow managers	Taverna and Spotfire Miner	Taverna is an open and free platform with a very active user community. The Spotfire Miner product supports the definition of workflows to collect, prepare, and analytically enrich data prior to visualization via other Spotfire facilities that drive rich clients or web pages.

Table 12-5   Metrics Workflow Technologies

Orchestration can be viewed as the glue that integrates the end-to-end stream of activities that makes up the lifecycle of a metric. With a purpose-built solution, you don't have to build one yourself. Some technologies provide orchestration for a subset of the activities, which can save you time and effort. If you are considering building your own solution, keep in mind that, like stereo systems, if you populate your solution with components from different sources, then integrating those components and ensuring compatibility are your responsibility. Software integration is more difficult than stereo component integration due to the relative lack of standardization in the software world, but the concepts are similar as are the pros and cons.

The next section presents a case study to illustrate the experiences (good and bad) of a company that implemented three common strategies for automating its metrics program.

Case Study

The three most common strategies for automating a metrics program are, in order, using spreadsheets, using in-house talent, and purchasing a purpose-built solution. As it happens, there is one enterprise that has tried all three. The following paragraphs chronicle its journey as the scale and scope of its metrics efforts evolved over a period of approximately four years.

ACME Corporation (not its real name) is a large, public, multinational pharmaceutical company that is highly regulated by a number of country, state, and even local jurisdictions. ACME is audited frequently by both internal and external auditors.

Into Action

The case study for ACME Corporation describes three very distinct stages of metrics program maturity:

- Spreadsheet chaos
- Homegrown solution
- Purpose-built solution

You can try experiencing the same evolution on a micro scale by picking one data source and implementing metrics first in a spreadsheet, and then in a simple database solution using free and open components such as MySQL and the R language. You will be able to see some of the trade-offs between the ease and familiarity of spreadsheets and the accountability and multiuser support of a database-centric solution. You will also gain insight into the amount of effort it takes to create a homegrown solution. This insight might help you to determine whether purchasing a purpose-built solution would be cost effective.

Metrics are not unknown to ACME. Its manufacturing and quality control units have been using Six Sigma (www.isixsigma.com) for years. Its corporate unit has been implementing the Balanced Scorecard Model (www .balancedscorecard.org) for years. However, security metrics are unknown as we begin our journey.

LINGO
Six Sigma is a quantitative analysis discipline whose goal is to reduce defects in the output of business processes. A core strategy used by Six Sigma is to reduce variability in process output, thereby making it more consistent and predictable.

Spreadsheet Chaos

ACME has a very large corporate network with many Microsoft Active Directory servers managing access to domains of laptops, desktops, printers, scanners, special devices, and networks all over the world. An internal audit for Health Insurance Portability and Accountability Act (HIPAA) compliance produced several negative findings regarding the management of user accounts. In the interests of space, this case study focuses on just one finding: user accounts are not reviewed regularly. Two undesirable consequences of this are

- Terminated employees still have access to the corporate network.
- Users accumulate privileges as their job responsibilities change.

In preparation for an upcoming external audit, the identity and access management (IAM) team decided to implement two metrics:

- **Account mean time between reviews (AMTBR)**   This metric is measured in days and is computed using information from a service management system that tracks when each user account is reviewed.

- **Account mean group membership (AMGM)**   This metric is measured in number of groups and is computed using information about accounts and groups from Microsoft Active Directory servers.

ACME has over 90,000 user accounts, so automation is a clear necessity. The following strategy for implementation was adopted by the IAM team:

1. Extract CSV files from the service management system such that each CSV file consists of one row per account ID. Each row consists of the following fields:

   - **AccountID**   The employee Account ID
   - **ManagerID**   The current manager of the employee associated with Account ID
   - **BusinessUnitID**   The current business unit associated with the manager
   - **TSLR**   Time since last review for Account ID

2. Extract CSV files from each Active Directory server such that each CSV file consists of one row per (AccountID, GroupID) pair. Each row consists of the following fields:

   - **AccountID**   The employee Account ID
   - **GroupID**   The Group ID of a group to which the Account ID belongs
   - **ManagerID**   The current manager of the employee associated with Account ID
   - **BusinessUnitID**   The current business unit associated with the manager

3. Load all of the CSV files into two sheets in an Excel spreadsheet—one sheet for the CSV files from the service management system and one sheet for the CSV files from the Active Directory servers.

4. Using Excel pivot tables, compute the following metrics:

   - **AMTBR by Manager**   The mean TSLR for each ManagerID
   - **AMTBR by BU**   The mean TSLR for each BusinessUnitID

5. Computing the AMGM metrics requires two steps in the spreadsheet:

   - Compute a count of groups for each account. In a spreadsheet this can be accomplished via a pivot table, which will yield a resulting table with four columns: AccountID, ManagerID, BusinessUnitID, and GroupCount.

- Compute AMGM metrics:
  - **AMGM by Manager**   The mean of GroupCount for each ManagerID
  - **AMGM by BusinessUnit**   The mean of GroupCount for each ManagerID

6. Generate bar graphs that show relative values for AMTBR and AMGM metrics by business unit and by manager within each BU.

7. Manually compile results into a PowerPoint deck and distribute it for review.

The steps to extract CSV files took ACME three weeks due to the large number of Active Directory servers and the need to create an extraction script. Spreadsheet and PowerPoint deck creation took a week due to the large number of files and the training that was needed to work with Excel pivot tables.

The IAM team's intention was to run this report once per month. This would result in (hopefully) a favorable monthly trend that would, at the very least, show an auditor that the problem is being successfully mitigated. The IAM team's second objective was to identify lagging BUs and managers or, alternatively, to inject some friendly competition and drive improvement.

The iterations after the first month did indeed take less time to create—on the order of two to three fewer days of staff time each iteration. Also, the friendly competition took hold, with requests from (and approval for) BUs to generate their own intra-month results to track and drive progress before monthly status meetings.

So, each BU obtained its own copy of the spreadsheet and began to annotate its Account IDs and Group IDs with additional information that was used to count or not count them in the calculations. None of this new information was fed back to the person with the master spreadsheet. Each BU had results that did not match the results generated for the monthly meetings. Additionally, the owners of the Active Directory servers were receiving multiple, uncoordinated requests for the same data.

To make matters worse, other metrics were being defined and managed by other staff with their own spreadsheets, with equal success in terms of interest. In fact, there was interest in integrating metrics across the spreadsheets.

Homegrown Solution

After about six months of chaotic spreadsheet proliferation and meetings that dedicated more time to how metrics were derived than to what actions they suggested, ACME realized that it needed to make a change. This was a big step because it required more formal coordination among several departments and, horror of horrors, software developers.

In Actual Practice

The following is a summary of some of the lessons learned from ACME's spreadsheet metrics efforts:

- Spreadsheets are fantastic tools to initiate a metrics effort. They are familiar to users and capable of generating quick and useful results.

- Spreadsheets are inherently single-user tools. Coordination across multiple users is difficult at best.

- Proliferation of spreadsheet copies is the enemy of accuracy and, ultimately, trust in a metrics program.

- Spreadsheets primarily automate calculation. They do little to automate design, collection, communication, and orchestration.

- Any tasks that are not automated are subject to human error.

- Any tasks that are not automated are a distraction from more fruitful tasks such as interpreting results, developing remediation strategies, or performing new lines of quantitative analysis.

- Errors undermine trust in metric results.

The fact is that many companies, even big ones, start out with tiny, underfunded metrics programs. Spreadsheets are the natural way to get started.

A metrics program was formally announced and staffed. Regular meetings were held to discuss which metrics would be supported by the new solution. Based on the metrics, required datasets were identified and the appropriate owners of raw data were contacted to generate mutually acceptable data extraction strategies.

A metrics developer, familiar with database, programming, and web technologies, joined the team. The developer identified candidate technologies to use, based on existing enterprise agreements already in place at ACME. The developer then began development, and two months later demonstrated a web prototype to the group. Minor adjustments were made and production use for the initial set of metrics was initiated within the next four weeks.

A monthly metrics run was scheduled and synchronized to have results ready for regularly scheduled monthly management meetings. The first meeting went extremely well.

Much discussion about the metric results ensued, leading to the requirement that the commentary should be captured as annotation to the month's results. Would it be possible to add this to the existing metrics website? Absolutely. The developer added the capability to the website for each manager to enter annotation pages. There is no inherent way to link these pages to a particular metric dashboard element, but this is easily accomplished by manually editing a couple of database tables, which takes the developer only a few minutes each month. It can be automated later.

The next meeting went well, but some discrepancies between the same metric across different BUs were identified. These discrepancies had something to do with counting security incidents. After some discussion, it was discovered that one BU was counting each password reset request as a security event, while other BUs were not counting them at all. It was decided that both more detail in metric specification and convenient access to these specifications were required. The developer stepped up to the task and began to develop an online catalog.

The third meeting also went well, and a new feature was requested. As before, the developer added a quick and dirty solution that requires developer-level knowledge to completely work, but, again, not much time is needed. Catalog development was delayed. This pattern was repeated often in the ensuing months.

Eventually, ACME became concerned about what would happen if the developer were to get sick or quit the company. What started out as a small, informal application development effort had blossomed into a fairly critical program on which multiple BUs rely.

Purpose-Built Product Solution

At this point ACME had a decision to make: stand up a formal application development effort internally or try to find a commercial off-the-shelf (COTS) product. ACME reasoned that, due to the experience with their own internal metrics efforts and (also) due to the shortage of internal application development resources, they would have the expertise to effectively evaluate commercial metrics applications.

ACME assigned a knowledgeable metrics consumer to work with the developer to create and rank a list of functional requirements for the metrics system. These requirements addressed each of the five functional areas described in the previous section: design, collection, calculation, communication, and orchestration. This document was used as a guide to evaluate approximately ten commercial products at a high level and three in detail. ACME conducted trials with two finalists.

The commercial software market for managing metrics programs is new enough that there are significant differences between the products available. ACME selected the cloud service called MetricsCenter. There are four differentiators offered by MetricsCenter that were likely the primary drivers in ACME's decision:

- **MetricsCenter Catalog**   This catalog (briefly described earlier in this chapter) comprises a set of standards and an online repository of specifications regarding metrics.
- **Integrated analytics**   The R language is embedded as an optional capability for enriching results from slicing and dicing with modeling for levels of confidence, forecasting, cluster analysis, and other useful analytics.
- **Anonymization**   Metric results can be stored in a manner that makes it very difficult, if not impossible, to associate them with a given user account.
- **Community and benchmarking support**   MetricsCenter provides the ability to select certain metric definitions and results to be shared anonymously with fellow members of a trusted community.

ACME began to leverage the MetricsCenter Catalog and integrated analytics immediately. While the anonymization and community features were originally intended to support cross-enterprise metrics sharing, ACME is large enough to make use of these features across business units within the same organization.

We've Covered

Some representative technologies that are commonly used to implement the automation workflow of any metrics program, whether it is specifically targeted at security or not

- Listed by function
- Both commercial and open source tools

The strengths and weaknesses of common technologies in light of requirements

- Integrating your own solution versus purchasing a purpose-built solution
- Specific strengths for metrics management

A case study that illustrates a range of programs, automation efforts, and experiences associated with establishing a metrics program in a range of companies

- Spreadsheet phase
- Build-it-yourself phase
- Purpose-built tool phase

Endnotes

1. CIS Consensus Security Metrics, http://benchmarks.cisecurity.org/en-us/?route= downloads.metrics.

2. Cloud Security Alliance (CSA), http://cloudsecurityalliance.org.

3. NIST, *Recommended Security Controls for Federal Information Systems and Organizations*, Special Publication 800-53, Revision 3 (Gaithersburg, Md., August 2009), http://csrc.nist.gov/publications/nistpubs/800-53-Rev3/sp800-53-rev3-final.pdf.

4. MetricsCenter Catalog, www.metricscenter.net/index.php/mc-catalog.html.

5. Tom Baeyens, "The State of Workflow," TheServerSide.com, May 1, 2004, www.theserverside.com/news/1365159/The-State-of-Workflow.

PART VI

Creating the Best Environment for Healthy Metrics

CHAPTER 13

Define a Communications Strategy

We'll Cover

- Techniques for communicating the value of the security program more effectively

- Recommendations on keeping a clear and consistent message

- Tips on how to tailor your message to specific audiences, including advice on how to communicate well and share more using multiple communication formats

I f you've ever had an experience similar to any of the following, you understand how challenging it can be to communicate about security:

- You try to schedule a meeting with a business unit to discuss security initiatives or work you need them to do, but are rebuffed repeatedly.

- After publishing weekly reports to an executive staff group for several months, you try to engage group members to talk about the reports, but discover that they haven't been reading them at all.

- You hold a meeting with a security committee group and find yourself derailed 5 slides into a 60-slide deck, totally off course onto an irrelevant subject and unable to finish all the slide material you wanted to review with the group.

- After presenting security awareness material to a group, you receive no questions but lots of blank stares.

A common communications mistake is to concentrate so much on the content of what we're going to say that we don't pay enough attention to how we're going to say it. This chapter is intended to help you avoid that mistake. Content generation is the focus of much of this book, so this chapter is meant to direct your focus briefly to the context of your message and how it is delivered, with the aim of achieving the most effective communication to obtain all the benefits of information security metrics—enhancing visibility, driving change, and improving the program.

What Do You Want to Communicate?

Security metrics often play a big role in communicating various messages to security stakeholder teams. For example, when a chief information security officer (CISO) meets with stakeholders, the agenda typically includes reviewing program accomplishments, providing an update on overall security posture and status, discussing security issues, and perhaps asking for additional headcount or budget. Security metrics can play a role when discussing each of these areas. They can provide evidence to support assertions that goals and objectives have been achieved; they can be used to support presentations of current risk posture; they can be used to show how widespread or severe a security issue is; and they can show how much more investment may be required to meet risk tolerance expectations of the company or organization.

As the CISO or as a team member supporting the CISO, you'll want to take one of two approaches. If you have a message you want to communicate, you can gather and share metrics that support your message (assuming that after gathering the data, you find that it actually does support your message). Alternatively, if you have been gathering data and are now ready to report, you'll want to package up that information in a coherent message that makes sense and is ready for consumption by your audience. You can start with one or the other; which you start with simply depends on what situation you find yourself in.

Tip

Make metrics a part of the work fabric by incorporating them into office posters, screen savers, hand-outs, and so forth. Don't just dust them off for monthly meetings.

Keep Your Message Consistent

It's important to communicate the same message to all audiences. This helps to eliminate confusion and shows the rest of the company that the information security team is well organized and aligned. Ensuring that each of the individual team members understands what to say to upper management about the team's work can provide a big-picture context that further enhances their understanding of the impact of their work on both the overall organization and the customers of the organization. It also helps to ensure that the team is not promising one thing but delivering another, simply due to miscommunication. Communication "sideways" to peer groups and stakeholders in the information security program is just as important.

Tip

Security communication should be no different from regular company communication. To determine how best to format security communication, follow the company culture. In a culture where professionalism, brand alignment, and "fitting in" is important, make sure to use standard company communication tools and formats. In this case, security communication should look no different from regular company communication. On the other hand, in a more eclectic company environment, you may want to find a way to make the security messages stand apart from other company messages in order to be noticed.

Communicating large, strategic changes and business initiatives from the CISO down to the teams is critical as well, so that the teams can incorporate the knowledge of the changes into their plans. Failure to do this creates gaps in both planning and execution.

IMHO

Especially in situations where a security team is distributed internationally and team members are in a variety of regionally disparate offices, it's important to keep communication open and consistent. Team members who work remotely, work internationally, or are from a recently acquired or merged company can be most effective in their jobs only if they receive the same, consistent communication that everyone at headquarters receives.

Keeping a message consistent throughout an organization may sound simple but in practice may not be that easy. There are reasons for various roles and hierarchies in any organization, and what might be most appropriate to share at some levels may not be appropriate or understood at others.

Into Action

Communicating the following types of information can be useful in ensuring that, to the right degree, everyone who needs to be informed is on the same page:

- Program goals and objectives (and any changes or feedback made to these, either from the top down or from the bottom up)
- Company/organization goals and objectives (and any changes or feedback made to these, either from the top down or from the bottom up)
- Company/organization business strategic initiatives, changes, and announcements

Managers may receive this type of information during management meetings, and they, in turn, can communicate to staff team members during team meetings or in e-mail. Or if managers receive e-mail communications outlining this type of information, they can share it by forwarding the e-mail or by summarizing the key points during a team meeting or in a separate e-mail.

Know Your Audience

How you communicate with an internal team within your organization differs from how you communicate with a team from a newly acquired company. To effectively communicate your key messages to key audiences, it's important to understand the background of your audience and to tailor your message accordingly. Communicating with an audience in China is very different from communicating with an audience in Israel, for example. Communicating goals and setting policies will be different if your audience is more mature folks with decades of experience versus new college grads with little experience.

Acquisitions

If you are responsible for the information security program at a company that performs acquisitions as part of its business strategy, then you may find yourself meeting with teams from newly acquired companies on a regular basis.

Most likely, someone from your team is involved in the planning phase of an acquisition. This may be an opportunity to learn about the company as a future stakeholder of the information security program, as well as one of your first opportunities to communicate security messages. During the initial assessment process, you will be setting the standard for the security culture and requirements post-acquisition.

When communicating security messages to a team from a newly acquired company, it's also important to understand your company's overall approach to acquisitions—does your company prefer to integrate new acquisitions into the same corporate infrastructure and transfer all of the acquired company's information into your company's applications, or is its approach to let acquisitions run very independently of the parent organization? How

In Actual Practice

If your team is not already involved in the planning stage of an acquisition process, contact the business strategy team that is responsible for performing acquisitions and ensure that the information security team is included appropriately. Learning about the business model and security posture of the potential acquisition will be key to modifying the overall information security strategy to accommodate for any newly acquired risks.

your program and messages will be perceived will differ depending on the overall approach and how well the approach is communicated to the newly acquired company and explains the supporting functions of both companies. The messages from the information security program should fit in with and support the overall company approach to the acquisition.

International Audience

Another situation in which you will want to tailor your information security messaging to best communicate with your audience is when you are communicating with international teams. People from different cultures will react to particular communication methods differently, so it will be worth your while to research common business and communication practices prior to meeting with people from other cultures and countries. Practices such as hand gestures, courtesies during mealtimes, seating arrangements (in restaurants and in conference rooms), and style of dress can differ dramatically depending on the region. Even communication styles as subtle as how comfortable a particular group of people may be with saying "no" (or how it's done) may differ in different places. It's important to be informed of and accommodate cultural norms both to show respect for your international

Into Action

Be aware of the following important communication issues before you meet with international colleagues:

- Cultural practices and norms during meals, including seating arrangements, hierarchies, when to do what, which party is responsible for payment, and so forth.

- How to handle conflict, offer opposing opinions, and say "no." (It's important to understand both how to perform these practices and what to look out for when observing others act.)

- The relative importance of spending time with colleagues in and outside the office.

- Respectful and disrespectful sounds, behaviors, and gestures.

This type of information commonly can be found in travel guidebooks. Reference books that provide tips on how to do business in specific countries and cultural contexts are typically located in the Travel or Business section of a bookstore or library.

colleagues and to avoid any inadvertent offensive behavior. Doing your research ahead of time to learn cultural practices and norms will also be helpful for getting your security messages and points across.

Communicate Well

In this section, I discuss ways to communicate well, including the use of visual displays and remote communication technology and the benefits of media training.

Information Security Is Complex: Visual Aids and Remote Technology

Information security is complex and has a variety of distinct components, as discussed in Chapter 1. This multifaceted complexity can make it difficult to convey your message clearly, especially in the context of a 30- or 60-minute meeting with executives.

Your Plan

Creating or using a visual display of a standard industry framework can be effective, and you can use colors to highlight which areas of a program you want to discuss in greater detail, as well as to identify which areas are doing well or poorly. There are many such frameworks to choose from—you may want to review several and then pick one that you believe is a good platform for supporting the messages you want to convey about the information security program. An important key to remember is to be consistent, and stick with one framework once you've chosen it. As you meet with the same audiences repeatedly, having the same framework for reference will ensure that your communications become smoother over time. As your audience becomes familiar with the way in which you structure the program and highlight particular points, they will focus more on what you are saying than on trying to figure out the framework and how it fits into the rest of the program.

Another consideration is to create a visual display of how your team works with and relates to other groups throughout the organization. Typically the information security team sets policies and guidance for other teams to carry out operationally. Especially when setting the stage for discussions regarding driving change and leading other teams to perform security work or optimize security work, this type of visual aid can be helpful for showing the context of how security works as one member of a larger cross-functional team as opposed to independently.

Using visual graphical displays instead of long lists of items as visual indicators can assist in communicating the complexity of the program. You want your audience to spend its time listening to your key messages and understanding what the metrics you're presenting mean rather than trying to figure out what a list of items means.

IMHO

To convey the details of an important meeting accurately to remote offices and international teams (as well as to any local team members who may have been absent that day), I recommend recording a video of the meeting and posting it to a shared web portal or distributing it by e-mail. Communications technologies such as these can ensure that all team members are truly on the same page, hearing and seeing the original message exactly as it was delivered. This can reduce any confusion or message dilution that may occur from the bias or misunderstanding of the person carrying the message from the original speaker to another team member.

Media Training

If you spend part or much of your time as an information security professional communicating with various teams, consider taking a media training course. These courses are often designed to train executives who have to interface directly with the media on how to handle difficult situations, which includes teaching them what to say and what not to say. The folks who provide this type of training have performed or are informed by studies measuring communication techniques and their effectiveness. They cover many different forms of communication, including the impacts that body language, tone, and other non-content-related forms of messaging have on an audience.

Tip

Media Training Worldwide, Speak First, and Toastmasters are three resources you can look into for media training. I also recommend investigating local resources to help you in this area.

This type of a course or training session will teach you important tips such as how many bullet points are most effective on a PowerPoint slide (fewer typically is more effective), how to balance your visual presentation with your speaking points, how to structure the content you want to convey such that it is most likely to be remembered and make a longer-lasting impact, and so forth. Some programs will even videotape you as you present and then play the recording back so that you can watch yourself while the instructor provides real-time feedback on your presentation style and its effectiveness.

Share More

One technique that would help to further enhance the effectiveness of information security programs and the overall industry—a technique that is not typically incorporated today—is simply to share more information, more often. While the hackers and attackers that we are fighting against have effective forums for sharing and using information and techniques, there is still a cultural resistance in the security industry to creating better forums and technologies for effectively sharing security information both internally and with other information security professionals. As technologies become more sophisticated and complex, the "security through obscurity" method of protection becomes less and less useful. As we become more sophisticated in the detection, auditing, prevention, and protection technologies that we employ to protect and guard our businesses, employees, organizations, and customers, we must also incorporate the practice of sharing information.

Why is there a cultural resistance in the information security field to sharing in the first place? There are some valid reasons for this resistance, as described next. However, these reasons need to be evaluated in light of the benefits of incorporating more information sharing into our program practice, discussed a bit later, to determine whether the benefits outweigh the risks.

Why Not Share?

There are some very good reasons not to share information. You need to weigh these factors into your decision to share or not share information. Here I discuss a few reasons not to share.

One reason not to share information is that the information concerns an ongoing investigation, in which case it is not in our best interest to share. Sharing information prematurely in this type of situation may "tip off" the party being investigated or in other ways cloud the proceedings of the investigation.

Another reason not to share information is to avoid liability. If a lack of security controls exists and nothing is being done about it, and then a security-related incident occurs, any information pertaining to this lack may be used as evidence against the company or organization to prove that it did not do due diligence to prevent the incident from occurring.

Tip
If you're unsure about sharing information regarding an ongoing investigation or an associated liability, check with your legal team first and make sure to get their explicit approval before sharing the information.

A third reason for not sharing more information is to shield employees or customers from worrying about (or in some cases, even knowing about) security concerns.

A Few Good Reasons Why Sharing Helps More Than It Hurts

With the exception of the reasons just described, there are many good reasons for sharing information within an organization, particularly with stakeholders, but also with employees and customers when there is a good reason to do so. The benefits of sharing must always be weighed against the risks, which requires that you make the best decision for the program and for the organization based on your specific situation.

Sharing security information within an organization can raise the profile and enhance the credibility of the information security team. One type of information that is safe and very useful to share with program stakeholders, employees, and even customers (depending on how critical security is to the business or organization) is information about current events happening in the information security area. You might assume that you don't need to share this type of information because it is likely to be covered in the news media, but if stakeholders, employees, and customers hear it from you first, and are aware that you're addressing their concerns and letting them know if they need to take any action, the credibility of your team will be enhanced. When leveraged in combination with delivering other key messages, sharing this information can often complement other components of effective communication (such as security metrics) to show that the threats you're concerned about and trying to prevent are actually affecting similar companies and organizations. This way, you're sharing information about threats, but not as directly as talking about specific incidents that may have occurred at your company or organization.

IMHO

Something that security professionals occasionally complain about is not being included in preliminary discussions concerning business strategy, or not being informed when technology developments or changes are being made by the network operations team or IT team. The security team typically wants to be included up front so that it can perform security reviews and evaluations and design security into the project from the beginning. Similarly, employees and customers may resent receiving security communications that do not include reasons for a new security initiative or alert. Often security professionals fail to explain why a security control or prevention technique is being put into place. In some instances, providing some basic information about incidents that have already occurred provides context for the rest of the alert and helps to build trust with employees or customers.

Sharing information also plays a key role in information security awareness and participation. The more informed others within the company are about what information security professionals know, the more likely they will think in similar ways, thereby creating a culture of security in an organization. They are more likely to comply with security policies and guidance, integrating security into everything that they do. Sharing information builds trust and credibility, can align other teams with your goals, and can be carefully integrated into an information security program to enhance communication and further expand the influence and impact of information security metrics.

Sharing security data with other security teams at different organizations and companies is also very beneficial. This allows all teams involved to improve their benchmarking and to collaborate on ways to defend the "good" side. The hackers, cybercriminals, and fraudsters share their data with each other, so why shouldn't we?

The challenge to doing this is making sure that metrics are shared in a standard manner and that information is disclosed responsibly. It requires the right processes for getting permission from legal teams and scrubbing data to ensure that no sensitive, confidential, or proprietary data is shared inappropriately.

Communication Formats

This section describes a few of the primary communication formats the information security team may use to communicate with all stakeholders. Many other possibilities exist. The point here is that part of formulating your communications strategy is to choose the best format in which to deliver your message.

The 1:1

As the name suggests, in a one-on-one (1:1) meeting, only two parties are present. This allows for private, uninterrupted conversation. Many people feel more comfortable sharing information and concerns in this type of setting.

A 1:1 is a great setting to have a two-way conversation with a stakeholder in the information security program. It's an opportunity to ask a lot of questions, get feedback, and convey key messages. Both parties can bring to the table strategies to discuss and each can take away guidance from the other.

IMHO

It's important to keep up regular communications even when you're not asking for something or alerting your audience about a security issue. However, make sure to strike a careful balance when deciding how often to communicate; you don't want to hold a meeting that your audience deems to be pointless. That said, there's always something interesting going on in information security. Take advantage of regular communications to continue to emphasize and shed new light on your key messages.

A 1:1 is also a good way to begin to gather consensus or feedback on a particular topic before meeting with a larger group. Folks may feel more comfortable providing their honest feedback and concerns in a 1:1 setting, and you will have time before the group gets together to address their concerns. Conducting several 1:1 meetings with various stakeholders can help you to build toward a meeting where everyone concurs with a decision.

The Committee

In a committee format, several stakeholders in the information security program meet monthly or quarterly to discuss organization-wide security concerns. Several such committees may exist, each having a different purpose. For example, the focus of a committee may be centered on security-related topics, with multiple stakeholders involved, such as the risk team.

One advantage of communicating in a committee type of format is that everyone is in the same room at the same time, so everyone hears the same message and has an opportunity to voice their concerns in an open forum. For a group with a clear charter and purpose, this can save a lot of time compared to meeting with everyone 1:1 periodically.

Effective committees have charters and mission statements that are intended to keep the discussion focused and purposeful. Initial committee meetings can be used to draft and finalize these purpose statements. It's also useful to define a procedure for decision making, such as a voting process with rules that fit the group (for example, a simple majority may be required, a 2/3 vote may be required, or everyone may have veto power).

In Actual Practice

It's not always necessary to create a formal group to communicate in a committee type of format. Another way to structure a communication meeting that is somewhat like an expanded 1:1 meeting is to hold an "all-hands" meeting. This is useful for making an announcement, calling awareness to an issue, or gathering input from a larger group.

Additional Tips on Communicating Effectively

The following are some additional helpful hints to consider when you are defining your communications strategy:

- Don't "cry wolf." Regular announcements and alerts are key to appropriately informing employees and customers about what's going on in the security world, but characterizing security alerts and announcements with the appropriate level of urgency and priority is critical so that the recipients of the messages understand when to be concerned, when to take action, and what action to take.

- Avoid causing FUD—fear, uncertainty, and doubt. Planning for worst-case scenarios is part of a security professional's job, but these plans shouldn't be communicated to others in the organization simply to establish the security team's importance in the organization. Ensure that the guidance you provide is actionable, accurate, and clear.

- Ensure that your communications are two-way rather than one-way. Asking open-ended questions is a technique that you can use to obtain key information about future business strategy. Remember that the purpose of the information security team is to protect the information assets of an organization; the information security team is not the primary purpose for the organization's existence.

- Don't say "no" to a company priority if it means getting in the way of the critical path of the business; instead, figure out a secure way to do it. The company likely will not wait for you to make up your mind, but instead will forge ahead with its business plans.

- Deliver on your commitments. This will build trust with your key stakeholders and lay the foundation for future communications, requests, and efforts to drive change.

We've Covered

Techniques for communicating the value of the security program more effectively

- Communication from the information security team typically includes an update on accomplishments, status, issues, and requests.

- Take a professional approach to communicating what security does. Incorporate media training techniques into your communications strategy.

Recommendations on keeping a clear and consistent message

- Communicate the same message to all audiences.

- Information security is complex, so choose a framework and stick with it.

Tips on how to tailor your message to specific audiences, including advice on how to communicate well and share more using multiple communication formats

- Learn about your audience and tailor your message accordingly.
- Share information.
- Meet 1:1 or in a committee setting.
- Don't "cry wolf" or communicate FUD.
- Keep guidance clear and actionable.
- Don't say no; figure out a way to enable the company to conduct its business.
- Deliver on your commitments.

CHAPTER 14

Drive an Action Plan: The Importance of Project Management

We'll Cover

- Role of the project manager

- Managing changes to the project plan

- How to incorporate change: reporting and meetings

As discussed in Chapter 4, project management involves defining an end goal and identifying the activities, milestones, and resources necessary to reach that end goal. Finding a good project manager for a security project isn't easy. Because security project management touches so many diverse areas and requires working with so many different types of people in various roles, a particular way of thinking is required to manage all the variables and coordinate and direct the project plan. Putting together a project plan is relatively straightforward compared to driving a project effectively to completion. This chapter examines the role of the project manager in shepherding a security metrics project through to completion and in managing change.

Role of the Project Manager

An effective project manager in the area of information security must have some subject matter knowledge, but the critical knowledge is a good understanding of what needs to be done and how to measure it (metrics do play a role in driving projects to completion). Typically the project manager is not the person who decides what needs to be done and how to measure it. That is the job of the subject matter experts (SMEs). Rather, the project manager is the person who is responsible for drawing out this information from the SMEs through effective communication skills and then formulating a project plan that will accomplish what needs to be done and ensure that it is completed within the designated timeframe.

The best project managers are detail oriented and able to grasp dependencies. This role also needs to be proactive, as most of the groups being coordinated may depend on this role to drive them in the right direction. Project managers keep track of the milestones and timelines in a schedule so that the SMEs don't have to. A person in this role must frequently check in with the SMEs to make sure that the project is on track. Depending on the business strategy and resourcing available, a project manager will more than likely be managing several different projects simultaneously. Therefore, a project manager needs to be able to prioritize tasks and manage time, not only for themselves but for others involved in the projects. He or she must be able to take ownership of an issue and see it through to resolution.

In Actual Practice

Depending on the size of an organization, it may not have the headcount available on the security team to dedicate someone specifically to project management, or it may have one or more designated project managers, but not enough to take on the full project management load. In either situation, other members of the security team must assume some of the project management responsibilities. Because security work requires working with and coordinating efforts among many different teams, it is to a team's advantage to hire and retain personnel who have the skill set required of a project manager, in which case having team members help manage a project shouldn't be a problem.

IMHO

The best project managers do not implement process or documentation requirements just for the sake of generating activity to report. Implementing too many such requirements may be a sign of a poor project manager, and this type of behavior can result in a less-effective security effort. A project manager should take work off the plate of the SME, not put work on it.

Managing Change

Before a project begins, a project manager must facilitate project planning (as discussed in Chapter 4). After a project begins, a project manager should be prepared and willing to make changes to the project plan if necessary and, more importantly, know how to manage change and ensure that changes are properly communicated, planned for, and implemented. This section discusses two tools that a project manager has available to effectively manage change: regular reports and status meetings.

Reporting

One of the key functions of project management is to provide visibility. Project managers keep track of and communicate to everyone involved in the project the general status of the project. That way, individual SMEs don't have to worry about communicating to everyone what they are doing or spend a lot of their time requesting status information from other people. At any given point, there may be a huge amount of information about the current status of a project and how that status is projected to change as the project moves forward. The project manager must determine which of that information needs to be reported in order to effectively drive the project to completion. This often is more of an art than a science. In addition to figuring out which information to ask for and which information to send out, the project manager must also be mindful of how much time and effort will be required from the SMEs to produce this information. If the benefit of reporting the information is outweighed by the time and effort required from SMEs to produce it, then the project manager should not request the information.

Reporting on a security metrics project should be defined as part of the initial project plan, and updates should be given as progress is made. Once a security metric has been baselined and put in place, the report should also include an update on the metric's current status. This is especially important for metrics used to drive change (for example, we decreased the number of vulnerabilities by $X\%$).

In addition to security metrics, reporting should include information used by the reader of the report to make decisions. I believe the most important information to include is on issues and dependencies so your reader can make the decisions needed to manage them. Reporting should always take into consideration the audience.

Issues and Dependencies

Typical weekly project status reports include a summary of the past week's accomplishments, an overview of the schedule, a list of issues, and the next steps in the project plan. The issues list is the most important item on the agenda, because discussion of this list is how changes and delays are introduced into the schedule. Although issues may be anticipated, they usually are not planned for, and addressing them sometimes requires upper management to step in to make a decision.

Report Audience

Before starting to generate reports, a project manager must ensure that the right people are on the list of recipients. There may be different levels of reporting, from the very detailed reporting that is necessary to drive day-to-day work, to the high-level reporting that is necessary to apprise stakeholders of project achievements. When working with one or more different vendor partners, a project manager may generate one version of a report for an internal audience and another version of the report for the external vendor partners. (Similarly, if you work for a vendor partner company, a report generated for your team may be different from one produced for your customers. Internal reports might focus more on issues, whereas external reports might focus more on accomplishments.)

One valuable source a project manager can consult to guide the choice of audience for a report is the original project RASCI roles, discussed in Chapter 4.

Meetings

There are basically two types of meetings related to a security metrics project. Status meetings can highlight accomplishments and provide updates on current and past data for a particular security metric. Issue meetings can be used to discuss issues and make decisions to resolve or eliminate an issue.

Status Meetings

Many project managers host weekly meetings to discuss the status and issues of the projects that they're managing. The advantage of holding weekly status meetings is that SMEs have to dedicate only 30 to 60 minutes of their week to status updates, and they can plan well ahead of time to attend. If a particular SME communicates more effectively verbally than in writing, a status meeting can be particularly useful for the project manager as he or she is putting together regular status reports. The downside of status meetings is that if one or more key decision-makers cannot attend the meeting, the value of the meeting may be diminished or the meeting may even end up being a waste of valuable time.

Tip

An alternative to the status meeting is for the project manager to spend 15 to 30 minutes with each SME to gather their input, and then to send out a report to everyone with a summary of the information.

Issue Meetings

Project meetings may also be held to resolve one or more specific issues, perhaps ones that came to light in a status meeting. Issue meetings are often more targeted, more focused, and more productive. For issue meetings, it is critical that the issue owner and any key decision-makers be present to discuss the issue and put together a list of steps for resolving the issue.

Decision Making

During the implementation of any security project, problems and issues will arise. Different teams will have divergent perspectives on decision making. The project manager is responsible for resolving any such problems and issues to keep the project on track.

This section reviews each of the project planning components of the project management methodology discussed in Chapter 4 and describes the importance of shepherding each component throughout the project implementation.

Brief Objective Statement

The objective statement must be kept in mind at all times throughout the project and continuously be the primary project driver. Throughout the course of a project, many different problems and issues may be discovered, some of which are more easily tackled than the original project objective. To preserve precious resources and budget for the highest priorities, it is critical not to waste time on side problems and issues that don't need to be addressed to accomplish the original objective. Of course, sometimes new issues and problems will come to light or new goals will be discovered that affect the original project objective. In this case, a proposed change to the objective statement requires proper buy-in by all the stakeholders, in the same manner or following a similar process as that which prioritized the original objective in the first place.

Referencing the original objective statement can also be useful when trying to make decisions related to the project or when stakeholders disagree on which particular path to follow to move forward.

Note
Make sure the objective statement is well thought out and well written before the project begins. It's often midway through the project that teams implementing the project wish that the original objective statement had been discussed more thoroughly and written more clearly.

Roles and Responsibilities

This section reviews the roles and responsibilities that were defined and assigned during the planning phase.

Responsible

The person responsible for owning the project is usually the right person to go to when a key decision needs to be made during project implementation.

Approver

The Approver is typically an escalation point person to go to when various stakeholders are unable to come to agreement on the right way to resolve an issue or the right decision to make when the project is in progress.

Supporter

Supporters typically are not involved in the project for its entire duration, but rather are brought in at specific times to accomplish specific tasks. The project manager or project owner must be aware of the order in which steps need to happen and ensure that the Supporters are properly engaged and their time is booked so that delays caused by the unavailability of specialized support teams are minimized.

Consultant

Similar to Supporters, Consultants typically are not involved for the entire duration of the project, but rather are brought in at specific times to accomplish specific tasks. Sometimes Consultants are outsourced vendors, in which case there are extra process pieces to be aware of, including the statement of work (SOW), contract approvals, and finance processes for generating purchase orders and paying invoices. The project manager often can incorporate some of the planning into the SOW up front and then refer to the SOW when measuring the success of the project or of the consultant engagement.

Informed

The teams in the Informed role are specifically not responsible for performing any project-related tasks or making any project-related decisions. If it is appropriate for the Informed teams to provide any consulting or input for the project, then the teams ought to be in the Consulting role instead.

Milestones and Critical Success Factors

Measuring success over the course of the project is critical, and this is where assigning roles and ownership to milestones comes into play. For build work, this may include Go/No Go gates at critical points along the way.

Go/No Go gates can be put in place as part of a project plan. For each gate, specific stakeholders must provide formal sign-off to document their satisfaction with the milestones completed to date. Only after all of the stakeholders identified for any given Go/No Go gate have given their consent can the project continue to move forward. These gates are put in place to ensure that the project achieves the original objective and to ensure stakeholder buy-in before the project has a chance to go too far off course.

Throughout the project, the project manager must hold milestone owners accountable. This ensures that the work that needs to be completed at each stage is completed. Assigning roles to milestones up front helps to prevent confusion regarding who is responsible for meeting each milestone.

In Actual Practice

During project implementation, if multiple teams believe they are responsible for accomplishing the same task, defined roles and responsibilities can help to clear up confusion and resolve disagreements. Role changes may occur as the project progresses, but changes to the original roles and responsibilities should be made only after appropriate deliberation and with the consent from the appropriate stakeholders.

Vendor Partners

The RASCI roles, especially the Support and Consulting roles, can be useful in determining up front what types of specialized expertise are required. However, as the project progresses, it may come to light that additional specialized resources are required. In either case (known ahead of time or not), if the specialized expertise is not available within the company or organization, then coordination with outside vendor partners will be required. This typically involves writing a statement of work (SOW), reviewing it with the legal team, establishing a contractual relationship with the vendor, and working with the finance team to generate a purchase order and with the accounts payable team to pay the vendor. This introduces dependencies on the legal and finance teams, and it will be useful to include timelines in the project plan up front that take into account the time needed to perform the processes required by these teams to work with external parties.

Problem Statement

During the project, the project manager should routinely reference the problem statement, in addition to the goals and objectives, to ensure that the project is not getting derailed or too focused on a side issue. The project manager can also reference the problem statement as a way to check in regularly with the project plan. This way the project manager can track how much progress is being made to solve the original problem, as well as determine whether the project has been completed successfully.

Solution Statement

The question to ask when referencing the original solution statement for a project is, "Has the problem been solved with this solution?" In some cases, the solution proposed in the original solution statement may not actually solve the problem, in which case it may make sense to change the project altogether or initiate a completely separate project using a new solution approach.

Team Priority or Principle Supported

If resource availability changes during project implementation (for example, budget and headcount become scarce), or if a project turns out to need more resources than originally planned for, taking a look at the original statement of the priority supported can help in making the decision to keep, reduce scope for, or cut out a project.

Project Scope

At some point in a project, especially a successful project, it may become obvious that applying a particular solution does solve a particular problem. Related teams may hear about the positive result and want to use the same solution for a target outside of the original scope of the project.

Budget Note

To stay within the original resources and budget allocated for a project, it's important to keep an eye out for "scope creep" to ensure that the resources and budget are applied to the originally scoped targets as planned. The issue that arises when trying to solve related problems is that the effort tends to consume resources, whether those are time resources, headcount resources, external consulting resources, or dollars. This becomes a problem if the original project ends up not having enough resources and budget to achieve the original objective.

Like any other project changes, scope changes should be made consciously and with the buy-in of the appropriate stakeholders. They should also be accompanied by appropriate changes (increase or decrease, depending on the scope change) in resourcing and budget. It's a zero-sum game for set budgets.

Some organizations have a formal change-order process that is designed to prevent scope changes made unilaterally by SMEs (that is, without appropriate communication to and buy-in from all the stakeholders).

Change Details and Impacts

The important thing to keep in mind when making changes to existing technology or processes is to ensure that the teams that own whatever technology or process is being changed are appropriately engaged during the planning and execution phases of the project. The roles of the owners will be Informed or Consulted at the very least, and may potentially be Support or Responsible. These folks need to be kept in the loop during the project via regular reporting or status meetings, so that they can plan and respond appropriately to the changes that will affect them.

Risks of Not Implementing This Project

Risks of not implementing a project can be measured throughout the duration of a project implementation to continuously monitor the success of the project. For a risk that exists prior to a project's launch, measuring the risk before the project implementation, throughout, and after should show a decrease in the risk. For a risk that might arise if the project is not implemented, measuring the risk should show that the risk does not materialize. If it does, that is a signal to change the project or speed it up.

Dependencies or Risks

Dependencies should be identified and planned for during the project planning phase. Any teams related to these dependencies should be notified before the project begins and again before they will be directly affected.

Metrics and Success Measures

Of course, metrics and success measures are critical to tracking the progress and ultimately the completion of a project. This is often where security metrics come into play, especially when the objective or goal of the project is to drive change throughout the company or organization and increase its overall security posture.

Some project managers and owners leave the definition, gathering, and reporting of metrics and success measures as the final step of the project. When the final deadline is approaching, sometimes the folks involved in the project are scrambling to identify and report success measures and metrics that will "prove" that the project was indeed successful. Metrics and success measures that are pulled together hastily at the very end of a project and with little thought tend to be less meaningful than those identified at the beginning of a project, and may be more wishful thinking than actually prove the success of the project.

IMHO

Sometimes a project ends, and then someone asks about project metrics. In cases where metrics were not originally considered, there is usually a scramble to put something together to satisfy the requestor (upper management or other). Defining success criteria and metrics at the start rather than at the end of a project is always best.

I recommend defining metrics and success measures at the beginning of a project. These, like any other project component, can change along the way, but for the purposes of achieving the initial goals and objectives of the project, they require some thought and planning up front. This helps to ensure that there is real, measurable, believable, and compelling data to show that the project has indeed been completed and added value.

Major Deliverables and Deadlines

The major steps component is the bulk of what constitutes a project plan. As mentioned in the "Roles and Responsibilities" section, it is critical to assign each step or task to a specific owner (group or individual) in order to attribute proper accountability and ensure that the steps are getting done, and by the right people. Reporting along the way will keep stakeholders up to date on which steps are being executed, and which are causing issues.

Budget

If a project has a fixed allocation of budget and resources, budget tracking and reporting is critical. Otherwise, your project may run out of money, resources, or time before the project is complete. This risk can be mitigated through the use of a regular process for tracking and reporting. A solid change management process may even be as rigorous as to require a change order signed by the project sponsor for a change to be approved. Absent a change management process, there may not be enough accountability for project finances. Budget forecasting up front can be useful to estimate how much various consulting services, licenses, software, and hardware will cost. Depending on the length of a project, the amount actually spent is typically captured on a monthly basis, at which time an analysis can be performed to determine how much budget remains and which new items (not originally forecast), if any, can be purchased.

Information Security Resources

The teams required to implement the project should be included in status and issue meetings and receive regular reporting about the project. Teams in the Informed role may not be required attendees for project meetings and may not need to be included on every regular status report that is sent out, but should be informed about major project milestones and issues, particularly the ones that affect those teams. Consulting teams play a slightly larger role and need to be included in the meetings that involve discussions for which their subject matter expertise is required.

Reporting Formats

This section reviews recommended reporting formats for status reporting. The key to effective reporting, as previously mentioned, is to provide information that your audience will read and find valuable. Ultimately the project manager is responsible for trying to reduce cycles spent by all the people required to make the project happen, including shortening the time it takes to generate and to read reports.

Status Reporting

A status report is typically sent out on a weekly, biweekly, or monthly basis, depending on the needs of the project. The purpose of status reporting is to inform project stakeholders of the latest updates. A status report should include the following sections, as described next:

- Accomplishments
- Issues, Risks, and Dependencies
- Overall Project Timeline
- Next Steps
- Metrics

IMHO

Here are a few tips regarding status reports:

- Limit reports to no more than one page per project.
- Send reports in text-only format (or have a text-only accompaniment to a PowerPoint slide, Excel spreadsheet, or whatever format you choose). Anything in text format can be easily read on a BlackBerry, iPhone, or other smartphone, which increases ease of reading and therefore value.
- Structure reports about critical functions or projects in such a way that the accuracy of a report provided by an SME can be independently validated. This can be thought of as mini-auditing and will prevent inaccurate status reports, such as one from a programmer who reports that code is 65 percent complete for eight weeks in a row.

Accomplishments

This section of the report informs project stakeholders about recent progress in the project and publishes information about completion of milestones. A common error made by project managers or project owners when compiling this section is to gather the information from the SMEs and simply copy and paste it all together, without context. The result is often a list of tasks that may be incomprehensible to anyone reading the report, other than the person who wrote it. A more useful approach is for the project manager or the SME (or both, through discussion) to provide context about how the recent tasks accomplished fit within the overall scheme of the project. Connecting a set of small tasks to a larger milestone can greatly increase the value of the status report for readers.

Issues, Risks, and Dependencies

This section of the report is critical to ensuring that the project stays on track. Highlighting issues, risks, and dependencies that, if not addressed, will lead to project delays and a waste of precious time and resources puts pressure on the people who are responsible for those issues, risks, and dependencies to take appropriate action and ensure that the project moves forward as planned. This is the most difficult section to prepare. Depending on the cultural and political environment of the organization or company, people may be hesitant to say that they have discovered an issue, risk, or dependency, for fear that a delay in the project will be attributed to them. Therefore, it is important to foster an environment in which full disclosure is not only encouraged but rewarded. Ultimately, addressing the issue, risk, or dependency sooner rather than later will increases the likelihood that the project will be completed on schedule. Full disclosure applies to the project manager as well: if an issue has gotten to the point where fixing it or deciding what to do about it is beyond the scope of the original report audience, the project manager should escalate the issue to upper management.

The key to making this section valuable is to attribute an owner to the issue, risk, or dependency and hold them accountable for addressing it. If no one is responsible for fixing the issue, then it may take longer to solve.

Overall Project Timeline

This section typically contains information about high-level project milestones to provide context for the particular status report. Each deliverable and timeline may also include a color depicting its success (green, yellow, or red). If this is done well, it can aid the effectiveness of the Accomplishments section.

Next Steps

This section outlines the next steps and upcoming milestones for the project and can be a call to action for teams involved in implementing the project. This section is also most valuable when the next steps are linked to a particular team or individual who owns responsibility for completing the task.

Metrics

Project metrics may also be included in regular reporting. In this section, it is critical to provide context for metrics: What's bad and what's good? What change has occurred recently? Are the metrics mature and repeatable or are they still being performed in an ad hoc manner? How stable and reliable are these metrics?

Note

Customer acceptance is critical to any project. At some point, every project must be declared completed, and whatever the project deliverables are must be formally accepted as satisfying the project goals. One way to move forward in the case of projects that have not been done perfectly is to conduct postmortems to document lessons learned from the most recent cases.

We've Covered

Role of the project manager

- The best project managers are detail oriented and able to grasp dependencies.

Managing changes to the project plan

- Project managers must facilitate project planning prior to the start of a project, as well as manage change throughout the duration of the project.

How to incorporate change: reporting and meetings

- Reporting is key to facilitating visibility of a project.
- Reports should include information on issues and dependencies, be written in such a way that they will be read, and take their audience into consideration.
- Regular status meetings can be used to discuss project issues.

PART VII

Secret Sauce: Lessons Learned from an Enterprise Practitioner

CHAPTER 15

Improving Data Quality and Presentation

We'll Cover

● Making useful data out of useless data

● Raw data generators, technology systems, and multiple systems for data

● Refining a process to match what people do and refining data to match a process

One of the problems with existing metrics and metrics programs is that security practitioners like to buy security technology, install it, let it run, and then report raw data (while calling it "security metrics") that are produced by the technology. Sometimes the information that comes out of this type of reporting is useful, but often it isn't.

One example of commonly poorly reported "security metrics" is vulnerability data. In a typical scenario, security engineers purchase a vulnerability scanner, spend a lot of time configuring and deploying it on systems, and then are asked by management what the money has been spent on, what the value is of the product and any associated process, and how it's helping to improve the overall security of the company or organization. The security team responds by producing a weekly report that displays the number of Critical, Severe, and Moderate severity vulnerabilities identified by the scanner and perhaps some information about which IP addresses were affected or what percentage of IP addresses were affected. The question is, what value or meaning does this information communicate to the teams receiving the report?

● Should they believe the systems are secure, or not? If the numbers are high, does that mean the security team is doing poorly or that the organization is not secure?

● Should they believe the systems are more secure than they were the week before? Few report recipients would take the time to dig through their e-mail messages, pull up last week's report, and compare the two reports side by side to determine if the numbers changed. Perhaps the numbers aren't even changing.

The point is, don't take data generated by a security product at face value. Data reports that are produced by security tools often report raw technical data. In some cases, the reports may be presented in a pretty user interface, but either way, raw data straight out of a machine fails to include subject matter expertise and business environment context. As mentioned throughout this book, when people hear the word *metrics,* they tend to think *numbers,* but numbers alone are insufficient to serve as metrics. In order to be valuable, the numbers need context and meaning.

This chapter is intended to teach you about a better method of data reporting that involves process optimization and improving data quality. I'll discuss the effort required to obtain "clean" data, the importance of understanding exactly what the data is telling you, the need to reconcile data inconsistencies across disparate sources (are they using the same identifiers, units of measure, and classification schemes?), and the importance of documenting how raw data is transformed prior to computing metrics.

Data Cleansing

One way to get better data quality is to manually go through and cleanse the data that you've collected already. This typically requires the specialized expertise of someone who is familiar enough with the systems that are generating the data and the data being generated to be able to determine which data should be counted and which shouldn't.

IMHO

In my opinion, data cleansing covers a multitude of objectives:

- Making it accurate
- Making it complete
- Making it consistent
- Making it suitable for loading into a tool to automate regular and repeatable metric calculations
- Transforming certain fields to enable correlation with other data sources
- Making it unambiguous

Making Data Accurate

One basic reason for cleansing data is to ensure that the data is trustworthy. Presenting security metrics data that you believe is accurate is extremely important.

Eliminating False Positives and Negatives

Reporting data that contains false positives and false negatives without either removing them or calling them out is undesirable because it may lead to an inaccurate understanding of a situation. The existence of false positives in data can make a situation look worse than it actually is, particularly when collecting data about something like vulnerabilities. Unfortunately, many vulnerability scanning systems (at both the network layer and the application layer) are based on pattern matching, which results in less than 100 percent accuracy. This results in false positives. To eliminate false positives, someone must manually review the reported vulnerabilities and validate whether or not they are real, which can be a lengthy process. The existence of false negatives in data poses a greater danger because they lull a security team into believing that no vulnerabilities exist when in fact they do.

Vulnerability scanning systems can be tuned up or down to best fit the needs of an organization. Tuning to get the right number of false positives is kind of like fishing in the ocean with a net versus spear fishing. If you go fishing with a large net, you'll probably catch a lot of

LINGO

A **false positive** is a result that indicates a problem exists where none actually exists, such as occurs when a vulnerability scanner incorrectly identifies a vulnerability that does not exist on a system. A **false negative** is a result that indicates no problem exists where one actually exists, such as occurs when a vulnerability scanner incorrectly reports no vulnerability exists on a system that actually has a vulnerability.

fish, but you'll probably also catch a lot of other things that you don't want to catch (such as kelp, starfish, and dolphins). If you go fishing with a spear, you'll probably catch far fewer fish, but you likely won't catch anything else. Similarly, with vulnerability scanning tools, when your system is tuned to find more vulnerabilities (large net), you'll likely have

In Actual Practice

The best way to tune a system depends very much on the specific environment and context for vulnerability scanning. For example, scanning an outsourced service such as Google Postini will be different from scanning the computer infrastructure for a bookstore. Risk tolerance and the amount of resources dedicated to fixing the issue are both factors to take into consideration, especially as elimination of false positives typically requires the subject matter expertise to determine what's a real vulnerability versus what isn't. A small startup company that has few resources available for manually identifying false positives (or for fixing vulnerabilities at all) may have a high risk tolerance and choose to tune its vulnerability scanning system such that it finds fewer overall vulnerabilities. On the opposite end of the spectrum, a government agency that handles very confidential defense intelligence information has a low risk tolerance, allocates more resources for manually identifying false positives and fixing vulnerabilities, and chooses to tune its systems so that they find and report as many vulnerabilities as possible.

more false positives. When your system is tuned to decrease the number of vulnerabilities it finds (spear), you'll likely have more false negatives, meaning you're more likely to miss some vulnerabilities.

Eliminating Repeats

Another means of cleansing data to make it more accurate is to eliminate repeats of the same item in a report and to fix a lack of repeats in a report where they ought to exist. For example, suppose a vulnerability scanning system identifies a specific vulnerability, and that same vulnerability exists on hundreds of different systems within the company. Should that be counted as one vulnerability or hundreds? (Another approach would be to count it based on the number of procedures required to fix it.) This decision also depends on the specific business context and environment in which the reporting is taking place. If an organization has a very standard environment in which each system is built, configured, and deployed in exactly the same way, it might make sense to count it as one vulnerability (especially if the systems are all fixed in the same way too). However, in a more complex environment where many different technologies exist and there is not one standard way for managing the systems, it might make sense to count it as hundreds of vulnerabilities (especially if the systems are fixed individually or in small batches).

There are also ramifications for counting a repeat as one item or hundreds with regards to security metrics reporting. If a vulnerability exists on thousands of servers but is counted and reported once, the severity of the issue may not be properly realized or communicated. Without accounting for repeats accurately, remediation efforts may also be under- or overestimated.

Tip

Eliminating duplicates can be very difficult if the raw data generators have overlapping coverage. The additional resources and time required to perform this type of data cleansing will need to be accounted for in security metrics activities intended to solve this particular problem.

Hierarchies present another type of "repeat" problem. As an example, consider the problem of assigning vulnerability counts to a server that is running several applications that use the same library of functions. In this case, a containment hierarchy of objects exists: the server contains the applications, and the applications all contain the same library. If the library has a vulnerability, how do we assign a vulnerability count to each object in the hierarchy? In particular, what is the vulnerability count for the server, each application, and the library?

This is not truly a repeat issue but rather one of making a determination up front at which level of a hierarchy to report issues. If this type of a process is performed by different people or teams and everyone is not on the same page, there are bound to be manually created discrepancies. The point is not to obsess over *the* right answer. Your job is to help the reader of the security metrics have the best and most accurate understanding of the situation possible. Most importantly, you must make a decision that you can defend, document it, and be able to discuss any biases that might result from it.

Making Data Complete

In some cases, you will find that you have an incomplete dataset. Perhaps the person inputting data failed to put the data into the right system and the information is located elsewhere. Maybe that person went on leave without a backup plan, or this role didn't even exist, or perhaps it simply wasn't filled due to lack of budget or approved headcount. In some cases, you will be able to complete the dataset by going back to the original source or seeking out additional sources for the data, but in other cases, you may not be able to. If you have an incomplete dataset, my recommendation is to first speak with all the potential people who are inputting data to discover if they put the missing data in a different system.

Making Data Consistent

Another way to cleanse data is to walk through the process with several sample data points to ensure that the way in which data is being input and in which it flows through a system are consistent. You may have a problem if teams input data in different ways, or even if different people on the same team are not inputting data consistently. Another issue is when someone processes input data differently from someone else to achieve different results from the same input.

Once you have identified a discrepancy in the way that data is being input or processed, you might want to clarify the correct way to input or analyze data for the teams required to input or process the information. For example, the name of a field may not be clear or may be interpreted differently by various individuals. Renaming the field so it's clearer or publishing a playbook or a cheat sheet for the team to refer to can help to ensure the process is being followed in a more consistent manner.

Making Data Suitable for Loading into Software Tools to Automate Regular and Repeatable Metric Calculations

Another data manipulation exercise you may need to perform is when data needs to be transferred from one system to another. You want to ensure that the data format is compatible with the system that it is being uploaded to. You can check the instruction manual or with your vendor partner team to figure out what the appropriate data format is for uploading to a new system.

Into Action

Unfortunately, the solution to this problem may be to go through every ticket and reassign the tickets with ambiguous categories to more specific categories. This can take a significant amount of time, but the benefits can be seen in more than searching or reporting. It may highlight a defect in the process or, in the case of tickets for security issues that must be assigned to remediation owners, it may produce clearer ownership and, therefore, better security work (what is owned more often gets done than that which is not owned).

Showing Correlation Among Multiple Datasets

Often the best way to show correlation between two sets of data is to graph trend lines or distributions, creating a visual chart. The first step to doing this may to be to get all the sets of data into one reporting system (as just discussed in the previous section). Reporting systems are available that have been developed to perform this functionality. Archer is one I have used in the past.

Making Data Unambiguous

Sometimes data is categorized in a manner that is too general to be useful. When ticketing systems are built and categories are defined in drop-down fields for the purpose of useful reporting, there is typically a catch-all bucket defined. This may be called "Other" or "Company-wide" or something equally nondescript. When people who are responsible for filling out the tickets as part of an overall process perform this step, they may use this field more than it should be used, perhaps out of laziness (they don't want to review a long list of options) or perhaps because the ticket drop-down field is not up to date and simply does not contain the specific information they want to select. In any case, the number of tickets in this particular catch-all bucket can increase quickly, resulting in a large number of tickets that offer useless reporting.

Reporting Data from Multiple Systems

Most security metrics systems involve pulling data from one system into another (and for some, into yet another). This section discusses some typical systems in the flow, including raw data generators, ticketing systems, and asset management systems. Figures 15-1 and

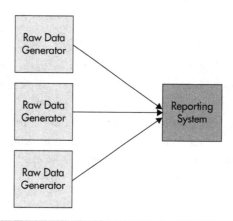

Figure 15-1 Multiple raw data generators feeding into a reporting system

15-2 show a couple of examples of how these systems might be set up to interact with each other.

One common setup for pulling data from multiple systems into a single system is to pull datasets from different systems into a single system used for reporting.

Raw Data Generators

Raw data generators are usually security technologies that are deployed for the purpose of doing some kind of security-related work. Examples include badging systems, camera systems, scanning systems, forensics systems, and auditing systems. Typically data pulled from a raw data generator is pushed into a separate system for reporting the data in a dashboard format (this separate system may be as simple as an analyst transferring data to an Excel spreadsheet and transforming it, or as complex as an enterprise-level dashboard reporting tool).

Ticketing Systems

Often security metrics involve data that is captured in ticketing systems that produce service tickets for the security team to handle an issue, such as incident response data,

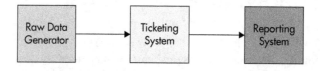

Figure 15-2 A raw data generator feeding into a ticketing system feeding into a reporting system

security architecture consulting data, and policy exception data. This type of data may be input by company employees who are outside of the security team, which usually involves requesting a service from the security team. As shown in Figure 15-2, data typically enters a ticketing system from a raw data generator (such as a security technology system) and exits the ticketing system into a reporting system.

The role of ticketing systems is to generate data for use in security metrics. It is up to the security practitioner to analyze the data that is generated from ticketing systems to determine if the quality is high enough for use in a security metrics project or if data quality needs to be improved first.

Tip

Another thing to consider with regard to keeping consistent meaning between tickets is which raw data generator to pull data from when obtaining data used for metrics. With multiple systems, there may be many choices. My recommendation is to evaluate your options for data quality and consistency prior to choosing which raw data generator to use in your security metrics projects.

Asset Management Systems

An asset management system typically is one of several raw data generators that feed into a reporting system. Correlation of data between the asset management system and any number of raw data generators usually is performed by a reporting system. Asset management systems may contain business-specific data about systems deployed in a corporate or production network environment. They often are useful for information security reporting because they contain a mapping from various systems to their owners. These owners are the teams that build and support the systems, who are also responsible for hardening and patching the systems—implementing the work that the information security team drives with a metrics program.

The security team is rarely the owner and direct manager of an asset management system—usually this is done by an operations or information technology team. The security team typically is a consumer of the asset management data.

Note

As more organizations begin to make broader use of cloud computing, the definition of what constitutes an asset of the organization is in flux. Data? Software? Hardware? The role of security metrics for cloud computing is covered in depth in Chapter 17.

In Actual Practice

The process of developing and maintaining an asset management system in a way that best supports information security reporting often makes more sense to the information security team than to the network operations team or IT team. The objective of the information security team is to be able to tie assets to a specific owner or manager for the sake of driving change, specifically to ensure that the systems are properly hardened and patched. The network operations or IT team is more concerned about getting the asset management systems up and running, and keeping them up and running, to support what the business needs. The team paying for the system likely will be in charge of choosing the vendor and overall design, which means the objective of the information security team may not be met.

In this case, the information security team needs to supply security metrics requirements to the network operations or IT team prior to the design choice. Alternatively, if the system is already up and running, the information security team should request that the network operations or IT team either rework the design to support metrics reporting or pay for it to be reworked.

Consistent Meaning

When multiple systems are linked to each other, involving one or more raw data generators sending data to a reporting dashboard, the meaning of the data sometimes gets lost in the transmission. Therefore, data sometimes requires manipulation in between the raw data generator and the reporting system to ensure that its meaning in the raw data generator is consistent with its meaning in the reporting system.

Poor data quality in the raw data generator will always translate to poor data quality in the reporting system (and poor metrics) unless the data is cleansed or manipulated to better represent the ideal process required to obtain the data in the first place.

Data, Processes, and People

Data is useless if nobody understands or reads it. Anecdotes and data are very different; however, sometimes anecdotes are able to convey a story and, therefore, meaning more effectively than data—especially if the data is not clean or presented effectively. Often the start of a metrics project reveals data discrepancies that originate from discrepancies in the processes. "Dirty" data may result from inconsistent or undocumented processes.

For example, consider a security team that sends weekly reports to upper management on raw data generated from a vulnerability scanning system. Suppose the data has not been checked for data quality and consistency, and it includes repeats and false positives. Someone reading this report may not understand the data in the first place without a written explanation of what he or she should take away from the data. Additionally, without being checked for data quality and consistency, the data may make the issue seem much more or less severe than the actual size of the issue being presented.

Contrast this with a report of vulnerability data that has been checked and the data quality improved by a responsible security practitioner. Perhaps in presenting this data, the security practitioner also includes a written narrative explaining the trend toward security vulnerabilities decreasing due to remediation efforts. An anecdote or story about a recent team that performed remediation efforts can showcase the good work being done in this area. This type of approach is much more effective in terms

> **LINGO**
> **Dirty data** is a very general term that may refer to (among other things) data that has unacknowledged correlation or undocumented origins or is biased, nonindependent, internally inconsistent, inaccurate, incomplete, unsuitable for integration with data from other important sources, or unsuitable for consumption by tools that automate computation and visualization.

of getting people to understand the situation and what needs to be done than the former.

Although the data collection and data manipulation performed by data collectors typically reflect accurately the processes that exist at the time the data collectors are implemented, over time processes change organically, and the data collectors do not necessarily change to reflect the new and up-to-date processes. This leads to dirty data.

When a data collector begins its work, the process for collecting data may be well or poorly defined. It may be mature or immature. When an issue arises, sometimes the issue is not with the data collection mechanism matching the process, but with the process matching people. In other words, the process needs to make sense to the people who are responsible for implementing it.

Tip
Before you replace an old data collector with a new one, run them side by side for at least three reporting cycles, so you can observe differences (if they exist) between the two data collectors. If you observe a difference and understand why, then you can replace the old collector. If you observe a difference and cannot account for it, that is a red flag; you should perform further analysis to find out why there is a difference between the systems.

The best processes are streamlined to be as simple as they can be, using the fewest steps possible to achieve the process's objective. Sometimes when processes come into being organically rather than purposefully, they end up having redundant steps or steps that don't add much value. Somebody at one point may have implemented a step that they believed would be useful, but it turns out that nothing is ever done with the data beyond that point. When there is a lack of fully automated reporting, fields need to be clear so that people entering information into those fields understand exactly what is being requested—this can help prevent "garbage" data from being input in the first place. Comments and context can be useful both in helping people to understand data that is presented in reports (when presenting metrics) and during the data collection phase, such as filling in fields in tickets as part of a process (when collecting data for metrics).

Working with Stakeholders to Perform Data Cleansing

Broken processes that lead to dirty data usually are not fully owned by members of the security team. To rework these processes to get better data, the security team must meet with stakeholders to discuss, clarify, document, and fix the processes. Most processes require more than one stakeholder team to perform various steps, and these teams might see the processes in different ways. It's important to meet with and interview each of the stakeholders to identify and document the process and the discrepancies. It's not easy to engage a stakeholder to bring up the topic of a broken process, especially when the process owner is under the impression that nothing is wrong. However, upon completion of data cleansing and process optimization, the process owner will be more confident in the consistency and effectiveness of the newly fixed process.

It's also important to meet with stakeholders as a group to review discrepancies. Healthy debates that ensue will result in determining the best way to perform the process.

Budget Note

The challenges involved in fixing dirty data and broken processes may result in delays (and cost of resource time) that were not originally anticipated or incorporated into a security metrics project plan. However, it is wrong to view the work required to clean up the data and processes as any sort of failure of the metrics project. In fact, identifying and fixing broken processes is a huge side benefit of the project. Working with stakeholders to remediate issues involving security-related processes results in better security overall.

When taking on this type of documentation and discussion facilitation work, it can be very useful to have a security team member in the room who has strong communication, documentation, and project management skills.

Fix the Process, and Then Automate

Security organizations that are anxious to get started with a new metrics program or technology deployment sometimes make the mistake of automating too quickly. Automation has many attractions. It may reduce the amount of hands-on involvement required from a member of the information security team, making more time available to focus on other, higher-priority work. Reducing the amount of human involvement might also reduce errors. Additional advantages of automating a manual process may include having all the data in a single, organized repository with consistent formatting and the capability to search and manage the data quickly. These attractions sometimes lead a security team to rush to automate a broken process before fixing it. The belief is that an automated process will save time and create efficiencies, and that there will always be a future opportunity to fix a broken process once it has been automated. However, fixing the process first and then automating achieves improved data quality much sooner.

Consider the scenario in which the information security team manages a process that is performed manually and is broken. A manual process typically involves hands-on involvement from a member of the information security team and may require data gathering and input into a system for managing, tracking, and reporting. Manual processes often involve collecting data from many different sources and storing it in a variety of formats. A process may be considered broken if it does not have roles and responsibilities clearly defined, is not executed consistently, or is either missing steps or includes steps that are not correctly executed.

Here's what usually happens when a security team decides to automate a process before it has been fixed:

1. Development work occurs to transform the manual process into an automated process. Now the team has the advantages of an automated process over a manual process, but the process is still broken.

2. The broken process continues to have negative impacts even after automation. Once these negative impacts have reached a certain threshold (which may come to light as a result of a risk assessment or an audit finding), fixing the process is given priority.

3. The process is reviewed to identify issues, and these issues are discussed. Roles and responsibilities and the steps required in the process are discussed with process stakeholders who are responsible for executing the steps in the process. Everything is documented to ensure that as team members change in the organization, the process

will still be performed consistently and correctly. (Documentation also ensures consistent and correct process execution in the case of outsourcing or offshoring the process work.)

4. The process is fixed.

5. After the process is fixed, additional development work takes place to translate the process fixes into the existing automated (broken) process.

The second, recommended approach achieves the same result in fewer steps. Fixing a process before automating has three key advantages: less work, better security, and improved data quality. Security organizations usually have more work than resources to do it. The recommended approach saves time, resources, and money because development work is done only once, instead of twice.

Under the first approach, as time passes while the process is still broken, steps may not be executed consistently or correctly, roles and responsibilities may not be clear, and the security work intended to occur may not be happening at the level desired by the

Your Plan

There is a better way to fix and automate a broken manual process, however. Starting with the same scenario from the previous example, the following steps are involved in the recommended approach:

1. The broken process negatively impacts the information security program. After these negative impacts have reached a certain threshold (which, again, may come to light as a result of a risk assessment or an audit finding), fixing the process is given priority.

2. The process is reviewed to identify issues, and these issues are discussed. Roles and responsibilities and the steps required in the process are discussed with process stakeholders who are responsible for executing the steps in the process. Everything is documented to ensure that as team members change in the organization, the process will still be performed consistently and correctly.

3. The process is fixed. The team continues to perform the process manually to ensure that no additional changes must be made.

4. After the process is fixed, documented, approved by key stakeholders, and manually operational, the development work to automate the process is performed.

information security team. Under the second approach, the process is improved more quickly. Even though the process is manually performed for a longer period of time, better security is achieved during that time.

Tip
When automating a system, run the new system side by side with the old one for a few cycles before turning the old one off completely.

Don't Wait for Perfect Data Before Reporting

Many information security teams try to get the most accurate data possible before they begin to report to anyone, even internally within the information security team. The benefits of this approach are clear—stakeholders will respond better to more accurate data, and having the most accurate data paints the clearest picture of the security situation. However, one potential major pitfall of this approach is that a team may become too focused on obtaining *perfect* data before reporting, in which case the work effort put toward getting better data may be never-ending, as data sources are constantly changing and updated, and the importance of timely reporting is overlooked. If a team waits for perfect data before it begins to report, it might never begin to report. Perfect data is almost never achieved, so it's better to report the data when the team deems that it is good enough to get its message across.

Tip
It has been said by statisticians that the first rule of statistics is that all data has bias; the question is whether you can correct for it.

The recommended approach with regard to data quality is to begin reporting right away (even if the data quality is poor at first) with the security team members who are responsible for owning the process and obtaining the data. This will often lead to the security team members responsible for cleansing the data to move more quickly in their attempts to improve the data quality, because they want to ensure that the data quality is good before the reporting reaches a larger audience.

IMHO
Generally speaking, I recommend that the security metrics lead share the initial reporting (with the lower quality data intact) immediately with the team that is responsible for executing the process.

Once cleanup is underway, these reports can be shared with the CISO to help escalate the data cleansing process. Another approach is to discuss with the responsible team a specific date for presenting the data reports to the CISO so that he or she is aware of the timeline and will still have the opportunity to obtain better and more accurate data prior to it being presented to management.

This model of showing the reporting (or scheduling a time to show the reporting) to a team's management can be extended beyond the information security team if the team depends on another group for obtaining quality data. For example, if the development managers are not consistently closing out the tickets when vulnerabilities are remediated, those vulnerabilities will still be counted as being present on the website and the reports will display a poorer security posture than actually exists. The security metrics project lead will likely get a positive response to take action from the development managers if the initial inaccurate data is displayed to his or her group or management.

In summary, reporting often improves data quality. This can be a continuous cycle that constantly drives better data, because the appropriate audiences are being exposed to the latest information.

We've Covered

Making useful data out of useless data

- Unfortunately, security technology reporting is usually not useful "out of the box." Better data quality requires cleansing the data produced by that technology, which includes removing false positives and repeats.

Raw data generators, technology systems, and multiple systems for data

- Many security metrics systems involve pulling data from one system to another. These types of systems may be raw data generators, ticketing systems, asset management systems, or reporting dashboard systems.

Refining a process to match what people do and refining data to match a process

- The best data comes from clean and simple processes that are clearly defined and well understood by the people implementing the processes.

CHAPTER 16

Resourcing and Security Metrics Projects

We'll Cover

- Obtaining buy-in to dedicate resources to a security metrics project or program

- Options for resourcing security metrics projects

- Recommended approaches that leverage politics and competition to support metrics programs

One of the most important benefits of any security metrics program is that it drives improvement and change in an organization. Before a security metrics program is in place, security is often viewed as a supporting cost center rather than a business driver. Getting people to do security work is not always easy. An organization that perceives the value of the security program to be low tends to prioritize security projects accordingly. When resources are required for a security project, the project often ends up at the bottom of the list of projects that a business unit must complete or work on during a quarter, half year, or year.

Can you relate to an experience where security work is given low priority and doesn't get accomplished quarter after quarter? This chapter describes how to use security metrics and reporting to solve that problem. Among other things, security metrics can demonstrate that the work of the security program is aligned with key performance indicators of the business as well as compliance mandates.

Note

Getting security professionals to focus some of their limited time and energy on metrics work is not always easy, either. This chapter is just as much about getting security personnel to spend time on metrics as it is about getting everyone else to do security work.

IMHO

Why is it often a challenge to get organizations to do security work? I believe it's because security work is usually different from the core competencies of the business units that need to do the work, and people are typically more comfortable with and prefer to do work that they're used to doing. For example, getting teams who are responsible for systems administration to deploy patches according to a service level agreement (SLA) set by the information security team can be tough. The key responsibility of these teams may be to ensure availability or to deploy new systems, and routine security work may not be part of what they initially choose to spend their time on. Many prioritization exercises may occur before installing patches makes it to the top of the list, and then only because vulnerabilities are being actively exploited.

The solution to this particular problem is clarity and guidance. Well-defined security metrics can help to clarify the work that needs to be done. If what needs to be done is very clear, and security practitioners are there to help guide the work (and, as discussed in Chapter 4, there are clear project plans, roles and responsibilities, and timelines), then prioritization will be less of an issue. On the other hand, poorly defined security metrics will only contribute to this problem.

Resourcing Options

Usually, a security metrics program requires two types of resources to be successful: expert resources from the security team, and resources from the business units that need to do the security work. For example, resources from the security team might be needed to provide requirements, guidance, and oversight for a patching project, and system administrator resources might be needed from an IT or network operations group to perform the patching work. Security is a team sport—the security work of any organization can't be performed by the security team alone, but requires support and assistance throughout the organization.

Either of these two types of resources may be outsourced. In Chapter 5, I describe the characteristics that make a particular type of work a good candidate for either offshoring

In Actual Practice

Just as the work needs to be shared, the rewards should be shared as well. Security metrics can show very clearly the progress that an organization makes in improving its security posture, and a big part of getting resources to do the work time after time is to share the rewards of the effort and make sure everyone in the organization knows about it.

The types of rewards given differ according to company budget and culture. Some organizations reward employees with cash bonuses or even paid vacations; others may use symbols of appreciation such as badges, certificates, toys, apparel, office supplies, meals, or plaques. A nice team meal or a set of T-shirts printed with the name of the successful initiative can go a long way toward showing people that their hard work is appreciated and is a good example of cultivating relationships between teams and team members.

or outsourcing. Routine, task-oriented work with mature processes can either be offshored or outsourced. Work needed to figure something out or to formalize a process (which is the case in many security metrics projects) can be outsourced.

Security Team Resourcing

Even within a security team, it can be hard to focus efforts on metrics projects. Security team members who are used to doing more traditional security work or are focused on more responsive, tactical activities may initially put up some resistance to doing the more strategic work of security metrics. Every security manager is resource constrained and would like to do more than they have time and resources to do. If they're not used to focusing some of their time on metrics and reporting, they may not immediately see the value of doing security metrics.

Security team members can be motivated to do security metrics work if they understand the value of having the data. For example, security metrics work that drives improvement is usually an easy sell to a security professional who inherently wants the organization to be more secure. Another example is if the security metrics work shows that the security team member is performing his or her job well. Different security metrics projects require varying skills from members of the security team.

In Actual Practice

Most security organizations I know spend the majority of their time responding to requests from the business. One of the big themes of this book is the importance of balancing reactive and strategic activities in a security program. Many organizations would benefit from moving toward a 50/50 split between responding to requests and proactively seeking out a greater understanding of the business issues and priorities.

Unfortunately, it's not always easy to stop responding to requests from the business or from everyday run-the-business type of work. One methodology may to automate or improve efficiencies in the process. Creating a web form or a ticket used to specify prerequisites and asking the right questions to get initial data on a request can cut down on unnecessary overhead time and save time cycles for team members. Another way to cut back on such requests is to define a standard of criteria that must be passed in order for a security review to occur. Raise the standards bar and fewer projects will make it through. A third methodology is to build a self-serve type of portal so more routine requests can be fulfilled by the requestor doing the research him- or herself, without needing to engage the security team as much.

Outsourcing to Obtain Metrics

Security metrics work can also be outsourced to third-party professional service providers. Sometimes, an easy way to incorporate metrics into an ongoing security program is to require the consultants to provide metrics reports.

Requiring weekly or project-long reporting as part of the contract deliverables requires that you define success criteria (and related metrics) up front. (Defining success criteria as part of your project management methodology was discussed in Chapter 4.) Having clear goals, objectives, success criteria, and metrics definitions is even more critical when work is being outsourced than when it's being done by the in-house security team.

LINGO
Typically consultants are brought in to perform a specific set of activities, and a **statement of work** outlines the deliverables to be completed and the deadlines for each deliverable.

If your security team works with other teams, such as IT or network operations, you may also want to become involved in the contract-writing stage when those teams are preparing to outsource work. For example, if system administration work is going to be outsourced, make sure that the contract requires the contractor to perform security "care and feeding" type of work (such as patches) in addition to maintaining and supporting the general infrastructure. Make sure to include reporting and metrics requirements in these contracts too.

Leveraging Politics and Competition

If a company or organization has many parallel lines of business, an indirect approach to getting people to do security work involves reporting security progress for each of the lines of business in comparison to each other. The most effective use of this technique includes communicating the report on a regular basis not only to the business lines involved but also to management overseeing all of the business lines. The leaders who make budget decisions about which teams get resources and which activities those resources work on are the people who need to see this reporting.

Tip
Different lines of business may have different numbers of systems, employees, and so forth. To fairly compare metrics between business units, some data may have to be normalized before it's reported. Chapter 15 covers data quality.

This type of reporting gives each business unit an opportunity to demonstrate its commitment to security and rewards business units who perform security work well. This motivates team members to help each other complete security work.

Be creative with how you present this information. Weekly reports by e-mail, charts on a bulletin board at company headquarters, and updates made on a company intranet site are all ways to showcase the progress that business units are making against each other.

Another way to encourage business units to do security work is to offer rewards or prizes for the "winner," or top five "winners." Perhaps the first business unit to reach a certain goal gets a trip to Hawaii or Las Vegas (or, depending on what the company budget will allow for, the local steakhouse). Maybe everyone gets a trophy or an iPod, or a donation made in their name to a charity of their choice. Figure out what is coveted (and affordable) and will fit your company's or organization's culture.

Note

The techniques previously mentioned should not be considered primary ways to get security work done. Rather, they should be used as motivational tools. Effective security metrics need to demonstrate tangible results and positive impact to a business unit.

In Actual Practice

Make sure the reporting you do is appropriately conspicuous. You want to make sure that the business units who are being reported on, especially those who aren't doing well, are aware that the rest of the business units and their leadership can see their metrics. This can be accomplished by posting results on a company bulletin board, whiteboard, or somewhere else visible in the office. In a more distributed environment, you can send the results via e-mail or display them on a prominent page on the company intranet.

Keep in mind that there is a fine line between highlighting the security postures of different business units and embarrassing those who perform poorly. An example of crossing the line would be to have each of the business unit leaders wear a T-shirt at the end of a quarter that displays the business unit's security progress. Additionally, depending on the company culture, this might be pretty tough to get people to buy into (and has the potential to damage your relationship with them).

Budget Note

Providing reporting is one of many steps that must be taken to convince a business unit to do security work. Additionally, the security team needs to engage with the business unit to understand why they are or are not performing the security work that they need to do. The security team may even be able to partner with business units that lack the resources to do all the security work and jointly present a resource justification case to leadership and decision-makers. Most business leaders don't have specific expertise in the security area and are willing to spend about the same amount that other business units are spending. They don't want their security spending to be too high (they may believe it is a waste of valuable resources), but they also don't want their security spending to be too low (they may be worried that they are not adequately protected). Comparison reporting at a resources and budget level can also support the effort to get an organization the resources it needs.

Remember that business units of different sizes and with different missions will need to be compared, and for this reason the metrics used must be normalized accordingly. One way to normalize is to present security spending as a percentage, as follows:

% of an organization's budget and resources spent on security (this can be per quarter, per year, or for a specific project)

Metrics as Justification for More Resources

One type of security metrics that has not been thoroughly discussed yet in this book is the type used to justify more resources. These may be as simple as metrics that track a few activities that teams are doing, especially customer-facing consulting teams or incident response teams. These teams cannot plan accurately how much or what types of work will come their way because they are in a consultative or response type of role.

Data and metrics reporting that shows that the resources available to these teams are not adequate to support the business need is one way to justify budget for more resources. Some examples of the metrics that provide visibility in this area include metrics that track the number of incidents or consultative requests that are received, the number of incidents or consultative requests that are actively being worked on, and the number of incidents or consultative requests that have been closed out or resolved.

Note

These metrics need to be tracked on a regular frequency to generate trend metrics for reporting. They can be tracked daily, weekly, monthly, quarterly, or annually.

This reporting can be as granular as makes sense for the organization. Some teams may choose to track by the hour what type of work teams are spending their time on (per project, or by type of work, such as project work or maintenance/run-the-business work). Security teams that are interested in understanding the performance of individual resources on a response or consulting team can track these same metrics per individual and trend that data over time.

Incident Response Metrics

Here is a set of metrics that captures performance of incident response work and can be used to justify a request for more security resources:

- Number of daily, weekly, monthly, or quarterly new incidents
- Number of incidents worked on (daily, weekly, monthly, or quarterly)
- Number of incidents closed or resolved (daily, weekly, monthly, or quarterly)
- Incident types
- Incident severity
- Incident priority
- Percentage of time spent on each type of incident per security response resource
- Number of incidents by business unit

For incident response work, the question to ask when presenting these numbers to key stakeholders is, "Is it acceptable to you that particular work is not being performed because there are not enough resources to respond to the number of incoming security incident alerts?" The number of security incidents that are not being responded to can be shown as the following simple calculation:

[(# new incidents per week) – (# incidents closed per week)]

This type of data can be nicely presented as a trend line over time (one data point per week for a month or for a series of months). Questions such as the following may be interesting to observe and analyze in this type of a graph:

- When and why does this line move up or down?

- If the line is trending down, does that mean the types of incidents are similar and the team knows how to respond appropriately?
- If the line is trending up, does that mean the incidents are higher in severity and take more time to respond to?

Graphs that show trends of two different measurements overlaid against each other can be used to show the correlation between two types of events. For example, if you fix more bugs, you may see fewer vulnerabilities over time. It's important when showing these types of graphs to also explain what the different lines are and what they mean.

Incident response metrics can be used to ensure that there are enough resources to handle the incidents that occur. In other words, incident response metrics can be used to justify a request for additional incident response resources for the security team. Metrics can be used to show that security team members whose core responsibility is not incident response are being pulled in to do some of the work in "all hands on deck" situations because the existing incident response team is not sufficiently staffed to handle them.

Security Consulting Metrics

The following is a set of metrics that captures performance of security consulting work and can be used to justify a request for more security resources:

- Number of daily, weekly, monthly, or quarterly new consults
- Number of consults worked on (daily, weekly, monthly, or quarterly)

LINGO
A **honeypot** is a system, a network, or an application that is set up specifically with the intent to attract attackers.

In Actual Practice

One clever way to measure the effectiveness of security controls is to set up a honeypot outside a zone with security controls and compare it to a similar system located in a zone that does have security controls. If your metrics demonstrate that the number of attacks on the honeypot is substantially higher than the number of attacks on the system within the secured zone, that indicates your security controls are effective at eliminating attacks on the system. You may be able to use these metrics to justify a request for additional security controls to reduce the number of attacks that do get into the secure zone.

- Number of consults closed or resolved (daily, weekly, monthly, or quarterly)
- Number of consults completed on time (as required by business unit customer)
- Consults types
- Consults severity
- Consults priority
- Percentage of time spent on each type of consult per security response resource
- Number of consults by business unit

For security consulting work, the question to ask when presenting these numbers to stakeholders is, "Is it acceptable to you that particular work is not being performed because there are not enough resources to respond to the number of incoming requests for security reviews?" The number of security reviews requested that are not being responded to within the terms of the SLA can be shown as the following simple percentage calculation:

[(# security reviews requested that are not closed within the specified SLA) /
(# security reviews requested that are closed within the specified SLA)]

This metric can also be nicely presented as a trend line over time (perhaps weekly over a month or a series or months, as with the incident metrics) with a meaningful story behind it. In the case of security reviews of new features and products, the following questions may be useful to observe and analyze in this type of a graph:

- If the number is increasing, is it because the business is moving and changing at a rapid pace and the security team is not adequately staffed to keep up?
- If the number is decreasing, is it due to architectural standards being put in place that are followed by teams throughout the organization, decreasing the amount of time that the security team has to spend reviewing any particular project or request?

Report Quickly

One key to getting off on the right foot when it comes to selling metrics work, either internally to a security team or externally to business units whose support is necessary to make a metrics program work, is to achieve some short-term quick wins and make sure the appropriate stakeholders know about them. Quick wins and some immediate results, even if they're not perfect, can go a long way toward convincing teams that the time their resources spend on this security work is worth it.

We've Covered

Obtaining buy-in to dedicate resources to a security metrics project or program

- Getting people to do security work is not always easy. Clear guidance, ongoing security involvement, and defined metrics can help alleviate this problem.

Options for resourcing security metrics projects

- Be creative when it comes to resourcing security metrics work. Security metrics work can be done by security teams, by nonsecurity business units, and by outsourced consultant teams.

Recommended approaches that leverage politics and competition to support metrics programs

- Security work often needs to be shared between different teams, and the reward for completing and doing a good job should be shared as well.

- Leverage comparison reporting to take advantage of natural politics and competition to drive security work.

- Metrics can be used to justify more resources either to assist the security team or directly for the team.

PART VIII

Looking Forward

CHAPTER 17

Security Metrics for Cloud Computing

We'll Cover

● What is cloud computing?

● Common business drivers that motivate organizations to move to the cloud

● The "new normal" for IT service delivery

● Common security metrics in the context of cloud computing

● Major cloud industry groups, especially the Cloud Security Alliance, and their efforts to describe cloud controls and related metrics

In the second decade of the 21st century, the world of computing is experiencing a revolution of sorts called cloud computing. After about a year of media hype and subsequent "cloud fatigue," IT professionals and other businesspeople are now contemplating what cloud computing means at a technical, business, and even societal level. This chapter focuses on cloud security metrics, drawing on knowledge you've already gained from previous chapters. In addition, this chapter examines how security metrics relate to cloud computing and discusses what resources are available today. Let's begin by quickly defining cloud computing and comparing what is new and not so new about the technology.

Cloud Computing Defined

In the United States, the National Institute of Standards and Technology (NIST, an agency of the U.S. Department of Commerce) provides the following broadly accepted definition of cloud computing:

> Cloud computing is a model for enabling ubiquitous, convenient, on-demand network access to a shared pool of configurable computing resources (e.g., networks, servers, storage, applications, and services) that can be rapidly provisioned and released with minimal management effort or service provider interaction. This cloud model promotes availability and is composed of five essential characteristics, three service models, and four deployment models.[1]

The following sections identify the characteristics, service models, and deployment models referenced in the preceding NIST definition.

Characteristics

The NIST definition specifies that cloud computing has the following five essential characteristics:[1]

- **On-demand self-service**   A consumer can unilaterally provision computing capabilities, such as server time and network storage, as needed automatically without requiring human interaction with each service's provider.

- **Broad network access**   Capabilities are available over the network and accessed through standard mechanisms that promote use by heterogeneous thin or thick client platforms (e.g., mobile phones, laptops, and PDAs).

- **Resource pooling**   The provider's computing resources are pooled to serve multiple consumers using a multi-tenant model, with different physical and virtual resources dynamically assigned and reassigned according to consumer demand. There is a sense of location independence in that the customer generally has no control or knowledge over the exact location of the provided resources but may be able to specify location at a higher level of abstraction (e.g., country, state, or datacenter). Examples of resources include storage, processing, memory, network bandwidth, and virtual machines.

- **Rapid elasticity**   Capabilities can be rapidly and elastically provisioned, in some cases automatically, to quickly scale out and rapidly released to quickly scale in. To the consumer, the capabilities available for provisioning often appear to be unlimited and can be purchased in any quantity at any time.

- **Measured service**   Cloud systems automatically control and optimize resource use by leveraging a metering capability at some level of abstraction appropriate to the type of service (e.g., storage, processing, bandwidth, and active user accounts). Resource usage can be monitored, controlled, and reported providing transparency for both the provider and consumer of the utilized service.

Service Models

NIST defines the three service models used in cloud computing as follows:[1]

- **Cloud Software as a Service (SaaS)**   The capability provided to the consumer is to use the provider's applications running on a cloud infrastructure. The applications are accessible from various client devices through a thin client interface such as a web browser (e.g., web-based email). The consumer does not manage or control the underlying cloud infrastructure including network, servers, operating systems, storage, or even individual application capabilities, with the possible exception of limited user-specific application configuration settings.

- **Cloud Platform as a Service (PaaS)** The capability provided to the consumer is to deploy onto the cloud infrastructure consumer-created or acquired applications created using programming languages and tools supported by the provider. The consumer does not manage or control the underlying cloud infrastructure including network, servers, operating systems, or storage, but has control over the deployed applications and possibly application hosting environment configurations.

- **Cloud Infrastructure as a Service (IaaS)** The capability provided to the consumer is to provision processing, storage, networks, and other fundamental computing resources where the consumer is able to deploy and run arbitrary software, which can include operating systems and applications. The consumer does not manage or control the underlying cloud infrastructure but has control over operating systems, storage, deployed applications, and possibly limited control of select networking components (e.g., host firewalls).

> **LINGO**
> **SPI** is an acronym for the three general delivery models for cloud computing: SaaS, PaaS, and IaaS.

Deployment Models

NIST defines the four deployment models used in cloud computing as follows:[1]

- **Private cloud** The cloud infrastructure is operated solely for an organization. It may be managed by the organization or a third party and may exist on premise[s] or off premise[s].

- **Community cloud** The cloud infrastructure is shared by several organizations and supports a specific community that has shared concerns (e.g., mission, security requirements, policy, and compliance considerations). It may be managed by the organizations or a third party and may exist on premise[s] or off premise[s].

- **Public cloud** The cloud infrastructure is made available to the general public or a large industry group and is owned by an organization selling cloud services.

● **Hybrid cloud**   The cloud infrastructure is a composition of two or more clouds (private, community, or public) that remain unique entities but are bound together by standardized or proprietary technology that enables data and application portability (e.g., cloud bursting for load balancing between clouds).

Cloud Computing, as Defined by ENISA

Given that IT transcends geographical boundaries, it is fitting to provide a non-U.S.-centric working definition of cloud computing from the European Network and Information Security Agency (ENISA):

> Cloud computing is an on-demand service model for IT provision, often based on virtualization and distributed computing technologies. Cloud computing architectures have:
>
> ● highly abstracted resources
>
> ● near instant scalability and flexibility
>
> ● near instantaneous provisioning
>
> ● shared resources (hardware, database, memory, etc.)
>
> ● "service on demand," usually with a "pay as you go" billing system
>
> ● programmatic management (e.g., through WS API)[2]

In Actual Practice

The hype around cloud computing might lead you to believe that this is brand new technology, but enterprises have leveraged on-demand utility computing, SaaS, web applications, and distributed or grid computing since 2002. Cloud computing is a natural progression from service-oriented architectures, the growth and trust in the Internet, utility computing, and virtualization. Through widespread adoption and familiarity with these technologies, enterprises are outsourcing computing capabilities to the cloud, expecting great cost savings.

Cloud Business Drivers

This brings us to the economics of the cloud. A simple but critical question to evaluate at this point, adapted to the context of a book about security metrics, is "Will the economic benefits of moving to the cloud outweigh the security risks?" Let's begin with some economic reasons why enterprises are moving to cloud computing:

- Enterprise data centers are large investments, with choices for streamlining and cost cutting mainly coming from consolidation efforts. A lot of time and money are spent on upgrades, patching, license management, troubleshooting, incident management, and so forth.

- Data center utilization is often poor because of the requirement to invest in hardware and software to handle peak loads instead of having a resilient architecture that allows enterprises to expand and contract commensurately with business processing needs (elasticity).

- Cloud vendors are demonstrating they can deliver infrastructure, platform, and software cheaper, better, and faster.

- Larger cloud vendors have better economies of scale than a single enterprise.

This list is not exhaustive, but it represents some of the business drivers that enterprises (and the vendors they depend on) employ to move to cloud computing. To come back to the question, "Will the economic benefits of moving to the cloud outweigh the security risks?" you will want to be able to answer that question with facts and data, and to do that you will need to employ good security metrics.

Understanding the business and economic reasons that underlie why your company is or may be moving to cloud computing is very important to you as an IT professional. Many of the benefits of the cloud have little to do with technology and everything to do with perceived cost savings. As an IT pro, you want to be on the same page as your business decision-makers and be ready to demonstrate the relationship between security metrics and the cost savings. For example, you may have data about applying critical security fixes in your environment. It might be very beneficial to be prepared to talk about the costs associated with deploying a critical security patch so that your company can evaluate whether leveraging cloud services is a way to drive down overall operational costs. Another example, which may seem very squishy, concerns business agility. Suppose your company develops new products or services in-house but wants to leverage cloud computing to deploy them far faster than it could before. From a security metrics viewpoint, your application development security metrics may really resonate with executive management if they demonstrate that secure in-house products and services can be deployed more quickly and at a cost savings by leveraging the cloud. Not to oversimplify, but the point of these examples is to be sure you consider how your security metrics relate to your company's budget considerations.

Note

Numerous cloud vendors offer one or more of the three SPI delivery models for cloud computing.[3] When your company engages one of these vendors, it is referred to as a *tenant* and usually is bound to terms and conditions outlined in a contract. Your company made a business decision about the capabilities of the cloud vendor and released a certain amount of control in exchange for those capabilities. For example, a cloud vendor may be able to do remote storage and backup faster, more reliably, and at a much lower cost that your company can. Perhaps the vendor uses best-of-breed technology that your company desires but cannot afford, and the vendor's personnel are experts at storage and backup, whereas your company would need to hire and train the right personnel.

In Actual Practice

The definition of a "tenant" in the context of cloud computing does not equal "customer." As an example, suppose your company leverages an SaaS offering, which in turn is hosted on a third party's cloud infrastructure or platform. In this case, both your company and the SaaS provider are tenants in someone else's environment. To your company, the data you store in the applications of the SaaS provider is most important. To your SaaS provider, if it is leveraging PaaS, then its application is what is most important; if it is leveraging IaaS, then its virtual machines, networks, and lower-layer services take precedence. In this example, it would be best to work with your legal department and contract experts not only to ensure that your contract with the SaaS provider clearly defines "tenant," but also to determine whether further due diligence is required if the provider is in turn leveraging other cloud services, to make sure you are not exposed to downstream risks. Regardless, the best practice would be to define "tenant" in your contract with the cloud vendor and not leave the interpretation open.

The New Normal

While cloud computing isn't technologically revolutionary, it is a new delivery model for IT services that presents a "new normal" we must adapt to. In this section, we'll look specifically at how metrics can be used to measure this new delivery model and thereby help us manage what is new or unknown. The following table provides some examples of what the "new normal" looks like compared to traditional enterprise computing:

Enterprise Computing	Cloud Computing
I have command and control over the data center.	Some or most of my computing processing needs are fulfilled by cloud vendor(s).
I have command and control over my data.	I'm still responsible and accountable for my data, but it's being processed outside of my control and I may have little visibility of where and how it is being processed.
I do background checks on all of my data center employees.	I may have no visibility of the hiring practices of my cloud vendor or its subcontractors.
I have control over data retention and disposal.	I don't know if my data is securely removed in the cloud, especially given the elasticity of the cloud and the ability to rapidly provision and de-provision resources.
My company's data and applications alone are running on my servers.	I am a single tenant in a multitenant environment, where my company's data and applications could be on the same physical server or the same virtual network as my competitors' data and applications.
I have established trust boundaries and my perimeter.	The highly leveraged nature of cloud computing means the trust boundaries have changed and some of the trusts are transitive to parties I am not aware of.

Don't interpret these examples to mean the new normal requires you to totally abdicate control. Remember, this book is designed to help you measure, analyze, and then manage. At a high level, the business (tenant) that is leveraging cloud services needs to think differently about who measures and reports, because the roles and responsibilities have changed and, specifically, the business doesn't have total command and control over its computing end to end. In the examples in the preceding table, the tenant is still responsible for its data, customers, and business requirements. But the tenant now needs information from its cloud vendor to complete the picture because it has leveraged some business process to a capability of a cloud vendor. If you are a tenant, you need to understand all the layers and know exactly which assets you own, which assets you touch that may not be on premises, and which assets you interface with both locally and remotely. This is the beginning to the process of answering the question of whether the economic benefits you might gain from cloud computing are worth the associated risks.

From a security metrics point of view, while cloud computing may become the new normal, with shared security responsibilities as the new model, some things haven't changed:

- Both you and your vendor will measure security. You now need to define who is doing what.

- Both you and your vendor will manage functional components of an information security program (see Chapter 1) and may agree to use an internationally recognized information security management system (ISMS) standard such as ISO/IEC 27001:2005, which mandates specific requirements so that the ISMS can be explicitly managed, audited, and certified to be compliant with the standard.

- Security work is never finished (see Chapter 2). Cloud computing should motivate both you and your cloud vendor to assess what the threat landscape looks like and what new or different security threats exist in the cloud.

Let's look at who's responsible for what in another way. The three SPI service models for cloud computing can be viewed as a stack, with platform building on infrastructure, and software building on both infrastructure and platform:[4]

Software as a Service (SaaS)
Platform as a Service (PaaS)
Infrastructure as a Service (IaaS)

Just as each layer builds on the previous one, similar to the layers in the ISO Open Systems Interconnection (OSI) model, security issues are inherited up the stack.[5] Generally, when thinking about roles and responsibilities, SaaS provides the most integrated functionality, with the cloud provider bearing most of the responsibility for security. PaaS offers a platform and assumes your company, the tenant, will build your own bespoke applications, which means application security is your responsibility. With IaaS, you have great flexibility but most of the responsibility for security, with the cloud vendor assuming responsibility only for infrastructure security.

Let's use an example to make this clearer. If your sales organization uses a cloud-based customer relationship manager (CRM) such as Salesforce.com or Microsoft Dynamics CRM, you are probably concerned about your customer data. You worry about how it is stored, how good the CRM's physical security is, whether or not the vendor uses encryption, and whether or not the vendor has good application and systems security. You will likely ask the vendor for information and assurances that its information security program is robust. You might even ask if it is ISO 27001 certified, meaning it has a standard set of ISMS components that you can compare to the components a competing vendor offers. In the

In Actual Practice

There is a lot of buzz around getting cloud vendors to demonstrate they have the requisite security controls in place. This might come in the form of ISO 27001 certification, American Institute of CPAs (AIC) Service Organization Control (SOC) 2 report (formerly called SAS 70 reports),[6] or BITS Shared Assessments.[7] There are two important points to make:

- All of these organizations are in the process of amending their certifications to account for cloud computing.

- While it is important to evaluate the security controls of your cloud vendor, it is not sustainable for you or the vendor to create custom questionnaires. For the vendor, this would mean filling out a questionnaire for each customer. And you, the customer, cannot audit and keep track of every vendor.

Just as industry bodies have arrived at agreed standards and auditing protocols, it's important for you to look for industry-accepted and standardized ways to evaluate a cloud vendor's security controls.

end, you expect the cloud provider to demonstrate its level of security to you. If you were creating custom applications on Google's App Engine or Microsoft's Azure platform, you would want assurances about the security and integrity of that platform, but *you* would be responsible for the security of the applications you created.

Security Metrics vs. Cloud Security Metrics

Up to this point, this chapter has discussed cloud security at a high level—the definition of cloud computing, the economic drivers that support cloud computing, and the cloud delivery models. I would like to turn our attention to a discussion of common security metrics compared to cloud security metrics. This section offers a way to think about common security metrics in a cloud context.

Let's begin by slightly restating the three main benefits of an information security metrics program outlined in Chapter 1:

- Cloud metrics provides visibility—visibility for the tenant both to the cloud provider and to itself.

- Cloud metrics educates and provides a common language for understanding the information security program as applicable to the cloud vendor and to the tenant.
- Cloud metrics motivates both the cloud provider and the tenant to improve.

The following table provides a structured way to think about common security metrics applied to cloud computing. Each column begins with a description of the column's content, after which two common security metrics are presented as examples, with corresponding suggestions about their relevance to the cloud.

Security Metric	Cloud Addendum	Vendor or Tenant?	Delivery Model	Target
Describes a common security metric.	*What is cloud specific about this security metric in a cloud context?*	*In cloud computing, there are multiple parties involved and a business process can be outsourced to one or more cloud vendors. In addition, the tenant is still accountable for the data and the information security and privacy risks associated with its data.*	*Each SPI delivery model, SaaS, PaaS, and IaaS, has different nuances and security responsibilities for the vendor and the tenant.*	*What is the acceptable range or value you want to achieve?*
Percentage of hosts that are up-to-date with critical security patches.	Here it might be important to know whether these hosts are at the cloud vendor site, on premises at the tenant site but interface with hosts at the cloud vendor, or both.	If you are a tenant, you need to understand all the layers and know exactly which assets you own, which assets you touch that may not be on premises, and which assets you interface with both locally and remotely. A vendor may be asked to report to customers on a metric similar to this on a quarterly basis in an effort to be transparent about its information security practices.	Depending on the cloud delivery model, responsibility for security generally lies mostly with the vendor for SaaS and mostly with the tenant for IaaS.	100%

(continued)

Security Metric	Cloud Addendum	Vendor or Tenant?	Delivery Model	Target
Application security incident: mean time to fix.	No tenant wants to be exposed to application security vulnerabilities from its cloud vendor, especially if the tenant has outsourced important business functions to the cloud. Further, this could impact the tenant's customers who have dependencies on services the tenant has outsourced to the cloud vendor. On the other hand, cloud vendors who provide infrastructure and platform services need to protect themselves from tenant application security vulnerabilities that could affect the infrastructure or platform.	Potentially both, depending on the deployment model.	This metric applies to the cloud vendor if it is responsible for the application. It applies to the tenant in a PaaS or IaaS delivery model if it has an application with a security vulnerability.	

The Cloud Security Alliance (CSA), introduced in Chapter 2, is spearheading an effort to create cloud-specific security metrics that uses a framework similar to the preceding table. The following section expands on the work that this nonprofit industry organization is doing because it has a direct bearing on security metrics.

Cloud Security Alliance

In April 2009, CSA issued version 1 of *Security Guidance for Critical Areas of Focus in Cloud Computing*, and today version 2.1 is available for download.[4] If you have not reviewed this document, it is worth reading. In addition to the guidance document, CSA has a number of working groups. One group in particular is related to our discussion of cloud security metrics—the CSA Cloud Controls Matrix (CCM) working group.[8] The vision of this group is to be the recognized global authority for information security controls for cloud computing. CSA formed the CCM working group after realizing that to fully leverage the benefits of cloud computing, trust must be built into the cloud ecosystem by solving key problems such as the following:

- Lack of visibility into cloud providers
- Risks that are not fully understood and managed, for both the cloud providers and tenants
- Difficulty of compliance attestation

The CCM working group was also formed under the assumption that cloud providers and tenants have a shared responsibility to optimize the governance, risk management, and compliance of cloud computing.

In September 2009, the CSA Cloud Metrics working group was formed and began creating cloud-specific metrics aligned to the domains described in *Security Guidance for Critical Areas of Focus in Cloud Computing*. As the Cloud Metrics working group evolved and the Cloud Controls Matrix working group published the first version of the CCM, an alignment between the two efforts became obvious.

The Cloud Controls Matrix also integrates with other CSA initiatives in addition to the Cloud Metrics working group, and with non-CSA initiatives. Here are summaries of other related activities:

- **CSA Consensus Assessments Initiative (CAI)**   Performs research, creates tools, and creates industry partnerships to enable cloud computing assessments. This group is focused on providing industry-accepted ways to document which security controls exist in SIP offerings, to provide security control transparency. On October 12, 2010, the CAI delivered the Consensus Assessments Initiative Questionnaire. This questionnaire, available in spreadsheet format, provides a set of questions a cloud consumer and cloud auditor may wish to ask a cloud provider. It provides a series of "yes" or "no" control assertion questions that can be tailored to suit each unique cloud customer's evidentiary requirements. This question set is meant to be a companion to the CSA *Security Guidance for Critical Areas of Focus in Cloud Computing* and the CSA Cloud Controls Matrix, and these documents should be used together.

- **CloudAudit**   An open standard and interface to allow cloud providers to automate audit assertions. The CCM provides CloudAudit with its Cloud Controls namespace, where CloudAudit answers the "how?" of audit assertions and CCM answers the "what?"

- **Trusted Cloud Initiative (TCI)** Will help cloud providers develop industry-recommended, secure and interoperable identity, access, and compliance management configurations and practices. TCI will develop reference models, education, certification criteria, and a cloud provider self-certification toolset. This will be developed in a vendor-neutral manner, inclusive of all CSA members and affiliates who wish to participate. A TCI assessor will use a combination of CCM–TCI mappings, Consensus Assessments questionnaires, and other tools as needed to cover the requirements specified in the TCI reference model. If supported by the provider, the TCI assessor will use CloudAudit-enabled tools to collect assertions.

- **Common Assurance Maturity Model (CAMM)** An industry initiative started by the contributors of the ENISA Cloud Computing Security Risk Assessment experts group, which includes ENISA, UK National Health Service, Amazon, Google, and Microsoft. The group has broad industry support and participation from key industry and standards stakeholders. CAMM is a methodology and solution for creating an independent maturity model-based measurement of the maturity of a cloud provider's security program. The Cloud Controls Matrix will map to CAMM's internal assessment controls, and providers can use CCM provider-specific controls to optimize their CAMM assessment scoring.

The CCM identifies security controls for the cloud that are applicable to all SPI delivery models, describe relevance to the cloud provider or tenant (or both), and are mapped to standards, regulations, and frameworks such as ISO, COBIT, HIPPA, and PCI-DSS. These controls help IT security and IT auditors leverage existing tools, processes, strategies, and frameworks to enable holistic cloud security. The link between these mapped control areas and the Cloud Metrics working group was a desire to describe a set of security metrics that could help cloud vendors and tenants alike demonstrate that these controls existed and were functioning properly. Indeed, any security management system, in the cloud or otherwise, needs metrics to report on the overall health and progress of the management system.

Even though the Cloud Metrics working group is aligned with the CCM, the group still needed to look at the control areas described and ask themselves, "What's important?" The group also knew that regulatory compliance would be a priority to most organizations. As you learned in Chapters 6 and 8, defining a target, understanding your context, and prioritizing are important steps to a successful security metrics project. The group also had a lot of different stakeholders with varying points of view creating metrics. To help them, they developed a metrics template and defined a simple lifecycle for a metric within the context of the Cloud Security Alliance and their direct link to the CCM.

CSA Cloud Metrics Working Group Template

The template that the CSA Cloud Metrics working group uses to create its metrics is presented here to show a real example of security metrics development in action. This template is a work in progress and will grow and evolve. The template addresses what the working group considers to be one of the problematic areas with security metrics—the lack of rich guidance and implementation information about a metric. To address this problem, the metrics template is detailed and allows for lengthy text in the Attribute Definition column.

Cloud Security Alliance Metric Definition Template

Author	Your name
Date	Date
Attribute	**Attribute Definition**
Name	The name of the metric.
Title	Short name or abbreviation.
Status	Possible states: Draft, Reviewed, Published, Under Review.
Audience	Choice of Operations, Management, or Executive.
Units of Measure	Units of measure such as incidents per month, vulnerabilities per server, or time in hours.
Targets	Values that enlighten interpretation of measurement results such as goal values, critical, normal, caution values, etc.
Description	A general description of the metric.
Objective	Succinct statement of the objective of the metric. Are there specific decisions for which this metric is useful?
Usage	Discussion regarding implementation experience such as use cases, scope, scale, or unintended consequences.
Implementation	
Automation	Amenability of this metric to automation. Choice of high, medium, or low followed by rationale.
Frequency	Suggested measurement interval for the metric, e.g., daily, weekly, monthly, etc.
Sources	A general description of data required to calculate the metric and where one might obtain it.
How to Calculate	A general description of how to calculate the metric plus a formula, if possible.

(continued)

Methodology	A description of any foundational models or assumptions associated with this metric. For example, if one were using linear regression to compute this metric, there is the assumption that errors are normally distributed.
Limitations	A general description of potential limitations in the implementation of this metric. What considerations are not taken into account with this metric?

Survey Interface

Question	For metrics that are calculated based upon survey responses, this is the question that would appear on the survey for this metric.
Answer	A description of the expected format of the answer, e.g., Yes/No, an integer between 0 and 100.
License	Usage restrictions.

Associations

References	Names of individuals or companies that contributed all or part of this metric definition. Also include either citations or URLs to other material that is relevant.
Tags	A comma delimited list of Contexts that are associated with this metric. For example, this field will hold a list of Control IDs from the CSA Controls Matrix, e.g., CO-2, DG-3, etc. Note that the CSA Controls Matrix will be used to automatically associate the metric with other standards such as ISO/IEC, PCI, HIPAA, NIST, and COBIT.

Cloud Relevance

Metric Collector	Who collects this metric? A cloud provider or tenant?
IaaS Relevance	Rating value between 1 and 10, 10 being most relevant.
IaaS Rationale	Rationale for rating assignment.
IaaS Sharing	Discuss the likelihood, motivation, and risks/benefits/costs of sharing this metric between provider and tenant.
PaaS Relevance	Rating value between 1 and 10, 10 being most relevant.
PaaS Rationale	Rationale for rating assignment.
PaaS Sharing	Discuss the likelihood, motivation, and risks/benefits/costs of sharing this metric between provider and tenant.
SaaS Relevance	Rating value between 1 and 10, 10 being most relevant.
SaaS Rationale	Rationale for rating assignment.
SaaS Sharing	Discuss the likelihood, motivation, and risks/benefits/costs of sharing this metric between provider and tenant.

Let's take a look at two important sections—Implementation and Cloud Relevance. These sections are important because they give you a place to discuss potential limitations of the metric, identify the source of the data needed, and indicate whether the metric is appropriate to share between tenant and cloud vendor. A metric may appear great on paper, but implementing it in real life requires some reality checks. For example, some data is too hard to gather or is in an unstructured format, and to implement the metric might require more effort than the business intelligence it provides. Further, in the Cloud Relevance section, the template asks you to describe who is collecting this information— the tenant, the cloud vendor, or both? Then the template asks you to rate on a scale of 1–10 how relevant the metric is to the three cloud service models (IaaS, PaaS, SaaS). The working group added this section to the template because it wanted to consider the main cloud delivery models and what would be the potential benefits, costs, and risks associated with sharing either the metric itself or the computed results.

Into Action

The following is a sample metric created using the Cloud Metrics working group template. You can use the blank column to create your own metric.

Cloud Security Alliance Metric Definition Template	
Author	Dan Crisp and Elizabeth Nichols
Date	8/25/2010 0:00
Attribute	**Proposed Definition**
Name	CloudServiceDataElementCount
Title	CSDEC
Status	Draft
Audience	Management
Units of Measure	Count of data elements used by a target cloud service.
Targets	None. This is an informational metric.
Description	The CloudServiceDataElementCount metric provides counts of the number of data items that have been outsourced to a cloud provider for a specific target service. The CloudServiceDataElementCount metric can report simply the count of all data items or the count of data items that hold PII or no PII. From this metric, one can derive the percentage of data items that have PII for a given service. Additionally, along with the CloudServiceUserCount metric, per-user, per-service metrics can be derived. If data elements are tagged with additional metadata that characterizes relevant regulations and compliance requirements, then metrics can be derived on a per-compliance/regulation basis.

(continued)

Attribute	Proposed Definition
Objective	The CloudServiceDataElementCount metric is designed to provide management with a simple tally of the number of attributes that are managed via a cloud provider for a target service. Additionally, it is designed to give insight into data sensitivity on a per-user and per-compliance/regulation basis.
Usage	Using CloudServiceDataElementCount conditioned by whether or not it holds PII, one can create a metric that characterizes the level of PII content for a cloud service. This metric, in turn, can be used to rank all cloud services based on their PII content. Similarly, by computing this metric on a per-compliance requirement basis, one can prioritize services based upon such criteria as local relevance of a regulation, penalties, review requirements, audit schedules and resources, etc.
Implementation	
Automation	This metric can be computed automatically based upon records kept about reviews. Since it does not change frequently, manual implementation is feasible.
Frequency	Update this metric across all services once per month or once per quarter, depending upon volatility of user base.
Sources	Generically, the required data for computing this metric will come from an Application Directory and the Data Dictionary for each service, or similar. Ideally the Data Dictionary will carry annotations for each data element regarding 1) optional vs. mandatory, 2) is it PII or not, 3) a list of associated regulations or compliance requirements.
How to Calculate	Compute this metric as a simple count of attributes for a given target service, sometimes aggregated on filters derived from metadata about each data item. Example metadata includes serviceName, isPII, piiType, and others.
Methodology	Simple count. For the cases in which the data dictionary is a SQL database, simple queries can generate values for this metric across many dimensions, e.g., isPII, piiType, etc.
Limitations	This metric does not necessarily reflect any information regarding the need, justification, or time to live regarding the PII data items associated with a service.
Survey Interface	
Question	
Answer	
License	CSA Use License
Associations	
References	
Tags	OP-02: Documentation SA-03: Data Security/Integrity DG-02: Classification DG-03: Handling/Labeling Security Policy

(continued)

Cloud Relevance	
Metric Collector	Typically the tenant collects this metric.
IaaS Relevance	Provider: 10 Tenant: 10
IaaS Rationale	To both providers and tenants, this information is critical. For providers, higher values of this metric imply greater resources consumption—storage, compute power, and network bandwidth. For tenants, this metric is a proxy for service popularity, visibility, and criticality.
IaaS Sharing	Sharing of this value is typically at the discretion of the consumer. Indirectly, the provider can infer estimates of this metric via traffic analysis of the services.
PaaS Relevance	See IaaS relevance.
PaaS Rationale	See IaaS relevance.
PaaS Sharing	See IaaS relevance.
SaaS Relevance	Provider: 10 Consumer: 10
SaaS Rationale	In this case, both the tenant and provider are completely aware of the service provided and all users and data involved.
SaaS Sharing	In this case, both tenant and provider are completely aware of the service provided and all users and data involved.

CSA Cloud Metrics Working Group Lifecycle

As stated earlier in this book, metrics are subject to change and need to be reviewed and revised on a regular basis. Figure 17-1 shows the lifecycle used by the Cloud Metrics working group for this purpose. The stages of the lifecycle are as follows:

- The Cloud Metrics working group creates and reviews the cloud metrics within the working group.

- Because the working group is aligned with the Cloud Controls Matrix, it requests the CCM stakeholders to do a review. When they are finished, a broad CSA review occurs. Finally, a general public review occurs.

- After public announcement, the working group makes the metrics available in an open and vendor-neutral manner.

- In an effort to ensure its metrics are usable, the working group asks either a cloud vendor or a tenant to implement the metrics and provide feedback.

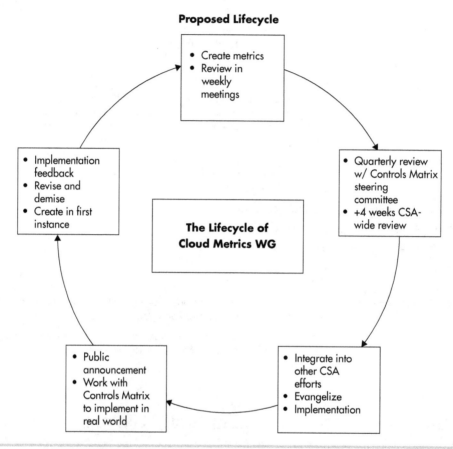

Figure 17-1   The proposed lifecycle of a metric, used as a guide by the CSA Cloud Metrics working group

- The working group reviews the metrics along with the changes in cloud computing and decides if each metric needs to begin the cycle again with a major revision or needs to be demised.

Final Thoughts

The need for security metrics in the cloud is not much different from the need for security metrics in general. Everyone in the cloud, vendor and tenant alike, will need to measure the effectiveness of security controls and show their accountability to each other and to regulatory bodies. In the past, there was little benefit for companies to share security metrics; indeed, there were risks in doing so. With cloud computing and a world of shared accountabilities across virtual, physical, and geographic boundaries, we need to find ways to share information between vendor and tenant and across industry in responsible ways. This implies we need to remove some of the roadblocks to success and work on areas such as common definitions for terms, common metrics deployed in a consistent manner, and a consistent reporting framework. Industry bodies such as the Cloud Security Alliance are helping to achieve these goals, and many security practitioners are volunteering their time and talent.

For information security practitioners, an important first step is to measure and get a baseline that is appropriate for your business and that describes what is the new normal for security in cloud computing. Businesses will need to make decisions based on facts and data, and your security metrics program can support important planning and decision making and drive beneficial changes in your organization.

We've Covered

What is cloud computing?

- NIST definition of cloud computing
- Essential characteristics for cloud computing
- Cloud service and deployment models

Common business drivers that motivate organizations to move to the cloud

- Core question, "Will the economic benefits of moving to the cloud outweigh the security risks?"
- Budget pressures, streamlining, and consolidation efforts
- Agility and the draw to cheaper, better, faster

The "new normal" for IT service delivery

- New delivery model for IT services
- Some comparisons between aspects of traditional enterprise computing and cloud computing
- Security metrics as a way to understand the new normal

Common security metrics in the context of cloud computing

- The value of developing metrics
- Structured way to think about common security metrics in the context of cloud computing

Major cloud industry groups, especially the Cloud Security Alliance, and their efforts to describe cloud controls and related metrics

- Cloud Security Alliance (CSA) and the *Security Guidance for Critical Areas of Focus in Cloud Computing*
- Cloud Security Alliance working groups, in particular the Cloud Controls Matrix and Cloud Metrics working groups
- ENISA's Common Assurance Maturity Model (CAMM)

Endnotes

1. P. Mell and T. Grance, "The NIST Definition of Cloud Computing," NIST Special Publication 800-145 (Draft), Jan. 2011, http://csrc.nist.gov/publications/drafts/800-145/Draft-SP-800-145_cloud-definition.pdf.

2. ENISA, *Cloud Computing: Benefits, Risks and Recommendations for Information Security*, Nov. 2009, available at www.enisa.europa.eu/act/rm/files/deliverables/cloud-computing-risk-assessment.

3. The OpenCrowd Cloud Taxonomy (http://cloudtaxonomy.opencrowd.com/) is a good resource to consult to see the diversity of cloud offerings available today.

4. A more complete discussion of the stack concept appears in the Cloud Security Alliance's *Security Guidance for Critical Areas of Focus in Cloud Computing*, V2.1, www.cloudsecurityalliance.org/csaguide.pdf, which is highly recommend reading for those interested in cloud computing security.

5. Both the OSI model and the cloud stack are *reference* models, which means that not everything fits neatly into one layer or another. This is especially apparent when you look at the large quantity of cloud vendors who provide services throughout the stack. It may not be easy to confine a vendor or offering in a single layer.

6. AICPA press release, "AICPA Publishes Guidance on Next Generation of SAS 70," Feb. 1, 2011, www.aicpa.org/Press/PressReleases/2011/Pages/NextGenerationofSAS70.aspx.

7. BITS Shared Assessments, www.sharedassessments.org and http://www.bitsinfo.org/.

8. CSA, "CSA Cloud Controls Matrix V1.1 is Released," https://cloudsecurityalliance.org/research/projects/cloud-controls-matrix-ccm/.

PART IX

Appendix and Glossary

APPENDIX

Templates and Checklists

P lease consider the following appendix a resource that you can use as a playbook when you are starting or improving your own Security Metrics Program. Here you will find summary checklists and templates used throughout the book for quick reference.

Chapter 1

The Three Benefits of a Security Metrics Program

- Measurement provides visibility.
- Measurement educates and provides a common language for understanding the information security program.
- Measurement improves. It improves an information security program in three key ways: it enables the best possible management of the information security program, it enables investment planning and decision making, and it drives necessary change throughout the organization.

Chapter 2

Best Practice Analysis

A security metrics program should ask the following questions in order to optimize the use of best practices implemented within the organization:

- How relevant to the organization's business model and business strategy is this best practice?
- What is the objective of implementing this particular control/best practice?
- What is the desired outcome of implementing this particular control/best practice?
- Are all the relevant stakeholders aware of and properly performing their role with regard to the implementation of this best practice?
- What's the actual result of implementing this best practice, and how does that compare to the desired outcome?

Chapter 5

Request for Proposal

When putting together an RFP, ask the potential vendor partners to include information about the following:

Professional Services Capability

- Evidence of their expertise and applicable experience
- References regarding their past history and proven track record
- Which service level agreements and availability requirements they adhere to

Terms

- Whether they comply with your organization or company's RFP format
- Whether they accept your organization's legal terms and service level agreements

Strategic Value Add

- What industry knowledge and expertise they bring to the table
- Evidence of relationships with emerging technology vendors and other thought leaders

Chapter 6

Metrics for High Risk Areas

Here are some Qualitative Metrics Questions related to various areas of high risk within an organization.

Qualitative Metric	Notes
Which areas of the organization have the greatest risk of information compromise?	This may be determined by performing an information security risk assessment.
Which information security–related areas of risk are high profile for my organization right now?	This may be discussed and determined by an enterprise risk group.
Which information assets are important to my company?	Interview business stakeholders.
Who is responsible for managing those assets?	Identify technical owners.
What is the lifecycle of those information assets?	Discuss with both business stakeholders and technical owners.

Metrics for Process Improvement

Here are some qualitative and quantitative metrics questions related to various areas of process improvement within a security program.

Qualitative Metric	Desired Outcome	Notes
Is this process defined and documented?	Yes	
Does each step in the process have clearly defined roles and responsibilities?	Yes	
Which steps or roles are unclear to or not agreed upon by the relevant stakeholders or process participants?	None	
Quantitative Metric		**Notes**
Number or percentage of steps in the process that all stakeholders agree upon	100%	This may be a count or a percentage.
Percentage of attempts to perform the process that are performed consistently	100%	Percentage—certain step-by-step measurement criteria may need to be specified for further definition of "performed consistently"; for example, "How often is the data capture involved in this process performed consistently?"
Percentage of SLA requirements defined for the process that are adhered to	100%	This may be measured as a percentage. A single process may have multiple SLA requirements defined, and this metric may be applied multiple times to a single process.

Metrics for Security Technology

The following table provides some recommended questions to identify targets for metrics work in the domain of security technology.

Qualitative Metric Questions	Notes
What is the scope of coverage for this security technology? What are the advantages and disadvantages to increasing or decreasing the amount of coverage?	Does the scope of coverage include only headquarters, or all remote offices? Does it apply only to the development network, or to the production network? Does it apply only to corporate, or to production?
What are the functions of this security technology? What gaps in capability exist? Which functions are being performed by multiple different security technologies (overlap)? How effective is the technology?	In answering these questions, you may discover that you are paying for and resourcing technologies whose functions overlap. To find out which technology you can eliminate, proceed with an assessment and comparison of the two (or more) products. Alternatively, you may discover that a particular technology no longer works well.
Are the ownership, roles, and responsibilities associated with both the deployment and the ongoing maintenance of this technology clearly security related? If not, is this technology and what it delivers a priority for the team?	If the answer to the second question is yes, then resources need to be allocated to the technology. If the answer is no, then the technology should be decommissioned.
What are the intended functions of this security technology? How well does the security technology execute those functions? (That is, is it doing what it's supposed to do?)	To begin answering these questions, refer to the original project deployment plan for the technology or the RFP materials used to evaluate the technology initially. The answer to the second question may be as general as High, Medium, or Low Effectiveness.
What additional functionality is this technology capable of delivering? Does that functionality align with the priorities of the information security program? What is preventing this functionality from being deployed?	Many security products have capabilities beyond what an initial project to deploy the technology may require. Sometimes a security technology is deployed for a particular purpose, but it may be able to do much more. In terms of maximizing dollars and an investment in technology, look at the capabilities of existing technology before going out and buying and installing new technology to do what existing technology can already do.

(continued)

Qualitative Metric Questions	Notes
Do the benefits of this technology deployment outweigh its ongoing maintenance cost, in terms of both annual licensing and team resources spent on maintaining the system? Are you spending in accordance with your priorities?	The first question is considered to be qualitative rather than quantitative because, depending on the situation, there may or may not be hard quantitative data with which to perform this analysis. Answering this question can at least start the thought process moving in the right direction. For example, do you have too many logs to actually review them? Is the resource burden too heavy to carry on? This speaks to the question of cost of ongoing maintenance. Oftentimes when a technology is deployed, folks may fail to think about how much it actually takes to keep it up and running. I have seen organizations buy and then not effectively use technology because proper maintenance costs (resources to support the processes required) were not taken into consideration.

Metrics for Non-Security Technology

Technology deployed outside of the information security program and with primary functions having little or nothing to do with security may still be a good target for an information security metrics project, if that technology deployment represents a significant amount of risk for your company or organization. The following table proposes a set of high-level questions that may be useful for identifying technology targets for your next information security metrics project that are not directly related to security.

Qualitative Metric Questions	Notes
Have there been security incidents related to this particular technology? If so, how many? How often? Why? (Side question: Are you sure you would know whether or not security incidents related to this technology have occurred?)	Repeated incidents involving a particular technology may be a good indicator that it is a worthy security metrics project target.
Does this technology manage personal information or transactional data? Is the data that is stored, transferred, or processed by this technology system appropriately protected for its level of classification in the organization? How effective are the security controls currently in place? To what extent are security controls prescribed by the information security team adhered to by the teams who use and manage the systems?	The second question assumes an information classification standard is in place. If not, developing one may be a good place to start.
Who has access to the system? Are appropriate access controls in place considering the classification and uses of the data contained in this system?	The second question assumes an information classification standard is in place. If not, developing one may be a good place to start.
Does this technology have authentication and authorization controls? If so, how do they function? Alternatively, how does this technology manage passwords?	Depending on the sensitivity of information stored in this technology, you may want to take a look at the authentication and authorization controls. An example metrics project may be to identify and strengthen authorization and authorization controls for the most sensitive data types throughout your organization.
Who are the end users of this technology? Are the users of this technology customer service representatives or system administrators? Employees or just executives?	Different end users require different levels of controls for protecting information stored in and managed by a technology.
Does this technology integrate with third-party partners or providers?	If so, you may need to conduct a vendor assessment (if one has not already been completed) to review the security of this technology fully.
Does this technology accurately reflect the company's or organization's data retention (or anti-retention) policy?	You can assess the compliance of this technology with data retention standards. A gap may indicate an opportunity for a metrics project.

Metrics for What's Basic?

This table provides a few questions that will help you analyze what basic components of an information security program you might be missing or what might need fixing in order to identify a target for a metrics project.

Qualitative Metric Questions	Notes
Which basic components of an information security program do not exist in the organization or are at a level of maturity lower than best practices dictate?	This question is about identifying gaps in the security program.
What units (product, corporate IT, customer service, etc.) of the organization lack one or more basic information security functions? Which functions?	These questions is similar to the first question but applies to more specific targets.
Based on recent news articles and mainstream trends in information security, which information security functions might management expect to have fully implemented? Are those functions currently at the expected level of maturity?	These questions is about identifying topics that may be on the mind of non-security professionals.

Metrics for New Technology

When you are looking to choose a new technology product to deploy in your environment, metrics used to assess and compare one vendor partner against another will be critical to making the right decision for your company or organization. The following table provides a few questions that might be incorporated into an assessment of a new technology.

Qualitative Metric Questions	Notes
How much does this technology cost, both up front and ongoing? What resources will this technology require for the build phase and for maintenance?	Cost will always be a factor. Managing how the information security budget is invested must be done carefully in order to properly fund the program priorities.
What are the functional requirements for this technology? What is it expected to perform and deliver?	Answering these questions will help ensure that you specifically evaluate the new technology to ensure it meets all of your requirements.
What are the service levels provided by the vendor? Do these meet your needs?	Answering these questions will help ensure you're getting the level of service you need from the vendor once the technology has been deployed.
Is the vendor financially viable? Will the vendor be able to sustain your needs in the short and long term?	Answering these questions helps you determine if the vendor will be around long enough for you to use their technology when you need it.
Does this vendor adhere to the legal requirements that you set forth?	Your legal team may require an answer to this question. This is a good question to ask up front.

Chapter 7

Meeting with Stakeholders

The following are some sample questions that you can ask when meeting with stakeholders to gather their input and incorporate it into your metrics project objectives. These questions are open-ended by design because they are intended to be starting points for a deeper, two-way conversation.

- What is your role relative to the target identified for this metrics project?

- What do you see as potential risks, issues, and dependencies that may impede visibility, improvement, and education in this area?

- From your history related to the target identified for this metrics project, what can you tell me about what has worked and what hasn't worked in the past?

- What are historical distance and time parameters in terms of changes for this particular metric? What is a reasonable objective based on what's been accomplished in the past?

- What do you believe would be a reasonable goal in terms of distance and time for what we need now?

- What changes will need to be made in order to achieve these objectives?

Chapter 8

Basic Prioritization Questions

- What do we need to accomplish?

- What is the highest priority

Here are some questions I recommend asking when considering compliance as a factor in a prioritization exercise:

- Is this project, task, or initiative directly tied to a regulatory compliance requirement that must be adhered to?

- If so, how important to compliance is this item?

- What negative impact on the organization's compliance status could result from not performing this project, task, or initiative?

- What are the negative consequences if the organization fails to comply in this area?

Risk Reduction Questions

As information security professionals, we are in the business of managing risk; specifically, if necessary, we must reduce the current level of risk in the information security area to align with the level of risk the company is willing to tolerate. How this alignment should be achieved is not always easy to identify quantitatively, but even very qualitative judgments with respect to risk reduction are useful during prioritization exercises. Assigning a priority level to a project from a risk-reduction perspective may be as simple (though not as easy) as asking the following questions:

- What type of attack or negative impact will this project, initiative, or task eliminate?
- What is the probability of this attack occurring if this project, initiative, or task is not deployed?
- Is that probability increasing or decreasing?
- What is the potential severity of this attack (estimated in dollars, if possible)?
- Is the potential severity increasing or decreasing?
- What is the risk reduction associated with deploying this project, initiative, or task? (Should be calculated by Probability × Severity if the attack or negative impact can be completely eliminated, or as a percentage if it only partially reduces the impact.)

Business Objective Alignment Questions

You can ask the following questions to identify top business objectives during your prioritization exercise:

- What matters to the top executives at your company?
- Is the task, initiative, or project being prioritized directly or indirectly associated with or supporting a top company priority, goal, or objective? To what extent?
- Will the company goal be negatively impacted if this item is not completed?

Of course, sometimes you may be prioritizing in-progress security metrics projects against new projects. In that case, the following questions may be useful:

- What's the point?
- Will we potentially do anything differently once we have this data?
- Does anyone look at this?

Especially for metrics projects involving reporting, the straightforward question "does anyone even look at this?" is very important for prioritization.

- Who is the intended audience for this metrics project reporting?
- Why don't they look at the reports?
- Do they understand the data?
- Do they care about the data?
- Do they understand what the data means for their team and for the overall organization?

Chapter 9

Identifying Key Audiences and Key Messages

This section presents a series of questions to kick-start your brainstorming process and help you to formulate the key messages that you'll want to convey to key stakeholders and sponsors.

- What's this person's area of responsibility? Why is this person important to information security?
- What's valuable to this key stakeholder?
- What are their security needs?
- For what purpose do you need their buy-in? What do you need them to approve?
- What information do you need from this person?

Stakeholder Analysis

The following are some recommended techniques for gaining a richer understanding of how to best communicate with the key stakeholders in your organization:

- Look up the key stakeholder or sponsor in your corporate directory. Their specific job title may provide insight into what they do.
- Look up the job title of the manager of the key stakeholder or sponsor in your corporate directory. This will help you to understand the broader role of the key stakeholder or sponsor.

- Related to the job title and role of the stakeholder or sponsor, find out what their budget responsibilities and contributions to revenue are, how long they've been with the company, and any cultural issues you may need to understand before presenting to the team or individual stakeholders. Understanding this will help you know how to best communicate with them and to understanding their history and biases, which can influence the scope of their responsibility.

- Visit a library or bookstore and take a look at professional development books and magazines written for this particular role. These resources may give you insight into some of the typical personality characteristics that you will want to be aware of before meeting with the stakeholder or sponsor.

- Look up the job titles of the person's peers (other people who report directly to the manager of the key stakeholder or sponsor). This will shed light on related topics that the key stakeholder or sponsor is likely to be familiar with.

- Look up the job titles of the direct reports of the key stakeholder or sponsor in your corporate directory. This provides additional detail on the stakeholder's or sponsor's areas of expertise.

Examples of Key Audiences, Key Messages, and Security Metrics

This table summarizes the examples reviewed in Chapter 9.

Key Audience	Key Message	Security Metric(s)
Chief executive officer (CEO)	Present information on security posture of multiple business lines	Comparative security score reporting
Chief financial officer (CFO)	Justify funding for the information security program	Benchmark data of peer companies
Chief risk officer (CRO)	Present an update on the status of regulatory compliance	Percentage of controls tested Percentage of controls failed
Chief technology officer (CTO)	Educate on risks of outsourcing and obtain buy-in for vendor security assessments Request remediation processes to manage vulnerabilities	Percentage of vendor security assessments resulting in a status of high risk Percentage of high-risk security assessments for which found vulnerabilities are remediated within an SLA defined by the information security team Percentage of security vulnerabilities per million lines of code

(continued)

Key Audience	Key Message	Security Metric(s)
Business unit (BU) leader	Drive further compliance with information security policy	Trend of audit results over time
Chief information officer (CIO)	Improve patching, secure build, and antivirus procedures	Percentage of patches deployed within SLA Percentage of new systems deployed according to standard secure build Percentage of systems in compliance with secure configuration standards Percentage of systems with up-to-date antivirus Percentage of unmanaged systems (and trends for each)
Director of physical security	Define a joint process for managing physical device and information loss related to laptop theft	Trend in number of laptops stolen by office location Trend in number of tailgaters by office location
Director of human resources (HR)	Promote a culture of security for company employees	Trend in number of social engineering–related security incidents Trend of percentage of employees completing information security training

Analysis: What Do You Need?

Here are some guiding questions that you can use to identify which teams you'll need buy-in from:

- Which teams will need to provide support?
- From which teams will you need resources and time to make your project happen?
- Which teams will be affected during the implementation and rollout of your project?
- Which teams will need to be informed about the project deployment and results?
- Which teams are the customers to whom you will be providing services?

Chapter 17

Template for Completely and Unambiguously Defining a Metric

The template that the CSA Cloud Metrics working group uses to create its metrics is presented here to show a real example of security metrics development in action. This template is a work in progress and will grow and evolve. The template addresses what the working group considers to be one of the problematic areas with security metrics—the lack of rich guidance and implementation information about a metric. To address this problem, the metrics template is detailed and allows for lengthy text in the Attribute Definition column.

Cloud Security Alliance Metric Definition Template

Author	Your name
Date	Date
Attribute	**Attribute Definition**
Name	The name of the metric.
Title	Short name or abbreviation.
Status	Possible states: Draft, Reviewed, Published, Under Review.
Audience	Choice of Operations, Management, or Executive.
Units of Measure	Units of measure such as incidents per month, vulnerabilities per server, or time in hours.
Targets	Values that enlighten interpretation of measurement results such as goal values, critical, normal, caution values, etc.
Description	A general description of the metric.
Objective	Succinct statement of the objective of the metric. Are there specific decisions for which this metric is useful?
Usage	Discussion regarding implementation experience such as use cases, scope, scale, or unintended consequences.
Implementation	
Automation	Amenability of this metric to automation. Choice of high, medium, or low followed by rationale.

(continued)

Frequency	Suggested measurement interval for the metric, e.g., daily, weekly, monthly, etc.
Sources	A general description of data required to calculate the metric and where one might obtain it.
How to Calculate	A general description of how to calculate the metric plus a formula, if possible.
Methodology	A description of any foundational models or assumptions associated with this metric. For example, if one were using linear regression to compute this metric, there is the assumption that errors are normally distributed.
Limitations	A general description of potential limitations in the implementation of this metric. What considerations are not taken into account with this metric?
Survey Interface	
Question	For metrics that are calculated based upon survey responses, this is the question that would appear on the survey for this metric.
Answer	A description of the expected format of the answer, e.g., Yes/No, an integer between 0 and 100.
License	Usage restrictions.
Associations	
References	Names of individuals or companies that contributed all or part of this metric definition. Also include either citations or URLs to other material that is relevant.
Tags	A comma delimited list of Contexts that are associated with this metric. For example, this field will hold a list of Control IDs from the CSA Controls Matrix, e.g., CO-2, DG-3, etc. Note that the CSA Controls Matrix will be used to automatically associate the metric with other standards such as ISO/IEC, PCI, HIPAA, NIST, and COBIT.
Cloud Relevance	
Metric Collector	Who collects this metric? A cloud provider or tenant?
IaaS Relevance	Rating value between 1 and 10, 10 being most relevant.
IaaS Rationale	Rationale for rating assignment.

(continued)

IaaS Sharing	Discuss the likelihood, motivation, and risks/benefits/costs of sharing this metric between provider and tenant.
PaaS Relevance	Rating value between 1 and 10, 10 being most relevant.
PaaS Rationale	Rationale for rating assignment.
PaaS Sharing	Discuss the likelihood, motivation, and risks/benefits/costs of sharing this metric between provider and tenant.
SaaS Relevance	Rating value between 1 and 10, 10 being most relevant.
SaaS Rationale	Rationale for rating assignment.
SaaS Sharing	Discuss the likelihood, motivation, and risks/benefits/costs of sharing this metric between provider and tenant.

GLOSSARY

audit   A formal check to determine policy compliance, typically performed either by internal auditors at a company or organization or by an independent third party.

availability   The degree to which information is available when it is needed by authorized parties. Availability may be measured as the percentage of time information is available for use by authorized websites. For example, a business website may strive for availability above 99 percent.

Balanced Scorecard (BSC)   A performance measurement framework that is intended to enrich traditional financial performance measures with strategic nonfinancial performance measures, thereby giving a more balanced view of organizational performance. Developed in the 1990s by Drs. Robert Kaplan (Harvard Business School) and David Norton. (For additional information, see www.balancedscorecard.org.)

black swan event   An event that is highly improbable and therefore likely to end up at the bottom of the list of priorities to address. See *The Black Swan: The Impact of the Highly Improbable* by Nassim Taleb for further reading on the Theory of Black Swan Events.

botnet   A malicious botnet is a network of compromised computers that is used to transmit information, send spam, or launch denial-of-service (DoS) attacks. Essentially, a malicious botnet is a supercomputer created by and managed by a hacker, fraudster, or cybercriminal.

charter   A document that describes the specific rights and privileges granted from the organization to the information security team.

cloud computing   As defined by the National Institute of Standards and Technology, or NIST, a model for enabling ubiquitous, convenient, on-demand network access to a shared pool of configurable computing resources (e.g., networks, servers, storage, applications, and services) that can be rapidly provisioned and released with minimal management effort or service provider interaction. This cloud model promotes availability and is composed of five essential characteristics, three service models, and four deployment models.

compliance   Adherence to a set of policies and standards. Two broad categories of compliance are compliance with internal policies (specific to a particular organization) and compliance with external or regulatory policies, standards, or frameworks.

confidentiality   The prevention of disclosure of information to unauthorized parties.

consultant   A subject matter expert who is contracted to perform a specific set of activities. Typically, a statement of work outlines the deliverables to be completed by the consultant and the deadlines for each deliverable.

core competencies   The fundamental strengths of a program that add value. They are the primary functions of a program and cannot or should not be done by outside groups or partners.

data cleansing   The actions performed on a set of data in order to improve the data quality and achieve better accuracy, completion, or consistency.

dirty data   Data that has unacknowledged correlation or undocumented origins or that is biased, nonindependent, internally inconsistent, inaccurate, incomplete, unsuitable for integration with data from other important sources, unsuitable for consumption by tools that automate computation and visualization, or lacking integrity in some other respect.

false negative   A result that indicates no problem exists where one actually exists, such as occurs when a vulnerability scanner incorrectly reports no vulnerability exists on a system that actually has a vulnerability.

false positive   A result that indicates a problem exists where none actually exists, such as occurs when a vulnerability scanner incorrectly identifies a vulnerability that does not exist on a system.

information classification standards   Standards that specify treatment of data (requirements for storage, transfer, access, encryption, etc.) according to the data's classification (public, private, confidential, sensitive, etc.).

information security   The protection of information and information systems from unauthorized access, use, disclosure, modification, or destruction. Also commonly referred to as data security, computer security, or IT security.

integrity   The prevention of data modification by unauthorized parties.

intercept of a line   Identifies the point where the line crosses the vertical y-axis. An intercept is typically expressed as a single value b but can also be expressed as the point (0, b).

metrics project distance   The amount of a change you want to achieve in your target measurement by the end of the metrics project.

metrics project timeline   How long you want to spend to achieve the metrics project distance.

mission statement   Outlines an information security program's overall goals and provides guidelines for its strategic direction.

objective desired direction   The direction in which you want the metrics project measurement to go to achieve the benefits of an information security metrics program, especially the benefit of improvement.

offshoring   Contracting work to resources in a different country (either third party or in-house).

online analytical processing (OLAP)   A specific type of data storage and retrieval mechanism that is optimized for swift queries that involve summarization of data along multiple factors or dimensions.

orchestration   The administrative oversight that ensures the workflow is executed as specified. It includes functions such as signing off on a metric definition, deployment of its implementation, scheduling its calculation at regular intervals, and executing and delivering updates. *See also* workflow.

outsourcing   Contracting work to a third-party vendor.

prioritization   An exercise in determining relative importance of tasks, projects, and initiatives.

project management   Defining an end goal and identifying the activities, milestones, and resources necessary to reach that end goal.

project scope   Indicates project coverage, typically by identifying the different regions, different networks, and/or different groups of people the project encompasses.

quartiles   Divide all of the observations into four equal groups, which hold the lowest one-fourth of all observed values (first quartile), the highest one-fourth of all observed values (fourth quartile), and the two middle fourths, one-fourth above and one-fourth below the median value (or the value that divides the set of observations into two equal halves).

RASCI   A project management methodology for assigning roles in projects that involve many people and teams. Each letter in RASCI stands for a different type of role, Responsible, Approver, Supporter, Consultant, and Informed, and each role has corresponding responsibilities.

Request for Proposal (RFP)   A document that an organization uses to solicit proposals for a project that has specific requirements. The organization can then use the responses to the RFP to evaluate and compare the proposals of multiple vendors.

sacred cow   An idiom for a practice that is implemented simply because it is "how it's always been done," without regard for its usefulness or whether it can help achieve a target goal or outcome.

slope of a line   A value that represents how fast the y values are rising or falling as the x values of the line increase.

Slope of line $= (y_2 - y_1) / (x_2 - x_1)$, where (x_1, y_1) and (x_2, y_2) are any two points on the line

stakeholders   Leaders responsible for critical decision-making and key supporters who will drive change throughout the organization.

threat analysis   An alternative approach to risk management that involves identifying and analyzing potential attacks, threats, and risks and preparing countermeasures accordingly.

workflow   A collection of rules that govern the relationship of steps required to complete a process. Relationships might include sequence order, branching conditions, looping, and number of repetitions.

Index

ISO (International Organization for
   Standardization), 47–48, 49
ISO/IEC 27001 standard domains, 9
issue meetings, 293
issues, 170
IT security. *See* information security

K

key audiences. *See also* audience
   becoming familiar with, 279–281
   BU leader, 206–207
   chief executive officer, 200–202
   chief financial officer, 200–202
   chief information officer, 207–208
   chief risk officer, 203–205
   chief technology officer, 205–206
   director of human resources, 210–211
   director of physical security, 208–210
   examples of, 370–371
   identifying, 369
   reporting, 292–293
   summary, 211–212
key messages
   BU leader, 206–207
   chief executive officer, 200–202
   chief financial officer, 200–202
   chief information officer, 207–208
   chief technology officer, 205–206
   considerations, 196, 199, 201
   director of human resources, 210–211
   director of physical security, 208–210
   examples of, 200–202, 370–371
   identifying, 212–213, 369
   summary, 211–212
key stakeholders. *See* stakeholders
keyloggers, 34
keys, 240
Kier (hacker), 42

L

language, common, 143, 167
LDAP (Lightweight Directory Access Protocol)
   repositories, 241
lexicon, 19

lifecycle
   Cloud Metrics working group, 353–354
   information assets, 147
   metrics, 264, 348
lifetimes, 171–172
Lightweight Directory Access Protocol (LDAP)
   repositories, 241
line of business, 325
linear regression, 66–67
lines of investigation, 65
LinkedIn, 158
list generation, 189–190
loading datasets, 244
log files, 241
logAffected metric, 74
logarithmic scale instance, 74
logarithms, 74–75
logical data modeling, 257, 258
logical extraction, 242

M

maintenance contracts, 108, 109
maintenance work, 107
malicious code, 30–31
malware, 32–33
malware kits, 33
management information bases (MIBs), 241
mathematical skills, 63–69
mean time to remedy (MTTR), 59–61
measurements, 20–25
media training, 282
medians, 63, 65
meetings
   issue, 293
   one-on-one, 285–286
   outsourced/offshore personnel, 139
   project management, 293
   with stakeholders, 225–226, 367
   status, 293
memberships, 109
merging data, 239, 240–244
MetricML Framework, 233
metrics. *See also* security metrics
   anonymization, 270
   collection technologies, 257–259
   design, 233–238, 254, 255–256

S

So many ways to prepare for exam day SUCCESS!

All-in-One—A complete exam guide and on-the-job reference

Study Guide—The #1 classroom-proven IT training and exam prep tool

Practice Exams—Score higher with the most effective self-test program available

Boxed Set—A great value on two books and three CD-ROMs—bonus CD-ROM available only with the set

Mike Meyers' Certification Passport—Concise coverage of only what you need to know to pass the exams

CompTIA certification apps by **Mike Meyers** available in Apple App Store

Follow us @MHComputing

Available in print and as e-books.

E-books available in multiple formats, including Kindle Edition with audio/video for the Study Guide

Learn more.  **Do more.**
MHPROFESSIONAL.COM

The Secure Beginner's Guides

SECURITY SMARTS FOR THE SELF-GUIDED IT PROFESSIONAL

The Secure Beginner's Guides offer trusted, hands-on coverage of current and emerging security topics. Written by experts in the field, these books make it easy to put security concepts into practice now.

Security Metrics: A Beginner's Guide
978-0-07-174400-3

Wireless Network Security: A Beginner's Guide
978-0-07-176094-2

Computer Forensics: A Beginner's Guide
978-0-07-174245-0

Web Application Security: A Beginner's Guide
978-0-07-177616-5

Available in print and e-book format.

 Follow us @MHComputing

Learn more. **Mc Graw Hill** Do more:
MHPROFESSIONAL.COM

Stop Hackers in Their Tracks

**Hacking Exposed,
6th Edition**

**Hacking Exposed
Malware & Rootkits**

**Hacking Exposed Computer
Forensics, 2nd Edition**

**24 Deadly Sins of
Software Security**

**Hacking Exposed Wireless,
2nd Edition**

**Hacking Exposed:
Web Applications, 3rd Edition**

**Hacking Exposed Windows,
3rd Edition**

**Hacking Exposed Linux,
3rd Edition**

Hacking Exposed Web 2.0

**IT Auditing,
2nd Edition**

IT Security Metrics

**Gray Hat Hacking,
3rd Edition**

Available in print and ebook formats

 *Follow us on Twitter @MHComputing*

 Learn more.  Do more.
MHPROFESSIONAL.COM

CPSIA information can be obtained
at www.ICGtesting.com
Printed in the USA
JSHW071500040223
37162JS00002B/21

9 780071 744003